D1237214

Illumination
and
Night Glare

Wisconsin Studies in Autobiography

William L. Andrews
General Editor

Illumination
and
Night Glare

The Unfinished
Autobiography
of Carson McCullers

Edited and with an
introduction by

CARLOS L. DEWS

THE UNIVERSITY OF WISCONSIN PRESS

The University of Wisconsin Press
2537 Daniels Street
Madison, Wisconsin 53718

3 Henrietta Street
London WC2E 8LU, England

Library of Congress Cataloging-in-Publication Data

McCullers, Carson, 1917–1967.
    Illumination and night glare : the unfinished autobiography of
Carson McCullers / edited and with an introduction by Carlos L.
Dews.
    256 pp.   cm.—(Wisconsin studies in autobiography)
    Includes bibliographical references (p. 225) and index.
    ISBN 0-299-16440-3 (alk. paper)
    1. McCullers, Carson, 1917–1967.   2. Women authors, American—
20th century—Biography.   I. Dews, C. L. Barney (Carlos Lee Barney),
1963– . II. Title.   III. Series.
PS3525.A1772Z74   1999
813'.52—dc21   99-19805
[B]

A review of life is not an orderly account from conception to death. Rather it's fragments from here and there.
—William S. Burroughs

The silence in the room was deep as the night itself. Biff stood transfixed, lost in his meditations. Then suddenly he felt a quickening in him. His heart turned and he leaned his back against the counter for support. For in a swift radiance of illumination he saw a glimpse of human struggle and of valor. Of the endless fluid passage of humanity through endless time. And of those who labor and of those who—one word—love. His soul expanded. But for a moment only. For in him he felt a warning, a shaft of terror. Between the two worlds he was suspended. He saw that he was looking at his own face in the counter glass before him. Sweat glistened on his temples and his face was contorted. One eye was opened wider than the other. The left eye delved narrowly into the past while the right gazed wide and affrighted into a future of blackness, error, and ruin. And he was suspended between radiance and darkness. Between bitter irony and faith. Sharply he turned away.
—Carson McCullers, *The Heart Is a Lonely Hunter*

Contents

Illustrations

Preface

In addition to the autobiographical text *Illumination and Night Glare,* this edition includes, per her instructions, the outline of McCullers's first novel, "The Mute" (published in 1940 as *The Heart Is a Lonely Hunter),* and the letters exchanged between Carson and her husband, Reeves McCullers, during World War II.

To assist the reader, this edition also includes a biographical introduction, a detailed list of the handwritten changes made to the typescripts of the autobiography by McCullers and those assisting her, a detailed list of the changes made by the current editor, a chronology of McCullers's life, a bibliography of books by or about McCullers, and an index.

Acknowledgments

For their trust, I thank Dr. Mary Mercer, Mr. Robert Lantz, and Ms. Floria Lasky. For her indispensable book, *The Lonely Hunter: A Biography of Carson McCullers*, and her constant support, encouragement, and advice, I thank Dr. Virginia Spencer Carr. For sharing their memories of Carson and Reeves, thanks to David Diamond and Jordan Massee.

Thanks to Cathy Henderson, David Coleman, and all the other very professional staff at the Harry Ransom Humanities Research Center, University of Texas at Austin.

For their constant support and encouragement, I thank Dr. Gregory Lanier, Chair, Department of English and Foreign Languages, and Dr. Richard Doelker, Dean, College of Arts and Social Sciences at the University of West Florida. Thanks also to the University of West Florida Foundation for a grant in support of this project. For their ever present support and patience, thanks to Linda Uebelsteadt and Deborah Burlison.

And, for the support only friends and lovers can provide, I thank Bret Pearson, Carolyn Leste Law, Sandy Whitehead, and William Lamar Polk.

Introduction

> Carson's heart was often lonely and it was a tireless hunter for
> those to whom she could offer it, but it was a heart that was graced
> with light that eclipsed its shadows.
>
> —Tennessee Williams

Carson McCullers, Georgia-born novelist, short story writer, and playwright, celebrated her fiftieth and final birthday on February 19, 1967, at New York's Plaza Hotel. During her week-long stay, McCullers received well-wishes, enjoyed meals from the hotel's kitchen, and granted interviews. In one interview, with Rex Reed, McCullers revealed her reason for writing an autobiography:

I think it is important for future generations of students to know why I did certain things, but it is also important for myself. I became an established literary figure overnight, and I was much too young to understand what happened to me or the responsibility it entailed. I was a bit of a holy terror. That, combined with all my illnesses, nearly destroyed me. Perhaps if I trace and preserve for other generations the effect this success had on me it will prepare future artists to accept it better.[1]

The life McCullers wished to "trace and preserve for other generations" began in Columbus, Georgia, in 1917, where she was born Lula Carson Smith, the daughter of Vera Marguerite Waters and Lamar Smith, a jewelry store owner. Lula Carson, as she was called until age fourteen, was joined by a brother, Lamar, Jr., in 1919 and a sister, Rita, in 1922. Carson attended public schools in Columbus and graduated from Columbus High School at sixteen. An unremarkable student, Carson preferred the solitary study of the piano. Encouraged by her mother, who insisted that her daughter was destined for greatness, Carson began formal piano study at age nine but gave up her dream of a career as a concert pianist after a childhood illness, later diagnosed as rheumatic fever, left her without the physical stamina necessary for the rigors of practice and a concert career. While recuperating from

1. Rex Reed, "'Frankie Addams' at 50," *New York Times,* 16 Apr. 1967: D15.

this illness Carson read voraciously and began to consider writing as an alternate vocation, although she did not immediately reveal her new-found art for fear of disappointing her teacher and mother.

In 1934, at age seventeen, Carson sailed from Savannah to New York City, ostensibly to study piano at the Juilliard School of Music but actually to pursue her secret ambition to write. Working various jobs to support herself, Carson studied creative writing at Columbia University and at Washington Square College of New York University. Back in Columbus in the fall of 1936 to recover from a respiratory infection that left her bedridden much of the winter, Carson began work on her first novel, "The Mute" (later published as *The Heart Is a Lonely Hunter*). Her first short story, "Wunderkind," was published in the December 1936 issue of *Story* magazine, edited by Whit Burnett, Carson's former teacher at Columbia.

In September of 1937, Carson married James Reeves McCullers, Jr., a native of Wetumpka, Alabama, to whom she was introduced by Edwin Peacock, a mutual friend, when Reeves was in the army stationed at Fort Benning. The marriage was simultaneously the most supportive and destructive relationship in her life and was from its beginning plagued by the partners' shared difficulty with alcoholism, their sexual ambivalence, and the tension caused by Reeves's envy of Carson's literary successes.

In April of 1938, Carson submitted an outline and six chapters of "The Mute" to Houghton Mifflin as an entry in a first-novel contest. On the strength of the outline she was offered a contract and a five hundred dollar advance. The book, retitled *The Heart Is a Lonely Hunter* and published in June 1940, is the story of a deaf mute to whom the lonely and isolated people of a southern town turn for silent consolation. The novel was the first articulation of the themes of loneliness and isolation that would recur in much of McCullers's work. An immediate and much praised success, *The Heart Is a Lonely Hunter* propelled McCullers into the literary spotlight of New York at age twenty-three.

Reflections in a Golden Eye, McCullers's second novel, first appeared in *Harper's Bazaar* in August 1940 and was published by Houghton Mifflin in 1941. Readers who expected a book like the author's first novel were shocked by the troubling story of voyeurism, obsession, repressed homosexuality, and infidelity set on a peace-time army base. *Reflections in a Golden Eye* received a mixed critical reception, and its author faced ridicule from the people of her hometown who saw negative reflections of themselves in the characters of the novel.

Carson and Reeves moved to New York in 1940 when *The Heart Is a Lonely Hunter* was published. Later that year, during an initial separation from Reeves, Carson rented a house in Brooklyn Heights, New York, with George Davis (literary editor of *Harper's Bazaar*) and the British poet W. H. Auden. This house, located at 7 Middagh Street, became the center of a bohemian literary and artistic constellation including Gypsy Rose Lee, Benjamin Britten, Peter Pears, Salvador Dali, Virgil Thomson, Aaron Copland, Leonard Bernstein, Kurt Weill, Paul and Jane Bowles, Richard Wright, and Oliver Smith. Carson and Reeves divorced in 1941, and many of the friendships made during her time in Brooklyn would endure for the rest of her life.

Following her father's sudden death in August of 1944, Carson, with her mother and sister, moved to Nyack, New York, where they purchased a house at 131 S. Broadway. McCullers spent most of the rest of her life in this house within sight of the Hudson River.

Despite her difficult relationship with Reeves and the anxiety of World War II (Reeves and his brother Tom, Carson's friend Edwin Peacock, and her brother Lamar, Jr., were all stationed abroad), the years 1943 to 1950 saw the publication of what are considered McCullers's finest creative works. In August 1943, *Harper's Bazaar* published *The Ballad of the Sad Cafe,* a lyrical story of jealousy and obsession in a triangular love relationship involving a bootlegging amazon, a hunchbacked midget and an ex-convict in a small southern mill town. The work was later published in 1951 by Houghton Mifflin in an omnibus edition of the author's work, *"The Ballad of the Sad Cafe": The Novels and Stories of Carson McCullers.* March 1946 saw the publication of McCullers's fourth major work, *The Member of the Wedding,* the story of a lonely adolescent girl, Frankie Addams, who wants to quell her sense of isolation and longing and find her "we of me" by escaping with her older brother and his new bride on their honeymoon trip. McCullers's theatrical adaptation of the novel, suggested by Tennessee Williams, opened on Broadway in 1950 to near unanimous acclaim and enjoyed a run of 501 performances. This adaptation proved to be her most commercially successful work and received both the New York Drama Critics' Circle Award and the Donaldson Award for best play of 1950.

Corresponding during his deployment in Europe during World War II, Carson and Reeves reconciled and remarried in 1945 upon his return from the war. The couple bought a home near Paris in April of 1952. While living there in the late summer of 1953, Reeves, depressed and drinking heavily, tried to convince Carson to commit suicide with him. Fearing for her life, Carson fled to the United States. Reeves committed suicide in a Paris hotel room in November 1953.

The final fifteen years of McCullers's life saw a marked decline in her health and creative output. Bedridden by paralysis from a series of strokes, McCullers was devastated by the commercial failure of her second play, *The Square Root of Wonderful*, which closed after only forty-five performances on Broadway in 1957, and the largely negative reception of her final novel, *Clock Without Hands* (1961). A more encouraging event in her final years was the success of Edward Albee's adaptation of *The Ballad of the Sad Cafe* in 1963, which enjoyed a Broadway run of 103 performances. Her final publication during her lifetime was a book of children's verse, *Sweet as a Pickle and Clean as a Pig* (1964).

In addition to a celebration of her fiftieth birthday, McCullers's trip in 1967 to the Plaza Hotel was a test to see if she could withstand the strain of travel, in hopes of visiting her friend John Huston at his estate in Ireland. Having passed this travel test, McCullers, accompanied by her housekeeper Ida Reeder, left for Ireland on April 1, 1967. On her return from Ireland in mid-April, McCullers began in earnest to write the autobiography she spoke of in her interview with Rex Reed. To capture the alternating joy and tragedy of her life, she titled the work "Illumination and Night Glare." Working from her bed in her Nyack home, McCullers dictated the draft of her autobiography to a corps of friends, family, and student secretaries from a nearby college between April 18 and her final stroke on August 15. It is impossible to determine the identities of all those who helped her work on the draft of "Illumination and Night Glare," but those who spent considerable time with McCullers during the final year of her life included her cousin Jordan Massee; her physician and friend Dr. Mary Mercer; her sister Margarita Smith; her housekeeper Ida Reeder; a boarder at her house, Kenneth French; a Jesuit priest, Peter O'Brien; a volunteer helper and artist, Stuart Sherman; and a number of paid and volunteer secretaries.

As McCullers described to Rex Reed, the autobiography she wished to write would not only provide future generations assistance in dealing with early success but would also give her the opportunity to reconsider her response to her own success at a very young age and how this response affected her life and later career. This autobiography would be far more straightforward than the implicit one often barely submerged below the surface of her fiction. Perhaps more than any other twentieth-century American writer, McCullers's life experiences shaped her fictional world; the line between her fiction and her reality was often blurred. As she once said, "Everything that happens in my fiction has happened to me, or it will happen eventually."[2] In addition to removing the protective veil of fiction and recounting her life in

2. Virginia Spencer Carr, *The Lonely Hunter: A Biography of Carson McCullers*, Garden City: Doubleday, 1975, 105.

her own words, this autobiography would be structured around and chronicle the moments of inspiration when the significant ideas for her fiction were suddenly realized—what McCullers calls her "illumina-tions"—and detail the "night glare" horrors of her strokes, failed rela-tionships, and the deaths of her grandmother, mother, father, and husband.

Two published accounts of McCullers's medical condition and her continued attempts at writing refer specifically to the final months of her life. Earl Shorris wrote for *Harper's* of a visit to McCullers in Nyack:

How painfully she spoke, gathering fractions of words in her throat, raising them through creakings to her soprano song, straining to woo and polish the sounds with her mouth. It was after the stroke; her hand was clubbed, she could not walk, she could not write, she could not read unless the type was quadruple-spaced. She had not learned to use the tape recorder that had been given to her; it seemed to have been born broken. But she was writing, dictat-ing to a secretary, somehow getting it down, proving at the least that the in-domitability of the human spirit, which is the resolving power of her work, was not artifice . . . .[3]

Stuart Sherman also recalled details of McCullers's writing during the final months of her life:

Everyday she wrote, but not manually. She made up sentences in the presence of a secretary, and the secretary copied those sentences onto paper. On some days sentences came hard and there were only a few of them after several hours' effort. But the effort was always made and some sentences were al-ways produced.

That year—the last year of her life—she was working on two books: her memoirs and a study of people who had "triumphed over adversity."

The memoirs were tentatively titled "Illuminations and Night Glare" and the study, "In Spite Of" (the latter's prospective roster included Helen Keller and Arthur Rimbaud!).

When I think of Carson as writer, when I think of Carson in the act of writing or (as she was ultimately compelled to do by illness and physical inca-pacity) speaking for transcription, I am now—as I was then—stunned into giving only the merest factual account of the process as I observed it.[4]

McCullers combined within "Illumination and Night Glare" the two projects recalled by Sherman. However, rather than considering Helen Keller and Arthur Rimbaud, the "In Spite Of" section of the autobiog-

---

3. Earl Shorris, "Books: Literary Life Among the Dinka," *Harper's*, Aug. 1972: 104–105.
4. Stuart Sherman, "Carson McCullers," *BOMB: Artists, Writers, Actors, Directors*, Fall 1990: 60–62.

raphy cites the suffering of Sarah Bernhardt and Cole Porter, among others. It appears that McCullers was attempting to include in what she knew would be her final work all those projects she had previously left undone.

The inclusion of details of her trip to Ireland, details of the filming of *The Heart Is a Lonely Hunter,* information on the release of the film adaptation of *Reflections in a Golden Eye,* and a mention of the scheduled amputation of her left leg all provide evidence that the bulk of "Illumination and Night Glare" was dictated between April and August of 1967. That the bulk of the autobiography was written so near the end of her life is singularly impressive given that fully seven years earlier, as biographer Virginia Spencer Carr writes, "many people thought she would never live to complete *Clock Without Hands,* or that she would be able to create any major work again."[5]

Besides Sherman's brief account of her writing and Shorris's recollection of the difficulty she had communicating, very little has been written about McCullers's work during the final year of her life. Most accounts include details of her continuing illnesses and dismiss these years as nonproductive. Those around McCullers near the end of her life recall little of her writing at the time; instead their memories are mostly of her difficult health.

As she suggested in her 1967 interview with Rex Reed, McCullers's life was blighted by a series of cerebral strokes caused by her misdiagnosed childhood case of rheumatic fever, her lifelong smoking habit, and her dependence on alcohol. The first stroke, in February 1941, temporarily impaired her vision and caused debilitating headaches. The second and third strokes occurred in Paris in the fall of 1947 and temporarily affected the lateral vision in her right eye and permanently paralyzed her left side. Comatose for forty-seven days after a final cerebral stroke on August 15, 1967, McCullers died at 9:30 A.M. in the Nyack Hospital on September 29. She was buried beside her mother in Nyack's Oak Hill Cemetery overlooking the Hudson River. A testament to her will to write and live, McCullers's autobiography remained forever a first draft.

In an appraisal of her life and work accompanying McCullers's front-page obituary in the September 30, 1967, *New York Times,* Eliot Fremont-Smith wrote of the impact of her first novel in what could also be an assessment of McCullers's lasting influence:

> It is not so much that [*The Heart Is a Lonely Hunter*] paved the way for what became the American Southern gothic genre, but that it at once encompassed

5. Carr, *Lonely,* 481.

it and went beyond it. . . . The heart of this remarkable, still powerful book is perhaps best conveyed by its title, with its sense of intensity, concision and mystery, with its terrible juxtaposition of love and aloneness, whose relation was Mrs. McCullers's constant subject. . . . Mrs. McCullers was neither prolific nor varying in her theme. . . . This is no fault or tragedy: to some artists a vision is given only once. And a corollary: only an artist can make others subject to the vision's force. Mrs. McCullers was an artist. She was also in her person, an inspiration and example for other artists who grew close to her. Her books, and particularly "The Heart," will live; she will be missed.

After the publication in 1971 of *The Mortgaged Heart*, a posthumous collection edited by her sister Margarita G. Smith, the bulk of McCullers's letters, manuscripts, and miscellaneous papers were sold to the Harry Ransom Humanities Research Center at the University of Texas at Austin. These papers included two copies of the 128-page typescript of "Illumination and Night Glare." Although considered for *The Mortgaged Heart*, "Illumination and Night Glare" has until now remained unpublished.

To supplement the sections of "Illumination and Night Glare" dictated during 1967, McCullers intended to include as appendices the outline of "The Mute" (*The Heart Is a Lonely Hunter*) and the letters she exchanged with Reeves during World War II.

Written in 1938 and published in Oliver Evans's biography *The Ballad of Carson McCullers* (1966) and in *The Mortgaged Heart*, McCullers's outline of "The Mute" is the most extensive she wrote for any of her novels and was responsible for garnering McCullers her first book contract at age twenty-three. The outline was written during the early days of her marriage to Reeves when the couple lived in Fayetteville, North Carolina. The typescript of the outline is also housed in the McCullers Collection at the University of Texas.

With the words "Insert war letters" in the typescript of "Illumination and Night Glare" McCullers indicated her desire to include the letters she exchanged with Reeves during World War II. Although there is some evidence that Carson wanted to include only excerpts from these letters, it is impossible to tell which letters Carson had in mind when she made the note, and since a list of letters Carson compiled with the help of her tenant, Kenneth French, is not clear, the letters between Reeves and Carson during World War II for which both sides of the correspondence exists are included as Appendix II of this edition. The inclusion of Reeves and Carson's war letters represents the first time any of Carson McCullers's correspondence have been published.

In addition to the text of "Illumination and Night Glare," the outline of "The Mute," and the World War II letters of Carson and Reeves, this edition also includes a detailed chronology of McCullers's life and a McCullers bibliography.

As an unfinished and collaborative work, "Illumination and Night Glare" presents an editor with a myriad of difficult decisions, including how to deal with the free-associative style of the narrative, the difficulty in discerning Carson's intention about what to include in the appendices she suggested, and the impact of McCullers's penchant for exaggeration.

Despite the nonchronological development of "Illumination and Night Glare," a chain of associations which support the structure of the narrative is visible. The major divisions or apparent issues of concern to McCullers when composing "Illumination and Night Glare" include her relationship with Reeves McCullers; her experience of creative inspiration (what she called her "illuminations"); her maternal grandmother, Mommy, and the early influence she had on Carson's life and childhood happiness; the influence of Carson's early study of music with her second piano teacher, Mary Tucker; and the central importance of others in her life—from her housekeeper Ida Reeder to her doctors and friends William Mayer and Mary Mercer, her neighbor and friend Marielle Bancou, and her more "famous" friends, from Gypsy Rose Lee, George Davis, W. H. Auden, and Richard Wright to Tennessee Williams and Edith Sitwell. In the final section, which appears to be the remaining content from the oft-mentioned book in progress, "In Spite Of," Carson briefly recalls fellow artists and sufferers of poor health and amputation, including Cole Porter and Sarah Bernhardt.

The composition of "Illumination and Night Glare" was strongly influenced by Carson's delight in exaggeration and storytelling. As described by her cousin, Virginia Johnson Storey, "Carson loved to take the truth between her teeth and run with it, a habit she never got over."[6] Perhaps because of her penchant for fabulation, "Illumination and Night Glare" is alternately a surprisingly honest and interestingly untrustworthy text. With a highly developed sense of what was impor-

6. Virginia Spencer Carr, "Introduction," *Collected Stories of Carson McCullers*, Boston: Houghton Mifflin, 1987, viii.

tant and not open for exaggeration and what was less important and therefore grist for the imaginative mill, McCullers includes in the text numerous obvious misrepresentations, exaggerations, and distortions, at times insisting on their truthfulness. At the same time, however, she provides details that contradict accepted versions of some events as published in previous biographies and that encourage revisionary scholarship on her life story.

In a brief passage in "Illumination and Night Glare" about the opening night of her play *The Square Root of Wonderful*, McCullers dictated, "I was wearing my beautiful two-thousand-year-old, this is the truth, Chinese robe, and as I passed the theatre I did not even have the nerve to pray." This passage underscores, as has been often noted and as her cousin noted in the quotation that frames this section, Carson at times was more concerned with making a story more interesting than in recording a story accurately. The robe emphatically described as two thousand years old, "this is the truth," was a robe given to Carson by her cousin Jordan Massee. The mandarin robe, made to be worn by men and which reached to the floor when Carson wore it, was peacock blue with white embroidery and was at most 150 years old at the time. According to Massee, Carson wore this robe "on all state occasions" and liked to exaggerate both its age and ceremonial importance.

Through the work of her previous biographers it has generally been understood that young Carson's talent at the piano was revealed in a sudden and untrained blossoming of her talent when she played tunes "by ear" at a very young age. As Virginia Spencer Carr relates:

> McCullers surmised at an early age that she was no ordinary child, her mother having informed her—or so the story went—that certain "prenatal signs" presaged that her firstborn would be a genius, a flowering awaited by Marguerite Smith with an air of buoyant expectancy. At age six McCullers confirmed the prophecy (in her mother's eyes, at least), by sitting down at the piano and playing with both hands a song she had heard for the first time that afternoon in a movie theater.[7]

In "Illumination and Night Glare" Carson details a considerably different version of the story of the revelation of her prophesied talent when she admits to practicing her premiere songs at the piano of her Aunt Martha Johnson. This significant admission that contradicts the long-held belief that Carson displayed an innate talent for the piano, interpreted by her mother as the revelation of her destiny of fame, can

---

7. Virginia Spencer Carr, *Understanding Carson McCullers*, Columbia, S.C.: University of South Carolina Press, 1990, 7.

be cause for reconsideration of how conscious the young Carson might have been of her importance to her mother and the expectations her mother placed on her as a result.

Perhaps the most significant omission from the autobiography, especially given the lengthy consideration Carson provides of her relationship with Reeves and the frank discussion of the reasons for their divorce, is Carson and Reeves's relationship with the American composer David Diamond. Although not a physical relationship, the intimate connection among Carson, Reeves, and Diamond was one of the strongest attachments in Carson's life. The lack of mention of this relationship in "Illumination and Night Glare" is particularly significant because, in addition to her piano teacher Mary Tucker, Reeves McCullers, Annemarie Clarac-Schwarzenbach, and Dr. Mary Mercer, Carson's relationship with David Diamond was instrumental in the development of her philosophy of loneliness and love which is the most important theme in her fiction.

After Carson and Reeves met Diamond in New York in 1941, the trio seemed destined for a triangular relationship like those later depicted most clearly in Carson's novels *The Member of the Wedding* and *The Ballad of the Sad Cafe*. Originally attracted to Carson, Diamond soon developed a relationship with Reeves, as well. Carson and Reeves also shared a powerful attraction to Diamond. Awaiting his divorce from Carson, Reeves lived with Diamond in Rochester, New York, for four months in 1941. The appearance to Carson of a successful relationship between Diamond and her soon-to-be-divorced husband only furthered her sense of betrayal and fear that she would be excluded. Despite the intensity of her relationship with him, Carson does not mention Diamond in the text of "Illumination and Night Glare," and he is mentioned by his first name only once in Reeves and Carson's wartime letters. Carson, in recalling the reasons for her divorce from Reeves, fails to mention the betrayal she felt when Reeves and Diamond moved to Rochester, leaving her out of the triangular relationship she desired. This omission is particularly significant given the importance of untenable triangular relationships in many of McCullers's works and the thematic debt these works owe to her experience with Reeves and Diamond. Reasons for the omission of Diamond from her autobiography might include Carson's reluctance to discuss her sexual life in print, the reduction of importance of the Diamond relationship given the intervening twenty-seven years, or simply her reluctance to recall the painful memories of the experience.

Ultimately whether Carson McCullers accurately related the tales of illumination and night glare in her life is of little or no importance. The telling of her stories, as she remembered them, as they influenced her, is more important than the veracity of the tales she recalled. As an autobiography, "Illumination and Night Glare" is a complex mixture of memory, latter-day self-revision, de-mythologizing, and re-mythologizing and is an attempt by its author to memorialize herself in a way that is true to her own self-perception though not always consistent with strict biographical record.

In addition to recapitulating in her own terms the significant events in her life, "Illumination and Night Glare" also provides for the first time details of Carson's thoughts on sexuality. Despite the appearance of sophistication regarding human relationships and sexuality, especially in *The Heart Is a Lonely Hunter,* and the previous attribution of Carson's worldliness to her mother's libertine spirit, Carson laments in "Illumination and Night Glare" her lack of knowledge of sexual matters and her reliance on textbooks for her knowledge about sex: "When I asked my mother about sex she asked me to come behind the holly tree & said with her sublime simplicity, 'Sex, my darling, takes place where you sit down.' I was therefore forced to read sex text books, which made it seem so very dull, as well as incredible."

Carson does not discuss her bisexuality or lesbianism directly yet does include details, though somewhat veiled, of her attraction to and relationship with Swiss heiress Annemarie Clarac-Schwarzenbach. In describing Annemarie at their first meeting, Carson wrote, "She had a face that I knew would haunt me to the end of my life, beautiful, blonde, with straight short hair." As another testament to the strength of their relationship, Carson also included in the manuscript of "Illumination and Night Glare" excerpts of tender letters from Clarac-Schwarzenbach.

In much more direct language than she used in recalling her relationship with Clarac-Schwarzenbach, Carson details her naive expectations and ultimate disappointment in the sexual dimension of her relationship with Reeves:

I told my parents I didn't want to marry him until I first had experienced sex with him because how would I know whether I would like marriage or not? In doing so, I felt I had to confess to my parents. I said marriage was a promise & like other promises I did not want to promise Reeves until I was dead sure whether I liked sex with him. Reading Isadora Duncan & "Lady Chatterly's [sic] Lover" was one thing but personal experience was another. Besides in all the books there were little asterisks when it came to the point of what you really wanted to know.

Once again recalling Carson's explanation to Rex Reed for writing "Illumination and Night Glare," the autobiography can easily be understood as Carson's attempt to explain her life, both her successes and her failures, to future generations. On a personal and emotional level, writing the autobiography was an opportunity for Carson to explain herself to herself. But beyond Carson's personal motives for writing the autobiography, the night-glare details of her experience chronicle the life of a southern woman artist of the first half of the twentieth century struggling with the anxiety inherent during a period of global, social, and political upheaval.

Perhaps more important than any of the specific content in the autobiography are the traces of Carson's personality found just beneath the surface of the narrative of "Illumination and Night Glare." McCullers's rare, cherished illuminations helped her survive the more frequent and lasting night glare because they provided her, like her character Mick Kelly in *The Heart Is a Lonely Hunter,* an inner room to which she could retreat to recover, create, and protect herself. As a journal of her travel to the private space of her inside room, "Illumination and Night Glare" provides the reader not only the details of the night glare which forced Carson to retreat inward but, perhaps more important, provides a chronicle of the inspiring illuminations which ultimately restored her soul. *Illumination and Night Glare* is a rare invitation to join Carson on a visit to her own inner room.

Over thirty years after she set out to trace and preserve the story of her life, McCullers's autobiography is available to serve as an inspirational and cautionary tale for future generations, as she intended.

*Illumination
and
Night Glare*

3.

Biography

Reeves ~~at his home~~ in ~~Westchester, while he was~~ [who was living] [Goldens Bridge] [for The winter]

~~taking courses at Columbia in N.Y. My parents~~

respected me for my frankness and with some re-

luctance, let me go. The sexual experience was not [or colored] [lights]

like D.H.Lawrence. No grand explosions, but it

gave me a chance to know Reeves better, and really

learn to love him. We treated ourselves to pink

champagne and tomatoes out of season, ~~and working~~

~~together We were pretty good cooks.~~ I also told

Reeves about the Mute, [" my working title for "The Heart Is A Lonely Hunter"] and he was as thrilled as

I was. It was going to be a marriage of love and

[writing for both of us.] ~~work. In the meantime, and~~ in Sylvia Bates' class,

I had actually had a [my first] story published in Story Mag- [(It is hard today to really the]

azine, which was called WUNDERKIND. Exhilarated [prestige & importance]

by this also, Reeves thought he himself would like [That Story]

to be an author. On September (check year) [1936] we were [Magazine had at]

married, and I went on with the Mute." [that time for young authors)]

~~After his brief series of courses; philosophy,~~

psychology, etc., he found a job in North Carolina

and we moved to Charlotte.

My life was following a pattern I have always

followed. Work and love.

The Mute, my first title, took me two years to

write, and they were very happy years for me. I

worked hard and loved hard.

[money for trip came from piano class - write]

[Green velvet suit + Buster brown shoes - write]

[1917 19 1936]

Page from the typescript of "Illumination and Night Glare." Used by permission of the Harry Ransom Humanities Research Center, the University of Texas at Austin.

Illumination and Night Glare
The Unfinished Autobiography
of Carson McCullers

[Illumination and Night Glare]

My life has been almost completely filled with work and love, thank goodness.* Work has not always been easy, nor has love, may I add. My working life was almost blighted at the time I was seventeen and for a number of years, by a novel I simply could not understand. I had at least five or six characters who were very clear in my mind. Each of these characters were always talking to the central character. I understood them, but the main character was unfocussed, although I knew that he was central to the book. Time and again I thought I would just write these characters as short stories, but always I was restrained, because I knew that this mysterious creation was going to be a novel.

Then suddenly, as I was walking up and down the rug in my living room, skipping every other square in the design, and worn out with the problem I had set for myself, the solution all at once came to me. The central character, the silent one, had always been called Harry Minowitz, but as I was thinking and pacing, I realized that he was a deaf mute, and that was why the others were always talking to him, and why, of course, he never answered.

*This edition of Carson McCuller's unfinished autobiography is based on the two typescripts of the work housed at the Harry Ransom Humanities Research Center at the University of Texas at Austin. Every effort has been made to follow the intent of Carson McCullers in the preparation of this edition of her autobiography to the extent those intentions can be discerned. All changes in the text have been noted (words enclosed in brackets in the text are corrections made by the current editor) and can be found in the list of emendations and corrections (Appendix III).

This was a real illumination, lighting each of the characters and bringing the whole book into focus. [Straightaway], Harry Minowitz's name was changed to Singer, as the name was more expressive to the new conception, and with this fresh understanding, the book was well begun. As a preface I wrote the following passage:

[The broad principal theme of this book is indicated in the first dozen pages. This is the theme of man's revolt against his own inner isolation and his urge to express himself as fully as is possible. Surrounding this general idea there are several counter themes and some of these may be stated briefly as follows: (1) There is a deep need in man to express himself by creating some unifying principle or God. A personal God created by a man is a reflection of himself and in substance this God is most often inferior to his creator. (2) In a disorganized society these individual Gods or principles are likely to be chimerical and fantastic. (3) Each man must express himself in his own way—but this is often denied to him by a tasteful, short-sighted society. (4) Human beings are innately cooperative, but an unnatural social tradition makes them behave in ways that are not in accord with their deepest nature. (5) Some men are heroes by nature in that they will give all that is in them without regard to the effort or to the personal returns.

Of course these themes are never stated nakedly in the book. Their overtones are felt through the characters and situations. Much will depend upon the insight of the reader and the care with which the book is read. In some parts the underlying ideas will be concealed far down below the surface of a scene and at other times these ideas will be shown with a certain emphasis. In the last few pages the various motifs which have been recurring from time to time throughout the book are drawn sharply together and the work ends with a sense of cohesive finality.

The general outline of this work can be expressed very simply. It is the story of five isolated, lonely people in their search for expression and spiritual integration with something greater than themselves. One of these five persons is a deaf mute, John Singer—and it is around him that the whole book pivots. Because of their loneliness these other four people see in the mute a certain mystic superiority and he becomes in a sense their ideal. Because of Singer's infirmity his outward character is vague and unlimited. His friends are able to impute to him all the qualities which they would wish for him to have. Each one of these four people creates his understanding of the mute from his own desires. Singer can read lips and understand what is said to him. In his eternal silence there is something compelling. Each one of these persons makes the mute the repository for his most personal feelings and ideas.

This situation between the four people and the mute has an almost exact parallel in the relation between Singer and his deaf-mute friend, Antonapoulos. Singer is the only person who could attribute to Antonapoulos dignity and a certain wisdom. Singer's love for Antonapoulos threads through the whole book from the first page until the very end. No part of Singer is left untouched by this love and when they are separated his life is meaningless and he is only marking time until he can be with his friend again. Yet the four people who count themselves as Singer's friends know nothing about Antonapoulos at all until the book is nearly ended. The irony of this situation grows slowly and steadily more apparent as the story progresses.

When Antonapoulos dies finally of Bright's disease Singer, overwhelmed by loneliness and despondency, turns on the gas and kills himself. Only then do these other four characters begin to understand the real Singer at all.

About this central idea there is much of the quality and tone of a legend. All the parts dealing directly with Singer are written in the simple style of a parable.

Before the reasons why this situation came about can be fully understood it is necessary to know each of the principal characters in some detail. But the characters cannot be described adequately without the events which happen to them being involved. Nearly all of the happenings in the book spring directly from the characters. During the space of this book each person is shown in his strongest and most typical actions.

Of course it must be understood that none of these personal characteristics are told in the didactic manner in which they are set down here. They are implied in one successive scene after another—and it is only at the end, when the sum of these implications is considered, that the real characters are understood in all of their deeper aspects.][1]

The next day I actually began the book: "In the town there were two mutes and they were always together." For a year or so I worked steadily and when my teacher, Sylvia Chatfield Bates, with whom I had studied writing for a semester at N.Y.U. wrote me that Houghton [Mifflin] was conducting a contest for a first novel, I wrote a detailed working outline of ["The Mute"] and submitted it to them along with the 100 or so pages I had already completed. That outline was a moral support to me, [although] I have never before or again worked so closely with an outline. That outline appears in the appendix. It did not win the prize, but [Houghton Mifflin] offered me a contract, which in my mind was almost as good, and so I returned to my writing.

Meanwhile, in 1937 in my nineteenth year I had fallen in love and married with Reeves McCullers. I told my parents I didn't want to marry him until I first had experienced sex with him because how would I know whether I would like marriage or not? In doing so, I felt I had to confess to my parents. I said marriage was a promise & like other promises I did not want to promise Reeves until I was dead sure whether I liked sex with him. Reading Isadora Duncan & "Lady

1. See Appendix I below for complete text of "The Mute" outline.

[Chatterley's] Lover" was one thing but personal experience was another. Besides in all the books there were little asterisks when it came to the point of what you really wanted to know. When I asked my mother about sex she asked me to come behind the holly tree & said with her sublime simplicity, "Sex, my darling, takes place where you sit down." I was therefore forced to read sex text books, which made it seem so very dull, as well as incredible.

I told my parents my plan was to join Reeves who was living in Goldens Bridge for the winter. They respected me for my frankness and with some reluctance, let me go.

The sexual experience was not like D. H. Lawrence. No grand explosions or colored lights, but it gave me a chance to know Reeves better, and really learn to love him. We treated ourselves to pink champagne and tomatoes out of season. I also told Reeves about "The Mute," my working title for "The Heart Is A Lonely Hunter" and he was as thrilled as I was. It was going to be a marriage of love and writing for both of us. In Sylvia Bates' class, I had actually had my first story published in 1936 in *Story Magazine*[2] which was called ["Wunderkind"]. (It is hard to realize the prestige & importance that *Story Magazine* had at that time for young authors.) Exhilarated by this also, Reeves thought he himself would like to be a writer. On September 20, [1937] we were married, and I went on with "The Mute."

After his brief series of courses; philosophy, psychology, in [N.Y.,] etc., Reeves found a job in North Carolina and we moved to Charlotte.

My life was following a pattern I have always followed. Work and love.

["The Mute,"] my first title, later was changed to "The Heart [Is] a Lonely Hunter" by my publisher, a title which I was pleased with, took me two years to write, and they were very happy years for me.[3] I worked hard and loved hard. Directly after "Heart" was finished in 1939, I immediately began another work which was "Reflections in a Golden Eye."

The pattern of love had begun when I was a child. I adored an old lady who smelled always of lemon verbena sachet. I slept with her and

2. "Wunderkind," *Story*, Volume IX, Number 53, December 1936.

3. Robert Linscott, McCullers's editor at Houghton Mifflin, suggested the title "The Heart Is a Lonely Hunter," taken from a poem, "The Lonely Hunter," by Fiona MacLeod, pseudonym of William Sharp.

cozied in the dark. Often she would say, ["Bring] up the chair, darling, and climb to the top drawer of the bureau," and there I would find some goody. A little cup cake, or once, to my delight, some [kumquats]. This first love was my grandmother, whom I called Mommy.[4]

Her life had not been a happy one, although she never complained. Her husband[5] had died of alcoholism after years of being tended by a strong man-servant who could control his sudden [fits.] However, Mommy never had bad feelings against alcohol. Once, towards the last of her illnesses, some ladies from the [Woman's Christian Temperance Union] came to call. [They] were so serious it looked like a delegation.

"I know what you're here for," Mommy said. "You're here to arrange about that badge, purple and gold, to put over my body, but I tell you now I won't have it. I come from a long line of drinking men. My father drank, my son-in-law [Lamar][6] who is a saint drinks also. How sad it makes me when I hear that [POP,] and I know that all his home brew has exploded. And I drink also."

The ladies said in shocked voices, "You could not Mrs. Waters!"

"I do every night—[Lamar] fixes me a toddy, and moreover, I enjoy it."

"Well! Mrs. Waters," the delegation said aghast.

When [Daddy] came into the room, Mommy said mischievously, ["Is] it time for my toddy yet [Lamar]? I think it would be delicious now."

"Would any of you ladies like to join us?" Daddy asked.

But already the WCTU were fleeing in horror.

"To tell you the truth [Lamar], those WCTU ladies are awfully narrowminded, although I guess it's wicked of me to say so."

"Very wicked," my Daddy said, as he poured her toddy.

She was supported by her father-in-law and her [brothers]. Her brothers came every day to her home for dinner at noon, but she had to ask them every time she wanted them to buy circus tickets for the children. It was a time and place when men did not think that women had good sense. Therefore, they themselves would order barrels of flour, salt-pork and other staples and have it sent to her house. They also ordered her children's clothes, which did not suit her at all, and very often did not even fit. Still, she was well provided for, perhaps too well provided for, for her taste.

4. Lula Caroline Carson Waters (1858–1923), McCullers's maternal grandmother.
5. Charles Thomas Waters (1860–1890).
6. Lamar Smith (1889–1944), McCullers's father.

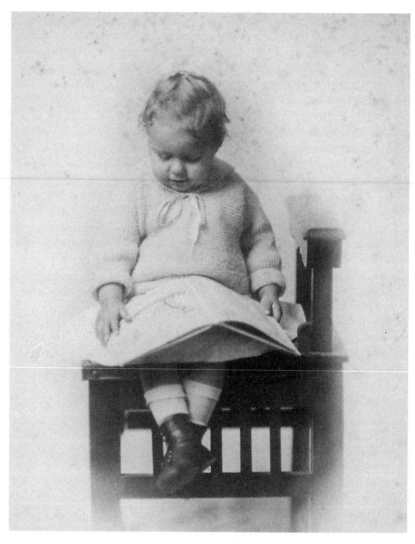

"The pattern of love had begun when I was a child." Lula Carson Smith, age 2. Used by permission of the Photography Collection, Harry Ransom Humanities Research Center, the University of Texas at Austin.

During Mommy's terminal illness, my brother[7], sister[8] and I were sent to Aunt Tieh's,[9] where we had five cousins. It was marvelous sleeping in the enormous sleeping porch. My eldest cousin[10] would tell us fairy tales about the glass mountain, Aesop's fables, and we would happily doze off. Aunt [Tieh] had a wonderful [scuppernong] arbor and many fruit trees. There was always [Tupelo] honey at the breakfast table and often ripe, peeled figs over which we would pour fresh, thick cream. On Sundays we always had ice cream, and I was allowed to churn it and of course, lick the dasher. I hardly realized it when the [gardener] told me that my grandmother was dead. So we were driven home in the old Dodge car by Aunt [Tieh].

At home, when I saw the wreath on the door, I knew that something strange and uncanny had happened. I flung myself to the floor in the hall and some moments later I had a convulsion. [When I was calm that afternoon] Mother wanted me to kiss my grandmother, but I said firmly, ["She's] dead isn't she, and you don't kiss dead people. [Kissing is for live people.]" Though my grandmother was dead, her spirit still lives with me, and I've always had a picture of her on my wall. A young, beautiful widow with five children.

Mother[11] and Daddy I also loved, but Mommy was someone always special to me. It was she who owned the house we lived in. It was a narrow house on 13th Street, Columbus, Georgia. [The floors creaked in the way of old houses.] She owned that house and the two properties behind it. It was in this house that I was born and lived throughout my early childhood. My parents and grandmother would not let me play with the neighbor's children, except Helen Harvey, the girl who lived across the street.

[missing text][12]. . . of Health & Beauty, which made my parents roar, considering all the convulsions I'd had. School was all right as I learned easily & went straight to the piano in the afternoon. I spent practically no time on homework. I passed every grade, but that was

7. Lamar Smith, Jr., McCullers's brother, born 13 May 1919.

8. Margarita Gachet Smith, McCullers's sister, born 2 August 1922.

9. Martha Elba Waters Johnson (1885–1953), McCullers's maternal aunt.

10. Virginia Johnson, McCullers's cousin, daughter of Martha Elba Waters Johnson and C. Graham Johnson.

11. Vera Marguerite Waters (1890–1955), McCullers's mother, known as Bebe by her family.

12. The first line of this page is missing from the typescript of the autobiography.

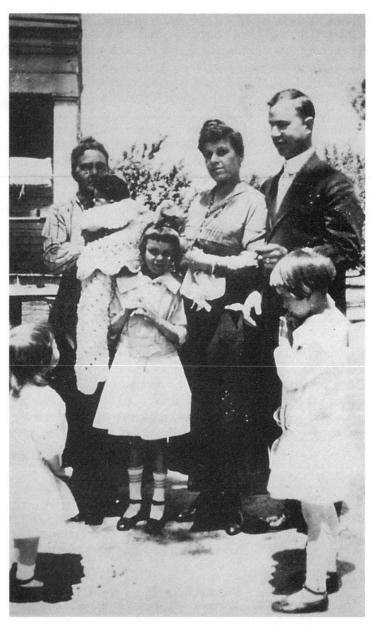

"During Mommy's terminal illness, my brother, sister, and I were sent to Aunt Tieh's, where we had five cousins." The C. Graham Johnson family. Used by permission of the Photography Collection, Harry Ransom Humanities Research Center, the University of Texas at Austin.

"This first love was my grandmother, whom I called Mommy." Lula Caroline Carson Waters (1858–1923), Carson's maternal grandmother. Used by permission of the Photography Collection, Harry Ransom Humanities Research Center, the University of Texas at Austin.

all. I liked to climb a tree in the backyard & sit in a tree house my brother & I had made. We had an elaborate signal system for the cook, who was awfully nice to fasten a string in a basket & bring up goodies. Years later when I was troubled I would still take refuge in that same tree house.

I had heard horrifying things about high school. I had heard, for instance, that when Miss Cheeves was dead her brain was going to be sent to the Smithsonian Institute Museum because she was so smart. Mother dressed me in a pink wool suit & I set out for that scary high school. It was not as bad as I thought. I still wanted to be a concert pianist so my parents did not make me go every day. I just went enough to keep up with the classes. Now, years later, the high school teachers who taught me are extremely puzzled that anyone as negligent as I was could be a successful author. The truth is I don't believe in school, whereas I believe very strongly in a thorough musical education. My parents agreed with me. I'm sure I missed certain social advantages by being such a loner but it never bothered me.

The first week at school I was literally captured by a girl when I was in the basement. She threw me to the floor & said "Say fuck three times."

"What is [it?"] I asked.

"Never mind what it is, you lily pure innocent, just say it."

All the time she was grinding my face against the cement floor.

"Well [fuck,"] I [said.]

"Say it 3 [times."]

"Fuck, fuck, [fuck,"] I said quickly, and she let me go.

I can still feel her foul breath on my face & her sweating hands. When I was released I ran straight home but did not tell my parents because I knew it was something ugly & wicked.

"What happened to your face?" my mother asked.

"Just one of the things in high school," I said. Although nothing else that dramatic ever happened to me, the dullness of school was a dreadful experience. When I graduated at 17, I didn't even attend all the ceremonies, but asked the principal to keep my diploma, as my brother would pick it up the next day.

However, my childhood was not lonely because when I was 5 years old [in] 1922, my Daddy bought a piano. My Aunt Tieh had a piano and I had touched it gingerly and even arranged a few chords, so when *my* piano arrived I sat down immediately and began to play. To my parents this seemed a miracle.

"What was I playing?" they asked me.

"A tune I had made up," I told them. [Then I swung into "Yes, We Have No Bananas."]

They decided that I ought to have a music teacher, and so they asked Mrs. Kierce[13] to give me lessons twice a week.

I did not much like the lessons, and still preferred to make up my own tunes. Mrs. Kierce was impressed, and very conscientiously wrote down the music. I studied with her until I heard a recital by Mrs. Tucker,[14] about ten years later, and I hoped that she could be my teacher. I discussed it with Mrs. Kierce, and she agreed with me.

The work I played for my new teacher was the 2nd Hungarian Rhapsody. She once said it was the fastest, loudest Hungarian Rhapsody she had ever heard, and she accepted me as a pupil. Not only as a pupil—I spent every Saturday at her home, and she started me on Bach, whom I had never heard before.

Mrs. Tucker was to me the embodiment of Bach, Mozart, and all beautiful music, which at age thirteen had enveloped all my soul. It was at a concert of Rachmaninoff that I met my first [grown] friend.

He was twenty-three and I seventeen and we could talk about all sorts of things together. Not only music, but he introduced me to Karl Marx and Engels, that was one of the things that furthered my thinking about justice. I had realized so often during the [Depression], when I saw [Negroes] rooting through the garbage pails at home, and coming to the house to beg, that there was something fearful and wrong with the world, but I had not in any way thought of it intellectually.

My new friend, Edwin Peacock, came every Saturday afternoon, and his visits were a joy to me. I was not ["in love,"] but it was real friendship, which has indeed lasted throughout all my life.

It was my joy to go to town to shop with my Mother and Grandmother. Then, one day when they had taken me to buy material; my Mother always made my dresses, my Grandmother my underclothes, my Mommy sat down on a stool in the drug store and said she didn't feel so well. Mother arranged for a taxi and told me to take her home and have Cleo, the maid, undress her and put her to bed.

"It's nothing," my Grandmother said, "just a little dizziness."

Feeling very important, I got Mommy to the taxi and took her

13. Mrs. Helen (Alice) Kendrick Kierce.
14. Mrs. Mary Tucker, wife of U.S. Army Colonel Albert Sidney Johnston Tucker.

"At first I wanted to be a concert pianist, and Mrs. Tucker encouraged me in this." Used by permission of the Photography Collection, Harry Ransom Humanities Research Center, the University of Texas at Austin.

home. Cleo and I both undressed her. However, in spite of her protests, it was not just a slight dizziness. It was Pernicious Anemia, and she died a year later.

I yearned for one particular thing; to get away from Columbus and to make my mark in the world. At first I wanted to be a concert pianist, and Mrs. Tucker encouraged me in this. Then I realized that Daddy would not be able to send me to [Juilliard] or any other [great] school of music to study. I know my Daddy was embarrassed about this, and loving him as I did, I quietly put away all thoughts of a music career, and told him I had switched "Professions," and was going to be a writer. That was something I could do at home, and I wrote every morning.

My first book was called "A Reed of Pan," and it was, of course, about a musician who really studied and accomplished things. However, I was not satisfied with the book and did not send it to New York, although I'd heard of agents and so forth. I was sixteen years old and kept on writing. The next book was called ["Brown River."] I don't remember very much about it except it was strongly influenced by ["Sons and Lovers."]

My grandmother had willed "to her gray-eyed grandchild" the only article of value that she had; a beautiful emerald and diamond ring. I put it on my hand just once, because I knew that I had to sell it. My Daddy, who was a jeweler in the town, sold it so that I was able to go to New York and take a course in creative writing and philosophy.

So, at last, I was leaving home and going to study. A girl I'd never met before was taking courses at Columbia, and she invited me to share her room with her. Daddy took one look at her and was dubious about the arrangements, because the girl had dyed hair, at a time when only ["fast"] girls dyed their hair. However, he let me go.

I [traveled] by boat from Savannah to New York, so for the first time I saw the ocean, and later, marvel of marvels, I saw snow.

My new friend lived upstairs over a linen shop. Immediately I noticed that she was seldom at home—in fact, she had a boy-friend with whom she spent the night. A man followed me upstairs and tried to put his arms around me but I pushed him away so violently that he ricocheted against the wall. So I was stuck there in that lonely room, with a sense of menace and a fear of strange men. [In the daytime I'd go to Macy's and just sit in a telephone booth where I knew I was safe. Then back to the horror of a sleepless night.]

Finally, I had the sense to go to the Dean of Women at Columbia, and ask her advice.

"How old are you?" she asked me.

"17," I said proudly.

"You're much too young to be living alone in the city," and she suggested a [Girl's] Club for students.

I got my belongings together and moved into the Parnassus Club. There, for the first time in more than a week, I slept. I slept for twenty-four hours.

A girl at the Club was practicing a Bach Fugue, and I felt completely at home. I made friends easily and thankfully. When my first and special friend told me that she was going to move to the Three Arts Club, I decided to join her.

Since my financial means were somewhat slender, I got a job with a magazine called [*More Fun and New Comics.*] Me, a tragic writer, editing the funny papers. The job was to be the ["front man"] for, as I soon discovered, the magazines were being sued. I was sincerely grateful when they fired me after a couple of months.

I coasted along when my Daddy sent me a small check. Then I was faced with the job situation again, and I found one with Mrs. Louise B. [Field], who insisted on calling me a Real Estate "salesman." I checked with customers about apartments in New York. The main part of the job, I remember, was getting sour cream for Mrs. [Field], which she would eat with a long ice tea spoon. But once, when I was reading Proust behind the ledger and got involved in a long Proustian sentence, Mrs. [Field] caught me. She picked up the ledger and banged me over the head with it. Her parting, venomous shot was "you will never amount to anything in this world," and banged me again with the ledger. So, under such circumstances, I was fired again.

Meanwhile, my friend Edwin in Columbus, had written me that while he was at the library he had met a young man and had invited him to his house for drinks. He said he was charming, and he thought that I would like him very much and we would get together when I came home. So in June of [1935] I went home and met Reeves McCullers[15] at Edwin Peacock's apartment. It was a shock, the shock of pure beauty, when I first saw him; he was the best looking man I had ever seen. He also talked of Marx and Engels, and I knew he was a liberal, which was important, to my mind, in a backward Southern community. Edwin, Reeves and I spent whole days together, and one night when Reeves and I were walking alone, looking up at the stars, I did not realize how time had passed, and when Reeves brought me home, my parents were distressed, as it was two o'clock in the morning. However, my mother was also charmed by Reeves, and he would bring her beautiful records. At that time he was a clerk in the army at Ft. Benning, Georgia. We both loved sports and often Reeves would borrow Edwin's bicycle and we would go off to the Girl's Scout Camp, about thirty miles away. Mother would pack a lunch and we'd ride side by side, stopping off now and then for a cold [Coke]. Chess was his great hobby, and after swimming in the brown, cool water, we would play a game, (he would always beat me.) Then swimming again and then the long ride home. I was eighteen years old, and this was my first love. He was going to New York to study, and I knew his departure would be sad for me.

I'd been writing for a couple of years and Reeves said he was

15. James Reeves McCullers (1913–1952), born 11 August 1913 in Wetumpka, Alabama.

Carson with her mother "Bebe," Vera Marguerite Waters Smith, and her father, Lamar Smith beside their home at 1519 Starke Avenue, Columbus, Georgia. Used by permission of the Photography Collection, Harry Ransom Humanities Research Center, the University of Texas at Austin.

going to be a writer also. Late that summer I developed a low-grade fever, and the [doctor] suspected Tuberculosis, so I was kept at home. It turned out to be a childhood attack of Rheumatic fever, but was never properly diagnosed, as [such.]

Reeves left at the beginning of the school year in early September, having bought himself out of the army. At the same time his Aunt had left him some money which he very generously wanted to divide with me, but I refused and told him he would need it to get through school. I did not realize the lost quality of Reeves until he was truly lost.

In the meantime, with Reeves gone and Edwin my only friend, I lived in the thought of his return at Christmas time. Fearful & ill, I spent my time writing and hoping and waiting for Reeves. He came back at Christmas and for the first time we drank Sherry instead of the beer we had always drunk together. Occasionally he drank whiskey. No, I never recognized the lost quality of Reeves McCullers until it was much too late to save him or myself. He had a splendid constitution and I would not have recognized alcoholism in those days. We had never made love sexually because I told him I did not want that experience until I was clear in my mind that I would love him forever.

After the Christmas holidays Reeves persuaded me to join him in New York. I was much better, although I still had the low-grade temperature. I told my parents I was going with him, and so we went to his apartment in Westchester.

As soon as I arrived there Reeves dropped out of school, and we spent two months together. I told him I felt he should have a job before we married, so we went down South again. He went to Charlotte, North Carolina, while I stayed in Columbus. Finally, he wired he had a job and was coming to get me. When I think of my parents' patience and understanding I can only marvel.

"She's the most truthful child I've ever known," my father always said, but now that I'm an adult, I wonder at their patience & understanding.

So Reeves and I were married in 1937 in the living room at home, and went to Charlotte to begin married life.

My cousin insisted I was married in a green velvet gown and oxfords. Could be? I can't remember. There was nobody at the wedding but Edwin and the immediate family. Edwin played the Bach double concerto for violins softly during the ceremony, and [Mother] wept as [mothers] are supposed to do, and [Daddy] blew his nose. After the ceremony we had the usual chicken salad and Champagne.

The first days of my married life were happy although I made the usual bride's mistakes. I cooked a beautiful chicken, after carefully removing all the pin feathers, and put it in the oven, not realizing it also had to be cleaned. When Reeves came home he [said, "What] in the world is this awful odor in the house?"

Absorbed in "The Heart Is A Lonely Hunter," I had not noticed anything. Reeves opened the windows, turned on the electric fan and [said,] "Baby, what is it?" I told him I was cooking a chicken and it seemed to be rotten. It took a little time before we realized my mistake; I had neglected to clean the inside of the chicken. He just laughed and said, ["We'd] better eat at the S & W tonight." In spite of that experience, married life was both exhilarating and a comfort. Every day when I'd finish my work, I would read it out loud to Reeves, and at one point I asked, ["Do] you think it's good?"

He said, "No! I don't think it's good—I know it's great."

The outline, which I more or less [stuck] to, was a moral support to me. In this respect, I must say, I had never written so detailed an outline, and that was only done because of the Houghton Mifflin contest.

I looked forward to Saturday, because that was the day I cleaned

"It was the shock of pure joy when I saw him: he was the best looking man I had ever seen." Carson and Reeves McCullers at the time of their marriage. Used by permission of the Photography Collection, Harry Ransom Humanities Research Center, the University of Texas at Austin.

the apartment instead of writing. Reeves gave [me moral support] and wrang out the wash which was too heavy for me.

We had no [other] friends and were content to be alone. On Saturday night, the house shining and my pencils sharpened and put away, we went to the wine store and bought a gallon of Sherry, and occasionally Reeves would take me to the S & W, which was an inexpensive restaurant in town. I could feel in Reeves none of the unhappiness or dissatisfaction that later [led] to his ruin and death.

Our aim in life during those days was to go to New York, and often we would just look at the parked cars with New York license plates and dream about the time when we, too, could go to the magic city.

At 4:00 AM one morning, after about two years of marriage, and with my full consent, Reeves indeed set out for the city, while I waited at home. Home was not a pleasant place without him. I was more aware of the miserable surroundings after he left.

It was a one family home, divided into little rabbit warrens with plywood partitions, and only one toilet to serve ten or more people. In the room next door to me there was a sick child, an idiot, who bawled all day. The [husband] would come in [and] slap her, and the mother would cry.

"If I ever get out of this house," I would say to myself, but the words dwindled after the scream of the sick child, and the poor mother's useless efforts to calm her. I hated to go to the toilet because of the stench. I know my parents would have helped if they had seen me in such misery, but I was too proud.

After one day of job searching Reeves returned. He had found nothing, but he said he had some leads.

A month later we went to New York, as I had gotten some money from Houghton Mifflin who had finally published "The Heart." At that moment, Reeves had accepted an invitation to sail a boat to Nantucket, (he was a good sailor) with a friend called Jack,[16] whom we had met a few months previously. After the poverty we had suffered, I hesitated to take a train, so I took a bus alone and went to stay temporarily with Miss Mills, whom I'd met in one of my writing classes. She found me a cheap boarding house somewhere on the West side, where there, cut off and lonely, I passed the day that my first book was published.[17]

Meanwhile, I got a mysterious telegram from Robert Linscott, whom I vaguely recognized as one of my publishers, to meet him the next day at the Bedford Hotel. My solitude was lightened. It was June, 1940, and I wondered what dress I should wear. Since my work had removed me quite from the world of fashion, I saw that none of my old clothes would do. I went to [Klein's] and in the heat and clamor of that store I bought a summer suit. So next day I was all ready for Mr. Linscott.

In the meantime I had started a third novel; I guess that once started, I was unable to stop writing. It was to be a book about a Jew from Germany. I wanted advice desperately so I had written to [Erika] Mann[18] asking for her help. She was very kind and set up an appointment with me, and it worked out that since both she and Mr. Linscott were staying at the Bedford Hotel, we were all able to meet each other for the first time that day in her room.

We discussed the publication of "Heart," and I told Mr. Linscott I'd already written a second novel.

"One thing at a time, my dear," he said.

16. John Vincent Adams.
17. 4 June 1940.
18. Erika Mann, eldest daughter of Thomas Mann.

He invited me to come to Boston to stay with him and his family, and I promptly accepted. He was the best editor at Houghton Mifflin and he gave me good advice. At this same meeting I discussed the plans for my new book, and Miss Mann gave me welcome advice also.

While we were thus engaged a stranger came into [Erika's] room. She had a face that I knew would haunt me to the end of my life, beautiful, blonde, with straight short hair. There was a look of suffering on her face that I could not define. As she was bodily resplendent I could only think of [Myshkin's] meeting with [Nastasya Filippovna] in the "Idiot," in which he experienced "terror, pity and love." She was introduced by [Erika] as Madame Clarac.[19] She was dressed in the height of simple summer fashion, that even I could recognize as a creation of one of the great Paris [couturiers]. I did not know that a dear friend of hers picked out all of her clothes, as [Annemarie] wouldn't have cared or noticed.

She asked me to call her [Annemarie] right away, and we became friends immediately. At her invitation, I saw her the next day and she said, "You don't know what it means to be cured of this terrible habit."

"What terrible habit?" I asked.

"Didn't anybody tell you about me?"

"No," I said, "What's there to tell?"

"I've been taking morphine since I'm eighteen years old."

Knowing nothing of morphine or the effects of the habit, I was not as impressed as I should have been.

She skipped abruptly to her wanderings in Afghanistan, Egypt, Syria and all the Far East. Fascinated as I was, I was bewildered.

"I love you well enough to ask you to promise me that you will never take dope."

"Dope?" I said, as it was the last thing that would ever occur to me.

Then she turned the conversation to her mother who had said when she was seventeen that she was a dope fiend, a communist and a lesbian.

I asked how it all happened and she told me that it was in Germany, during the years just following World War One. She had left home because her mother had beat her regularly. She would run away but her mother would catch her and bring her back. At home she lived in a castle with her mother and an idiot brother, who could barely

19. Annemarie Clarac-Schwarzenbach, Swiss heiress, journalist, explorer, daughter of Alfred Schwarzenbach, owner of Switzerland's largest silkweaving company, and Maria Renée Schwarzenbach, daughter of the Supreme Commander of the Swiss Army during World War II.

"She had a face I knew would haunt me to the end of my life." Annemarie Clarac-
Schwarzenbach. Used by permission of the Photography Collection, Harry Ransom
Humanities Research Center, the University of Texas at Austin.

speak. That was her environment. Her father wanted to help her, but
he was too much dominated by her mother, who, by the way, is said
to be the richest woman in Switzerland. She finally ran away for good,
and made friends with a distinguished German family.

I asked her how long it had been since she'd given up morphine,
and she answered "today."

We were out so late that night that Reeves was worried and furious
with me when I came back.

"By God!" he [said.] "What were you doing all night?"

"Just talking."

"Are you in love with [Mademoiselle Schwarzenbach?"]

I said, "I don't know."

Quick and powerful as a panther Reeves slapped me on the face,
and when I was trying to [struggle up,] he slapped me again. It was the
first time I had ever been slapped in my life, and I was too surprised to
speak. Later, I begged Reeves to try to get a job so he wouldn't just be

hanging around the apartment all day wasting time. The apartment, by the way, was on West 11th Street near the docks.

He said he intended to get a job. Untrained, and in the Depression I knew it would be hard for him, but I knew also he ought to try. He would go to bars to drink, and then come back home and read. The utter uselessness of his life depressed me, and that complete moral depression lasted until his death. I was writing all the time which must [have gotten on] his nerves. I really don't know how I stood those months.

Then [*Harper's Bazaar*] bought "Reflections In A Golden Eye," for $500.00, and every morning I went to their office to work with the editor. George Davis was gifted, charming and corrupt. At one point he said, ["Since] you don't get along with Reeves and live in such a miserable apartment, why don't you live with me?"

My prudery came through and I said, "Like brother and sister of course," which made George burst into roars of laughter. Next day he told me he'd had a dream that we were actually living in the same house; he saw it as an old [brownstone] in Brooklyn Heights. He asked me if I would go with him and look for such a house? So we went to Brooklyn, talked with the [agency,] and found a simply charming old [brownstone] on [Middagh] Street. We signed the lease together, and after I'd set Reeves up in a better apartment, I felt free to move in with George.

Meanwhile, George had a dear friend, the great poet W. H. Auden, who was also looking for rooms. We happily invited him to move in, and he had two friends; the very distinguished musician Benjamin [Britten], and his friend Peter Pears. In turn they had good [friends:] Louis [MacNeice], Christopher Isherwood, Richard [Wright,] Aaron [Copland,] Jane & Paul [Bowles]. Thank goodness the house was commodious. Everyone had their own room and there was a large parlor, a big dining room, and Gypsy Rose Lee, a friend of George's and mine, found us a cook. Everyone went out of his way to give us gifts, as though we were some kind of a multiple bridal [party]. Our many friends were so happy for us that they furnished our home down to the grand piano, which was donated by Diana [Vreeland]. At last, after all the years of apartment misery I was living in a comfortable, even luxurious house. My room was of Empire green, very simple and with a small dressing room adjoining. We all paid our share of the expenses, so the house was not too costly.

[Wystan] Auden, who at heart is a school teacher, talked with me about [Kierkegaard], and for the first time I heard the [Dichterliebe].

"Then one day someone suggested that I go to Yaddo, an artist's colony near Saratoga Springs, New York . . . It was to become a haven to me for a number of years." Group photo at Yaddo, 1941, *top row, standing,* Newton Arvin, Nichola Marcicano, Nathan Asch, Philip Rahv, Michel Seide, Karol Rathaus, Carson McCullers, Malcolm Cowley, unknown, Langston Hughes, Kenneth Fearing, unknown, Leonard Ehrlich, Jean Liberte; *bottom row, seated,* Mrs. Asch, Francis Mingorance, Merle Marcicano, Katherine Anne Porter, Helen Kuo, Juan Mingorance, Nathalie Rahv, Elizabeth Ames. Photograph courtesy of the Corporation of Yaddo.

Somewhat exhausted by all these new ideas, I would take refuge at Gypsy's place, where one of the most complicated things was, if you go out in the yard and find some lovely greenish apples, "I will make a strudel tonight."

On her visits to New York my mother met and loved Gypsy, but she didn't care for [Annemarie.]

In spite of, or because of the stimulation of Brooklyn Heights, I was eternally home-sick. Then one day someone suggested that I go to Yaddo, an artist's colony near [Saratoga Springs,] N. Y. It was quiet; lunch boxes were sent to the inhabitants in the middle of the day, and we only met at dinner. It was to become a haven to me for a number of years. The old town of Saratoga was dear to my home-sick heart, with the old United States Hotel, The New Worden Bar where every afternoon I would go in the Yaddo station wagon and have cocktails. I

Carson and Tennessee Williams in Havana, Cuba, 1955. Used by permission of the Photography Collection, Harry Ransom Humanities Research Center, the University of Texas at Austin.

met there many distinguished people; Katherine Anne Porter, Eddy Newhouse, John Cheever, Colin McPhee, the great authority of Balinese music, and many others. During that same summer I met William Mayer, who was to be my friend and [doctor] until his death.

Summer passed into fall and we would all go for long walks together. In the autumn weather tinged by coolness, and often with a beautiful harvest moon, Eddy Newhouse, who was a [*New Yorker*] story writer, insisted that I write something for the [*New Yorker*]. So one day I wrote a story called "The Jockey." It took, as I remember, two days, and Eddy was pleased with it; so was the [*New Yorker*]. I can think of scads of rejections from the [*New Yorker*] in later days as the [*New Yorker*] has a certain style, which, I must say, is not my style. Still they paid by the word and paid better than anybody else, so when they offered me a contract to write for them exclusively, I accepted it.

My agent situation, at that time, was as they say in the news, very fluid. First, I had an agent, Maxim Lieber, who suddenly joined the Communist party and went away to Mexico, leaving my files in great disorder. Then at the beginning of the next summer I had a letter from a playwright I had heard about but never met. He was Tennessee Williams, and he said that he was in poor health and was afraid he might be dying, and wanted to meet me before that happened. I answered the letter, and soon joined him in Nantucket.

That summer of 1946 was magnificent. It was a summer of sun and friendship. Every morning we would work at the same table, he at one end, and me at the other. He was working on "Summer and Smoke," and I was beginning "The Member of The Wedding," as a play, which had been published in novel form in 1946. I told Tennessee about my relations with Reeves. By accident, there was at Skonset, Margot [von] Opel, the wife of the Opel industrialist, and the friend of [Annemarie's] who had always selected her clothes. Tennessee and I had "Spuds Carson" almost everyday; that was my recipe, and it consisted of baked potatoes, mashed with butter, onions and cheese. After a long swim it was good fare. Then to break the monotony of the bill of fare Margot invited us to supper, and as she was a marvelous cook, it was always a [haute]-cuisine affair. Margot raised her own suckling pigs and Tennessee, [possessed] by some devil, fed them whiskey which made them go wild. So then we had wild shoats and hogs, and when peace was finally restored—a delicious dinner.

I was a good swimmer, but Tennessee was excellent; swimming so far out that sometimes I was actually afraid he might drown. In the late sea-lulling afternoon I would play the piano or Tennessee would read poetry; Hart Crane was his favorite poet. It was Tennessee who introduced me to his agent, [Audrey] Wood, whom I found overbearing, but put up with until I could decide on another. Then my lawyer, Floria [Lasky], who [has] been my close friend and legal advisor for twenty years finally found me a suitable agent. There are no words of praise that I can find suitable enough for Floria [Lasky]. She just took me on when an out and out nut[20] was suing me for $50,000. There was a legal procedure in which Tennessee and I appeared and swore that I'd written "Member of The Wedding" at his house in Nantucket. Naturally, I won the case. We never had to fight another case on any subject, but our meeting cemented an enduring friendship with her and her family.

The meeting with Margot made me remember [Annemarie] and the war years. In 1941 Reeves had joined the 2nd Ranger Battalion, which is a task force whose methods were influenced by the Commandos.

Before going overseas in 1943, he wrote me a pleading letter to join him at the port of embarkation, so that our emotional troubles

20. Greer Johnson.

could be reconciled. Carried away by the tide of war I joined him, and spent a few days with him at Ft. Dix. Then he was sent to England where he went three times on special missions to Normandy. I worried ceaselessly about him and wrote him every day. He also wrote as frequently as possible. (INSERT WAR LETTERS)[21]

In the middle of these years of fury and disaster my father suddenly died of a Coronary Thrombosis. He died in 1944 at his jewelry store. He had in his hand a copy of the [*New Yorker*] that he was going to bring home to mother, as it contained one of my stories. My mother called me on the phone and I met my sister, who was in New York, and together we returned home.

A grotesque and horrible thing happened at my father's funeral; it [was as weird] as something out of Flannery O'Connor. The regular preacher at the First Baptist Church was on a holiday, so that's how the mistake must somehow have happened. The minister questioned [Mother] about the service she wanted, and she insisted on the 2nd Psalm, which she thought was the 103rd Psalm. However, [Mother] in her distress, did not listen to the minister but insisted on what she thought was the "Lord is my Shepherd." She was dead wrong, but the relief minister not knowing the family circumstances and having protested all he could, proceeded to read instead that dreadful Psalm, "The Psalm of the Sinners." My father's family had come down for the funeral, and it was decided that [Mother] should live with Rita and me in a house in the suburbs of New York.

I knew of such a place, as I had visited Henry Varnum Poor and Bessie [Breuer] in New City, New York. So I asked them to look for a suitable place and they found one in Nyack, New York.

Mother sold the family jewelry store and was therefore able to pay cash for the Nyack house. We moved to an apartment in Nyack, which was next door to the house I live in now, and shall probably live in the rest of my life. This house that mother had bought is a three story, beautiful, old Victorian house with a garden.

Having settled in the house, I was able to turn again to the war news, which was bad, as I had just heard that Reeves was wounded. I couldn't help but feel glad because that meant that he would be withdrawn from the firing line. Still I wondered how bad his wounds were

21. McCullers indicated in the typescript of the autobiography to insert at this point the letters she and Reeves McCullers exchanged during World War II. See World War II correspondence of Carson and Reeves McCullers below.

"... it was decided that mother should live with Rita and me in a house in the suburbs of New York." Margarita Gachet Smith. Used by permission of the Photography Collection, Harry Ransom Humanities Research Center, the University of Texas at Austin.

Carson in Nyack. Used by permission of the Photography Collection, Harry Ransom Humanities Research Center, the University of Texas at Austin.

until I learned from his brother, Tom, who had just returned from England, that he'd been wounded in the arm and would be home soon.

As soon as he returned to Nyack, he immediately started a barrage to make me marry him again.

I said, ["Second] marriages are so vulgar."

Naturally, I was happy to see him, but I said, ["We're] much better as friends, without marriage." Marriage, however, was his motive.

I talked to Henry Varnum Poor, the great artist, and asked him his advice, and he said he could not give it to me. I also spoke with Dr. William Mayer, my [doctor] and psychiatrist, and he could only say, ["Men] don't change essentially because of a war."

I had been hoping that there would be some sort of a miraculous change in Reeves because of his experiences. He was covered with campaign ribbons and when we walked down the street everyone looked at him. I, of course, was enormously impressed. He was so darn sweet that I forgot the reasons for my divorcing him in the first place.

I went to stay with a friend of mine, Caroline H.,[22] whom I'd known at the Three Arts Club, and while I was living there, I wanted to visit Nancy,[23] another friend from the Three Arts Club, but Reeves was mysteriously reluctant to let me go until one day as we were riding on a 5th Avenue bus, eating cherries, he said that he and Nancy had been lovers, but he didn't care anything about her. I couldn't reconcile the two statements.

The reason I really divorced Reeves was that one day my father, who knew how careful I was about money, called me at Yaddo that my bank account was very seriously overdrawn. It was a mystery to me because I had only written a few small checks, but I told Daddy I would come home and clear up the misunderstanding. When I arrived, the cashier at the bank said "that it was a very clever forgery, and who in the world did I know who would forge my name?"

Since Reeves was the only person who had access to my checks, and since two friends had told me that their checks had not been honored, it was clear that Reeves was a very sick man and needed more help than I could give him. When I faced him with this accusation, he denied it completely and imperturbably. I went to a lawyer and told him the story, and we were divorced at City Hall almost immediately. It was then that George offered me a home in Brooklyn. The year was 1940.

The war was on and Reeves enlisted in the Rangers and I went

22. Perhaps Carolyn Haeberlin, a fellow resident with Carson at the Three Arts Club.

23. Perhaps Nancy Warren, another resident of the Three Arts Club.

home to Georgia, exhausted by the emotional strain. How beautiful was the old-fashioned home, and the holly tree that is the handsomest one in town. I had brought records and books with me. "Reflections In A Golden Eye" was just published, and this, with the attendant publicity made a quite a stir in town and especially at Ft. Benning, the Army Post nearby. Everybody accused me of writing about everybody else, so that I must say I didn't realize the morals of the Post were that corrupt. I want to say now that all of the characters were completely imaginary, as was also the case with "The Heart Is A Lonely Hunter."

The [Ku] Klux Klan even called me and said, ["We] are the Klan and we don't like nigger lovers or fairies. Tonight will be your night."

I naturally called my Daddy and he quit work and came with a policeman to stand vigil over me. At the same time I was attacked with a very violent pneumonia in both lungs and [erysipelas]. I was unconscious for days and only later I said, "Daddy were you and two policeman going through the [shrubbery] around the house while I was sick?"

He explained the circumstances, as I'd completely forgotten the threatening call from the Klan.

At that time another strange and horrifying thing happened to me. It was my custom to get up with my father at 6:00 AM, [tote a few tokens] of coal for the fires and have an oatmeal breakfast with him. One morning Daddy said, "Darling, will you see what time it is." I looked at the clock, but though my vision was perfect, I could not understand the numerals. I went back to the table and sat down.

I said, "Daddy, I'm afraid I'm sick."

My speech was a little halting too, but I was able to say, "I guess it's just a sudden nervous breakdown. I think you'd better call Dr. Mayer." Dr. Mayer was a dear friend of mine who practiced in New York, and whom I'd met several years before.

So Daddy reached him in his office and William prescribed just quiet and more quiet. No drugs, alcohol or anything toxic; just rest. I stayed in bed for a few days, and with the [doctor's] permission, I went out in the yard. When I tried to read I realized the pages meant nothing to me. Mother blamed it on [*Crime and Punishment*] which I'd been reading and took it away, but no book made any sense to me. I was soon able to call the [doctor] and ask if this was to be permanent, and he assured me it would not be. So I rested those dreadful months praying that my senses would come back to me.

Then a marvelous thing happened, I conceived "A Tree, A Rock, A Cloud," and soon I got to the typewriter and began to write. It seemed that the horror disappeared almost as quickly as it came. I remember when I finished "A Tree, A Rock, A Cloud," I burst out crying with thanksgiving and emotion, but the sinister illness that haunted my life all during my youth till the time I was twenty-nine had asserted itself. I lived in a constant fear of strokes.

After I had recovered, and the recovery was complete, I returned to Brooklyn, and wrote a few articles to cover my medical expenses; including "Brooklyn Is My Neighborhood," which was published in [*Vogue*] in March of 1941.

Sand Street in Brooklyn always had tender memories for me, imbued as it was with the recollections of Walt Whitman and Hart Crane, and it was at a bar in [Sand] Street, in the company of W. H. Auden and George Davis that I saw and was fascinated by a remarkable couple. Among the customers there was a woman who was tall and strong as a giantess, and at her heels she had a little hunchback. I just observed them once, and it was not until some weeks later that the illumination of "The Ballad of the Sad Cafe" struck me.

What are the sources of an illumination? To me, they come after hours of searching and keeping my soul ready. Yet they come in a flash, as a religious phenomenon. "The Heart Is A Lonely Hunter," had such an illumination, beginning my long search for the truth of the story and flashing light into the long two years ahead.

On a Thanksgiving Day where again I was living in Brooklyn Heights, the day had started miserably; never very sensible about pounds and arithmetic, I had bought a small turkey and the guest list was about twenty people. After some dirty looks at me George just picked up the turkey, took it out of the house, and exchanged it for an enormous bird more suitable for the occasion. I remember we had as our guests Aaron [Copland], Gypsy Rose Lee, a whole contingent of the Russian Ballet as well as our usual household. Just as we were having Brandy and coffee there was the sound of fire engines. Gypsy and I lit out to find the fire which was nearby. We didn't find it, but the fresh air after the long, elaborate meal cleared my head and suddenly, breathlessly I said to Gypsy, "Frankie is in love with the bride of her brother and wants to join the wedding."

"What!" Gypsy screamed, as until that time I had never mentioned Frankie or my struggle to solve "The Member of the Wedding." Until that time, Frankie was just a girl in love with her music teacher, a most banal theme, but a swift enlightenment kindled my soul so that the book itself was radiantly clear.

"What!" Gypsy screamed again. "What were you saying?"

But not able to explain it to her I only said, "Oh! Nothing."

I frequently spent the night with Gypsy as she was great company;

witty, kind, very sensible, and utterly true to herself. Sometimes I would go to the theatre with her, but usually I went to bed early, as I was an early riser. Several times at about dawn someone would knock softly at her door and she would let the person in. He was a rather measly looking person, but behind him there were always two strong men, who had the look of bodyguards. He was introduced to me as Mr. Wexler.

"Who's her?" [he] asked in a tone of trepidation.

"A friend of mine."

I went back to bed and looked at the silver light breaking in the city dawn. Then I looked down and saw a car as long as a hearse, and there were two more strong men at the entrance. I could not help but wonder.

Finally one day I said to Gypsy, "Who is Mr. Wexler?"

"He's a very lonely man," she [said.] "He squealed and was sent to Sing Sing. Do you understand that? He's just come out."

"How did you happen to know him?"

"He was very kind to me in my youth; made my mother straighten my teeth, and things like that."

"But who is [he?"] I insisted.

"If you must know he is Waxy Gordon, the [gangster."]

I never heard of him, but didn't ask any more questions. A few weeks later he was shot down near Gypsy's neighborhood.

The blessed light of "The Ballad of the Sad Cafe" started me writing again, and so I went home to Georgia to be free of any distractions. It was hard for my mother to understand my homesickness.

"You have the most distinguished friends of anyone I know and yet you just want to stick here with your father and me."

I loved my home with its garden and the old familiar furniture. I had a few friends in Columbus, Helen Harvey and Kathleen Woodruff, and several others, but mostly I got up at 6 AM and worked all morning. I had a piano in my own bedroom and spent most of the afternoon playing it or reading. Occasionally a friend would come and get me and we would go out together, but on the whole Columbus gave me that same tranquility and calm that was so necessary to my work.

I was waiting, of course, as the world was waiting. Waiting for news of the war. Now and then a service man from Ft. Benning would come to call on me. Once when one of these officers said, "How would you like to fly down to the Gulf of Mexico and come back for dinner," the horror of the proposal must have been reflected in my face, for I am deathly afraid of heights; I just tamely turned the conversation to the ice tea and sandwiches we were eating.

[Edwin Peacock] was in Alaska, Reeves at a point unknown. I waited for a telegram and every telegram made me tremble.

[Erika] Mann had persuaded [Annemarie] to go to a hospital in Westchester, where hopefully the doctors would be able to treat her addiction. I'd been home only a day or so when a wire came. It was not the wire I had been dreading about Reeves, but an almost equally upsetting one. "Have escaped from Blithe View. Staying at Freddy's,[24] (Freddy was an old mutual friend.) What shall I do now?"

I packed my still almost unpacked bags and went by train to Freddy's apartment in New York. Since Freddy had no room for such sudden accommodation, he had draped a sheet between his studio where he saw his clients and [Annemarie's] cubicle. When I arrived [Annemarie] was playing Mozart, the same Mozart over and over. She wanted me to call various people, including Margot [von] Opel, and even, so irrational she was, Gypsy Rose Lee.

I tried to calm her but she was in no mood to listen. I went to sit with Freddy and discuss the situation. As we were quietly talking [Annemarie] rushed into Freddy's bathroom, banging the door. As Freddy and I sat there perturbed and frozen, we saw a thin trickle of blood come through the door sill of the bathroom. Freddy tried to lunge his way into the bathroom and he said to me, "Find a doctor."

I rushed downstairs in search of a doctor, and in my confusion I collided with a special delivery man who said, "What's the hurry?"

[I] said, "Tell me a doctor near here because a friend has just tried to commit suicide."

He rushed passed me leaving me to hunt for a doctor myself. After knocking at apartment doors I finally found one, but when I went to his office, he was out. Then I went back to Freddy's to find what I could do next. When I entered the apartment there were about ten policemen there and [Annemarie] turned on me and said, "Why did you call the police?"

"I didn't," I said, but I was too upset to try to explain further. They were going to take her to Bellevue and she was resisting. I talked desperately.

"Haven't you police officers ever known anyone who was hurt or [crippled?] This girl is far from home, a stranger here, in the middle of a war, unable to get home and distressed. Haven't you ever had a friend or relation who has been so distressed that they momentarily wanted to take their own [life?"]

Meanwhile, her own doctor who had been called was sewing [Annemarie's] wrist and she was clutching me with her good hand.

24. The identity of Freddy is unknown.

"If you have any pity, and I'm sure you do, I would let this girl be free in the hands of her own physician, who will do better. Since he is German and speaks her language he will treat her with kindness and understanding."

I must say her doctor gave me a strange and malicious look because he had no idea what had really happened or who I was.

Freddy said to me, "Go home, darling."

As I went out the door [Annemarie] followed me, "Thank you, my liebling," she said and she kissed me. It was the first and last time we ever kissed each other.

Much later Freddy told me that the officers had to drag her downstairs as she held desperately to every bannister. I couldn't have stood that.

Once she was in Bellevue she was the kindest and most cooperative of patients. She saw to the needs of the other patients and encouraged them, but she wrote me that she could not live a hospital life, and therefore decided to leave America and go to Lisbon. After that she did not know what she was going to do. She eventually joined the Free French and worked with de Gaulle forces in the Congo where a statue of her was made by a native. John La Touche,[25] who was a mutual friend, mentioned that statue and said he wished he could have taken it home to me, but the natives had worshipped it as a sort of tribal [deity].

To my great relief she wrote she was going to return by way of Lisbon to Switzerland. There she hoped to work and live in a little peasant's house her father had bought for her, which she always considered as home. We'd exchanged many letters and she was always speaking of new travels, involved in the war as she was, and I was always hoping to God that she would stay home and work. All the letters of the last few years had been clear, completely rational and there was no trace of any taint of morphine. Indeed, I don't think she could [have] gotten it even if she had wanted to. Although she had experienced many horrible times, which she would refer to me, such as when she wrote from the Congo: "I have seen an old ugly woman who has killed and eaten her husband," she must have been completely cured of her addiction. Her letters were powerful and poetic.

"When I came up the Congo from Leopoldville, seven days on a small river boat, I got very frightened looking day and night at the jungle, it is just like an ocean of green, walls of green on both sides of the stream, green all around, and no open space, no horizon. Then I stayed some twelve days in a river post, where among the forty whites there were very few not hopelessly

25. John La Touche Treville (1917–1956), American lyricist and librettist.

drinking—they didn't react any more. Then I had some two hundred miles through the jungle in order to reach Molanda, and here I found a wide area cleared, planted, inhabited by only two whites. I got a big straw covered house all to myself, and at once I learned to react against this dreary, tired depression, in spite of the climate, in spite of loneliness, in spite of all,—it is like a stream of pride, and like learning the very first and simple rules of life."

From Switzerland she wrote the last of her many beautiful letters.

"Thank you forever. Should I return, I shall with your permission, translate ['Reflections In A Golden Eye.'] Carson, remember our moments of understanding, and how much I loved you. Don't forget the terrific obligation of work, be never seduced, write, and darling, take care of yourself, [as] I will. (I wrote, in Sils, a few pages only, you would like them,) and never forget, please, what has touched us deeply.
Your [Annemarie,] with all my loving affection."

I think there was a dichotomy in her relation; one part of her wanted to serve in the war as [a correspondent], and another part wished equally to go on with her poetry and live at her home in Sils Maria.

It was about this time that I had a telegram from Klaus Mann that [Annemarie's] bicycle had plunged over a ravine and she was knocked unconscious. She died in a hospital in Zurich without regaining consciousness.

I was living at Yaddo completely alone in a small cottage, and I was free to grieve and remember. I have talked much of her morphine addiction which was for some years dreadfully important to her, but I want to add that even in spite of that most crippling handicap, she became a Dr. of Philosophy at the University of Zurich, and at a time of crisis, she was always ready and willing to do even more than her part. I don't know of a friend whom I loved more, and was more grieved by her sudden death.

I was still working on "Member of the Wedding" when with a sudden voltage I remembered the hunchback and the giantess. There was a strong impulse to write that story, suspending "Member of the Wedding," so I went back to Georgia to write "The Ballad of the Sad Cafe." It was a torrid summer and I remember the sweat pouring off my face as I typed, worried that I'd broken faith with "Member of the Wedding," to write this short novel. When I finished the story I jerked it out of the typewriter and handed it to my parents. I walked for several miles while they read, and when I'd come back I could see from their faces that they'd liked it. It was always my father's favorite work.

Fall had finally come after the gruelling heat, and I would walk to a hill near my house and pick up pecans and put them in my leather jacket. The family looked forward to fruit-cake baking days which was a great occasion in my family as mother would bake about a dozen enormous ones and send them to relatives.

It must [have] been about this time when a fire completely demolished our home. I was reading Dostoevsky in bed when I heard a crackling sound. I thought it was my brother playing with his friends and so I said, ["Pipe] down [Brother], I can't even read."

Then the ceiling of my bedroom began to smoke and cinders fell down. I hopped out of bed and ran next door sounding the alarm. Nobody ever knew how it started except Lucille, who was our maid, and who might have put some trash in the stove before she went home.

For three or four months we were homeless and lived in an apartment in the city. Then the old house was rebuilt, and by then we were sick of apartments and were glad to get home.

In spite of the interruptions of the fire I was able to send my manuscript of "Ballad of the Sad Cafe" to the publisher, and it was included by Martha Foley in "The Best Short Stories of 1944."

I have used the word "illumination" several times. This might be misleading, because there were so many frightful times when I was totally "un-illuminated," and feared that I could never write again. This fear is one of the horrors of an author's life. Where does work come from? What chance, what small episode will start the chain of creation?

I once wrote a story about a writer who could not write anymore, and my friend Tennessee Williams said, "How could you dare write that story, it's the most terrifying work I have ever read."[26]

I was pretty well sunk while I was writing it, and was thoroughly glad when it was finished. If my patient readers will bear with me, let me recount the illuminations as they happened to [me: in] "The Heart [Is] a Lonely Hunter," after years of frustration, I was walking up and down a rug, when suddenly I realized that Singer was a deaf mute. In "Member of the Wedding," I had rushed out in the street because of the sudden fire alarm that Thanksgiving afternoon, and the wintry air after the heavy dinner had somehow, I don't know how, illuminated my heart. "Clock Without Hands," was more orderly and I had even written several pages of outline to guide me, so that there were one

26. "Who Has Seen the Wind?" the story which formed the basis of McCullers's play, *The Square Root of Wonderful*, was published in the September 1956 issue of *Mademoiselle*.

thousand illuminations instead of just one. "Reflections in a Golden Eye," came because quite at random when my husband had said there was a peeping-tom at the base nearby. At that time I was nursing Reeves with an infected foot, and when I went to the market I was so sleepy that I fell asleep leaning on the counter. The market man took me back home. "A Tree, A Rock, A Cloud," came after a long period of sickness in which I'd actually picked up a stone, looked at a tree and suddenly the magic illumination came. I will not write more about illuminations because they are so mysterious and because I don't understand them any more than my readers do. I'm just fascinated by them. I cannot explain them, I can only say that for me they come after months or years of struggling with a book, and there are more months and years following the illuminations until the work is completed.

I have been asked if I realize the quality of my work while I'm doing it. I would say that I'm so busy working that I'm no judge until it's finished. Then I have a fairly good idea, but of course, the critics might have quite opposite notions. I never read my reviews. If they're good they might give me the big-head, and if they are unfavorable I would be depressed. So why bother? Of course, friends filter in information that gives me a fairly accurate idea of what is taking place.

I have also been asked how I know that I have reached the end of a [book.] Since I usually write the ending long before the final chapters are anywhere nearly done, this gives me no trouble. In "Clock Without Hands" I wrote the last paragraph first, but in "The Heart [Is] a Lonely Hunter" I followed more or less in chronological order.

To come back to the "non-illuminations," the soul is flattened out, and one does not even dare to hope. At times like this I've tried praying but even prayers do not seem to help me. I remember the fallow times of other authors and try to draw comfort from them.

I want to be able to write whether in sickness or in health, for indeed, my health depends almost completely on my writing.

This has been a time of waiting for me. The doctors have all decided that my crippled leg must be amputated. They cannot do it right away because the hospitals are so full, and I must wait for my own team of doctors at Harkness Pavilion. So in the nights of glare I just cuss out the doctors for making me wait, and cuss out my leg for hurting so. I have read Sarah Bernhardt[27] and her superb gallantry and courage

27. Sarah Marie-Henriette Bernhardt (1844–1923), French actress.

have comforted me. They are going to chop off the leg so I can have more mobility and can get from the bed to the wheel-chair more easily. I've already made out a round of travels. First, to my doctor's home, Dr. Mary Mercer, with my faithful Ida Reeder who always [accompanies] me. Since I had such a grand time at Mr. John Huston's estate in Ireland this spring of 1967, and since he's invited me to come whenever I like, I am planning to visit him again as soon as my leg is healed. I just plan trips in my mind, and every single person whom I've broached about staying with them have been most welcoming. So after three years in bed, I will be able to travel again.

All the time during World War II, Reeves's letters were constantly harping on marriage. I was still reluctant about remarriage, although the subject was always uppermost in our letters. I think if I had just had a friendly, non-possessive relationship with Reeves, his life would not have ended in such disaster. But he was most determined to possess me. For instance, I was going to take a trip to England because my doctor said I needed a holiday, so I boarded a ship, but the first day out I saw someone, out of the corner of my eye, that looked a little bit like Reeves, and since I thought I was alone on the ship, I dismissed it and thought Reeves has really run me crazy this time so I'll have to go to an analyst when I get to London. The same apparition occurred on the second and on the third day there was a letter saying that he was on the boat, and that he was going to jump overboard unless I would reconcile with him. These threats and emotional blackmail became a daily pattern. If I wouldn't take him back he would kill himself; the same refrain. I was hesitant to give a curt and truthful answer. I was always so afraid he would actually fulfill his threats, which in the end he did. I had to handle him like a spoiled brat, conceding to everything, so that the dignity of our marriage was quickly being destroyed.

I thought very much about Reeves; first, he was the product of a broken home, but he even played on that for my sympathy. Another thing, not one of the McCullers family was honest. When I let his mother use my house in Nyack, when we were abroad, she took all of my lily of the valley. A bed that was more than a century old. She also helped herself to all my bulbs, and gave them all to her daughter. I guess Reeves came by his dishonesty honestly.

Being with Reeves spoiled all my pleasures on board, although I loved boats. When I got to London I finally persuaded him to go back home and stop following me. He went back and stayed with my mother.

When in London I met the wife of my publisher who was an analyst, and she proposed to cure me within six months.[28] I would have listened to anybody with such a proposition, and I was hypnotized at St. George's Hospital for reasons that were not too clear to me. Tennessee joined me in London and he felt the whole idea of hypnosis was highly irregular, but I was willing to give anything a try. Unfortunately, my doctor was a manic depressive and later committed suicide. My health was neither helped nor hurt by the experience.

While in London I wrote the long poem, "The Dual Angel," and I met my dear friend David Garnett and his family. Also, I became friendly with Dame Edith Sitwell, and it was a friendship that would last until her death. I went to lunch every day with her at the Sesame Club to which she [belonged. There also] I met many prominent people, such as David [Gascoyne][29] and of course, Sir Osbert Sitwell.[30]

After awhile I got very homesick for my mother, and Tennessee put me on the plane. I especially remember the stars on that flight and my bewilderment about what to do with Reeves.

No sooner had I returned home than Reeves started again about marriage. I don't know why I felt I owed such devotion to him. Perhaps it was simply because he was the only man I had ever kissed, and the awful tyranny of pity. I knew he was not faithful to me sexually, but that did not matter to me, nor am I an especially maternal woman. As I started to say before, we might have been far far happier as casual friends. But that's not the way it happened. For some reason, certainly against my will, we became deeply involved with each other again and before I really knew what had happened, we were remarried.

Restless as always, Reeves wanted to go back to Europe. I mentioned that he should take a job at home, but that made him more eager to leave than ever. So in 1946 we went to Paris.

First we stayed with Edita and Ira Morris at their splendid chateau near Paris. I tried to write, but somehow I did not feel very well and nothing I wrote seemed to satisfy me. Then one day I noticed that my lateral vision was affected. Immediately I sensed what it was, a second of those terrifying strokes. I went to the hospital in Paris and the doctor confirmed it. They said it was a very peculiar case, because they never

28. Katherine Hammond Cohen, wife of Dennis Cohen of London's Cresset Press.
29. David Gascoyne (b.1916), British poet.
30. Sir Francis Osbert Sacheverell Sitwell (1892–1969), poet, writer of fiction and autobiography, brother of Edith Sitwell.

Carson and Reeves in Venice, Italy. Used by permission of the Photography Collection, Harry Ransom Humanities Research Center, the University of Texas at Austin.

"The property was the most beautiful piece of land I've ever seen. It was called 'L'Ancienne Presbytere,' and was the place where the former curé used to live. An old stone house overlooking the small cathedral. The orchard had plums, pears, peaches, figs, green gage plums, and even small walnut trees which rattle in the wind." Used by permission of the Photography Collection, Harry Ransom Humanities Research Center, the University of Texas at Austin.

heard of a person having strokes at my age. The vision was never restored. After a short stay in the hospital, I decided I wanted my own home in France.

The property was the most beautiful piece of land I've ever seen. It was called "L'Ancienne [Presbytere,"] and was the place where the former curé used to live. An old stone house overlooking the small cathedral. The orchard had plums, pears, peaches, figs, green gage plums, and even small walnut trees which rattle in the wind. The house even had central heating of a sort, as an American had restored it and had lived there. We had a very good French couple to look after the household and a gardener. There was a fire place in every room and our dogs, we had five boxers at the time, loved to doze before the fire, between swift sorties to investigate other smells from Madame Joffer's kitchen. In true French fashion, the Joffers fed us enormously. First soup, then a [soufflé], then meat and salad, and a fruit dessert. I've tried to find the recipe for Madame Joffer's vegetable soup, the world over, but without success. It was a small house, but Reeves and I had separate bedrooms and there was a guest room.

At this time Reeves said he was writing a book, which delighted me, so I built him a studio in one of the [*dépendances*]. Every day he would go faithfully "to work" in his studio. I realized he was always rather tight at lunch, but didn't wonder too narrowly until I also realized that his studio was right over the wine and liquor cellar, which meant he only had to walk down a flight of stairs and bring up a jug whenever he wanted to. There was a further disappointment. I must say that in all of his talk of wanting to be a writer, I never saw one single line he'd ever written except his letters. Reeves' temper became more violent, and one night I felt his hands around my neck and I knew he was going to choke me. I bit him on his thumb with such violence that the blood spurted out and he let me go. The disappointment and the [dreadfulness] of those days might well have caused the last and final stroke from which I suffered.

I left L'Ancienne [Presbytere] for a few days to recover my balance and to visit my old friends, Richard and Ellen Wright, in Paris and while there, alone in the house, this final stroke happened. I was just going to the bathroom when I fell on the floor. At first it seemed to me that the left side of my body was dead. I could feel the skin clammy and cold with my right hand. I screamed, but no one answered, no one was there. I lay on the floor, helpless, from about eight in the evening all through the night until dawn, when finally my screams were heard. I was rushed to the American Hospital where my good friend Bob Myers took care of me. After a short stay, I was flown home and went to the Neurological Institute at Columbia Presbyterian Hospital. This was in 1947, and the effects of that stroke have never left me.

Mother, bless her heart, felt that steak would cure my stroke, so I had steak for lunch, steak for dinner, and even sometimes steak for breakfast. Finally, a doctor explained to her that diet had nothing to do with my strokes.

["It's] all so queer," Mother [said.] "Just so queer. Before Carson left for Paris, she was running upstairs, she worked up in the attic room, and I could hear her bounding up and chasing down for lunch, and I'm sure too much activity—she would go for long walks also—was part of the cause of her illness, but then who knows? But then Paris, where I hear they have wine three times a day, might have contributed. But then, I don't know."

Mother didn't know and neither did the doctors at the Neurological Institute know.

Finally, they discovered that I had a rheumatic heart condition as a child, and indeed too much running around put a strain on my heart so that it caused embolisms. Lying in the bed, completely paralyzed on my left side, unable to walk or use my left hand, I began to brood, and there were many times of nightmare glare.

Then suddenly, I thought back to the play, "The Member of [the Wedding,"] of which I had made a first beginning draft, and now I worked at it with total commitment. I made several minor changes, as one makes changes in transferring a novel to a play, but on the whole it was absolutely faithful to the novel.

My good friend, William Mayer, found a psychiatric nurse who helped me with the manuscript, and by the time I was able to go home I found a secretary to type up the script.

This was grand fun—the only trouble was the secretary had no sense of humor and when I was laughing I had to laugh alone, which is a bit ghostly I must say.

"Don't you think it's funny?" I would say to her occasionally.

"No," she would answer.

I kept on laughing alone.

Finally, my agent found two producers, Robert Whitehead[31] and Stanley Martineau[32] who saw the beauty of the manuscript, and were ready to go into production. One day a friend of mine, Bessie Breuer, brought a young girl to see me. She looked like Frankie, although she had never cut her hair, I could see her plainly in the part.

31. Robert Whitehead (b.1916), Canadian born Broadway producer and husband of actress Zoe Caldwell.

32. Stanley Martineau, sculptor and assistant producer of *The Member of the Wedding.*

"What experience have you had as an actress?" I asked.

"The Rabbit in [*Alice in Wonderland*] and a part in [*Sundown Beach*]."

Meanwhile we talked about the garden and I did not mention "Member," and she didn't either.

It was my first meeting with Julie Harris and soon as she left, I got on the telephone and called Miss [Audrey Wood.] Julie also had called her asking if there was any chance for her to play Frankie. So the producers approached Julie and officially signed her for the part.

Bob Whitehead went to Chicago, in person, to find [Miss Ethel Waters]. She was on her knees in her hotel room when Bob came in.

"I'm just praying that God will give me a good booking," she said. She had read the play and had turned it down, so it was up to Bob to convince her that "Member" was a good booking.

"To tell you the truth, I would never work for one of them little fancy [men."]

["Mrs. McCullers] is not a little fancy [man. She's] a very distinguished writer," Bob went on.

"But that girl Frankie swears and uses bad language."

It was the director, Harold Clurman[33] who was able to interpret the part of Frankie to Miss Waters. The laughter of the audience made Ethel realize that certain passages were very funny, and thanks to Harold she did an excellent job as Berenice.

Brandon de Wilde is another story. Our casting [director was] having dinner with some actor friends when she saw a little boy of seven or eight playing on the floor.

"Have you ever wanted to be an actor like your mother and daddy?" she [asked.]

Plainly Brandon had never thought about it, but with his [parents'] permission, he tried out for the part. Of all the actors he was the first to learn his lines, and he was the liveliest; playing Ghost with Julie in the dressing rooms. He had never set foot on the stage before, and the orchestra on opening night upset him because he was not prepared for it, so that he began to cry. Then after a few minutes he was master of his part, and the play as it was, a three part fugue, sang in the hands of this young genius.

Before opening, the producers wanted the opinions of various people, among them the man who had already signed the contract for the Empire Theatre. They asked what he thought of the play. He looked at Bob and Stan pityingly and said, "This will be the worst disaster ever to hit this theatre or any other theatre. God help us all."

33. Harold Edgar Clurman (1901–1980), American actor, producer and co-founder of the Group Theatre.

I had a funny feeling, a continual nausea all during the Philadelphia try-outs. Of course, I put it down to nerves & went about my business of going to rehearsal every morning & listening to the last [night's] conferences that Reeves would report to me, as I felt too sick to attend them myself. The Philadelphia press was good, but by no means ecstatic. I made one major 20 [minute] cut in the play that very likely saved [its] life.

But when the play finally opened at the Empire on [January 5,] 1950, it was an immediate and stunning success.

I was too scared to go to opening night, so I spent the evening eating [lobster] [Newburg] with Florence Martineau.[34] After supper we waited in the apartment. We waited and waited. Surely the play was over by now, we thought. Later we found that the audience rose, threw programs in the air and yelled and whistled with delight. Julie had to take thirteen curtain calls, and goodness knows how many Brandon and Ethel took. I would have loved to have been there that first night, and it served me right for being so cowardly. ["Member"] finally closed after five hundred and one performances, on March 17, 1951, after receiving many awards, including the "[Critics'] Circle [Award."]

The day after opening night I went home to Nyack immediately with my mother, who had been at the opening. She commented that I looked peaked.

"I feel like [hell]," I said.

"Don't use bad language, darling."

"But I do," I said.

So she called the doctor. He examined me, and after some tests at the hospital he told [Mother] that I was pregnant.

"But she can't be," Mother said.

I was surprised but pleased. However, I fixed my attention on the scene between the doctor and my mother.

"This is God's way of making up to her because of her ruined health," the doctor said.

Mother's scorn was loud and voluble. "You don't know what it is to have a baby," she [said. "It] will kill my child."

"Wouldn't you like to be a grandmother?"

"A grandmother while my child is dead? No! Besides I have a perfectly good grandson in Florida. I won't let Carson have this baby."

"What are you going to do about it?" [the] doctor asked.

"I'll do [something,"] she screamed, "something. I know what it is to have babies and you don't."

34. Florence Martineau, wife of assistant producer Stanley Martineau.

The doctor who had delivered about five hundred babies let that pass.

"I'll do something," she said again, "in the meantime you're fired!"

Mother quickly called Dr. Mayer, my [psychiatrist,] and he was as horrified as she was.

"Get her ready to go to the hospital [immediately.] I will make the arrangements."

That was on a Friday, and we had to wait until Monday for a room. The quarrel between Mamma and the doctor had upset me so, that I miscarried then and there. The miscarriage was not easy. Mother who had some outlandish fear that either they might put the baby back or do something that would kill me in the end, would not call another doctor. So I suffered until Monday, when a taxi took me to New York. The blood was all over the car by the time I got there, and Dr. Van Etten, the chief [gynecologist] at the Neurological Institute said to Reeves, "Why have you waited till now? Your wife is dying."

Meanwhile he was giving me transfusions. Then I was rushed to Flower Hospital and [William Mayer], who was always with me, was again with me holding my hand.

"So there was a member of the wedding," I said, "that I hadn't counted [on."]

After I was over the hump, William sent me to a [marvelous] hospital, where with the excellent food and care I quickly regained my [strength.]

Now it thrills me to know that Mary Rodgers,[35] the musician, and Marshall [Barer,][36] the [lyricist], have joined with me, as the author of the musical book, to do a musical or opera of "Member of the Wedding."

Mary said on the telephone, "I know opera is a dirty word but I'm afraid this work is turning into an opera."

"Don't make it too filthy," I said.

Mary is one of the few people I can really discuss things with on the telephone. I mean by that that she is never in a hurry.

At the moment she has five or six songs and is writing rapidly. Both Marshall and I have finished our work, and we are planning an opening for the first of the year. We have not started casting [and] I'm

35. Mary Rodgers (b.1931), American novelist and writer of short stories, children's and juvenile fiction, plays, screenplays, song lyrics, and libretti.
36. Marshall Barer, lyricist and collaborator with Mary Rodgers on Broadway musical *Once Upon a Mattress*.

just hoping that one of these days I will again see somebody on the back porch and be so excited that I will call my agent, who by the way, is Robbie Lantz.[37] After years of dissatisfaction, I have found him to be a marvelous agent and friend. He has sold all of my books to the films and has taken wonderful care of me for many years.

Although I've been bedridden for the last three years, my life is not without excitement. In June, of 1967, "The Heart Is A Lonely Hunter," will be filmed. Joseph Strick who so brilliantly directed "Ulysses" will direct [it.] In [September] of this year I'm expecting to see the first showing of "Reflections In A Golden Eye." Meanwhile [I'm] waiting eagerly to hear Mary and Marshall's work on "Member Of The Wedding."

When John Huston invited me to go to Ireland this year I joyfully accepted, and the visit was one of the happiest times of my life. John was the first person I told about the leg operation and he was the first to advise my following the doctor's orders in respect to the amputation.

"You'll move about so much easier," he said, "and it will be a blessing to be rid of all that useless pain."

I work hard every morning and read in the afternoon when I have the time, since friends are always dropping in. I usually go to the Plaza once or twice a year where I can meet with my business friends and give interviews. I simply love the menu there, and so does Ida, who of course, is always with me.

I have little cocktail parties specializing in Beluga Caviar with the proper onion, lemon, and egg. Friends are forever sending me goodies. Christmas is always a great time in my life as I always have a big party. Last year I had a beautiful one featuring [André] Girard's ["Painting in Movement,"] to the wonder and delight of all my guests. [André] has perfected a new way of showing his drawings in motion. He is a great artist and his pictures are superb and living on the screen. He has a new repertoire of pictures which he has promised to show to me very soon. He never minds my inviting guests to share them with me.

37. Robert Lantz (b.1914) literary agent, later named, along with Margarita Gachet Smith, as McCullers's literary executor.

"It is easy to blame Saint Subber, but I won't. He is the one who insisted I write the 'Square Root of Wonderful.'" Arnold Saint Subber. Used by permission of the Photography Collection, Harry Ransom Humanities Research Center, the University of Texas at Austin.

In 1954 I began to write a disaster not on purpose, God knows, but day by day, inch by inch I was falling into chaos. It is easy to blame Saint Subber,[38] but I won't. He was the one who insisted I write the "Square Root of Wonderful." But how could I know, because Saint is certainly one of the very finest of musical producers? How could I know a light comedy was just not his meat? But he was the most insistent and persevering man I'd ever known in my professional life. Every day he would come to 131 South Broadway, Nyack. I could see him with a whip in his hand all ready to shove me on. The play was about a writer who had married a foolish woman, and since my mother was failing in health and I wanted to preserve and recognize her most charming foolishnesses, which is fine in real life, but deadly on the stage, I had tried to capture her innocence. But the innocence turned out to be just dumbness and the unsuccessful writer was an extension of all my own fears of fallowness and failure. I was particularly hard on him as I sometimes get very hard on myself. He combined all the most unloving traits that were in me. My selfishness, my tending to gloom and suicide. In fact, he was a thoroughly bad actor. Why I wrote this crap is hard to realize; of course, I had no idea it was so bad. Not until the horrifying first night of the tryout in Philadelphia. Then like an angry hen defending [its] young I tried fiendishly to do something about it. Saint Subber was trying too, so that we had a change of six directors in all, one worse than the other.[39] Nobody seemed to realize it was just a bad play and so all the frenzied hiring and firing went on. It went on till the opening in New York.

As I don't go to openings, I certainly made no exception with this one. I skulked around the theatre waiting fearfully for news. I was wearing my beautiful two thousand year old, this is the truth, [Chinese] robe, and as I passed the theatre I did not even have the nerve to pray.

A couple who had walked out on the show said, "I wonder if she's a member of the play?"

When we went to the party given by the co-producer it was so painful I forget his name, Saint cried, the co-producer cried, and when the reviews were read from the [*New York Times*], they all cried double.

But me, I just sat there stony and crying inwardly, but never with a sob or a tear. At the risk of seeming to defend this utter failure,

38. Arnold Saint Subber (1918–1994), Broadway producer of *Kiss Me Kate* with Cole Porter and producer of Neil Simon's early plays.
39. Directors for the play included Albert Marre, Joseph Mankiewicz, Jose Quintero, George Keathley, and briefly, McCullers herself.

I must say the play read better than it acted. Finally after forty-five performances the play painfully expired on December [7,] 1957.

As this fiasco was not enough for me to bear, my dear friend John La Touche died suddenly of a heart attack at his summer home in Vermont. After I heard this news I had a letter from him postmarked two days before. I remember John's own courage when he had written a play called ["The Vamp"] and it had closed in similar circumstances. His equanimity was superb. I was at that time staying with him and his mother, and I wondered at his grace in the face of misfortune.

After John's death and the death of "Square Root of Wonderful" I felt that God had turned his back on me.

I had slept with my mother in twin beds for all the years that she had been delicate, but one day I was invited by my friends, Hilda and Robert Marks, to spend the night with them. Mother insisted that I should not call Ida and she said she'd be perfectly all right. With misgiving I [acquiesced] to her, and Ida, of course, would be there first thing in the morning.

"You've been confined to the house so long, darling," she [said. "Go] out and enjoy yourself."

I still worried about her in the evening and called and she said she was fine. Then early next day my cousin[40] came. He embraced me tenderly and said, "I have some bad news for you, darling."

My sister had been in the hospital with an appendicitis operation and my first thought was to her. "Rita?" I asked.

"No, darling, not Rita, it's your mother."

I said, "Is she dead?"

My cousin patted my hand and embraced me again.

I could only say, "What can I do?" But even as I heard my own voice, I knew the question was a foolish one. I called Ida at the house, and although she was crying she did say firmly, "Come home immediately, the funeral people are already arriving."

Ida had come to work very early and told mother she would bring her breakfast immediately.

"I'm hungry," my mother said, "[and] cold."

"Wait just a jiffy," Ida said, "while the stove heats up."

---

40. William Jordan Massee, Jr. (b.1914).

She came in with my mother while she was waiting and suddenly, very suddenly mother began to vomit blood. She died in Ida's arms. Mother was only able to gasp, "Thank goodness Sister[41] isn't here," and with her last breath she added, ["It] would be too much for her."

It was too much, almost too much. But my sorrow [led] to the happiest and most rewarding experiences of my life, which was my meeting with and love for Dr. Mary [Mercer.]

My cousin Boots[42] is a very remote cousin indeed. We claim kinship just out of love although there is a distant family relationship. My mother adored him and adored his father. His father[43] was one of the wittiest men imbued with a homespun, tall-tale humor that I have ever known, and Boots has inherited this same genius. He has one of the most beautiful apartments I have ever seen, filled with family possessions as well as his own "objects [d'art]." Whenever I want to give a special present to a friend I call on Boots and he always buys it for me. I can absolutely trust his taste. I used to love to spend the week-end with Boots, stay in his apartment and enjoy his fabulous collection of books and records. He has, I believe, fifteen thousand records and any worthwhile book you can name. I would go into the kitchen with him while he cooked supper. He is a topflight cook and open to [my] curious advice.

I remember one night he invited a very obese and extremely well-known Wagnerian opera singer to dinner.[44] He enjoys late meals and is not very prompt in serving them, so he had beautiful [hors d'oeuvres] which the singer looked at quizzically and asked, "What's this?"

["Just] a little something to nibble on before dinner's ready."

The opera singer was eyeing the dining room, she was not going to spoil her dinner by those tidbits, and so she waited and waited and waited. Finally, about eleven o'clock, Boots announced dinner and escorted her to the table. That night he was serving eggs benedict, but by the time he had seated her and gone around to his own place at the head of the table, he looked up and with horror he realized that the great singer had bolted the entire meal.

I loved twice told and thrice told stories, and so when Boots and I

41. Carson's family nickname.
42. William Jordan Massee, Jr.
43. William Jordan Massee, Sr. (1873–1961).
44. Margaret Matzenauer.

are together he tells me Marshallville[45] stories or more serious ones such as his friendship with Margaret Mitchell, and the tragedy that such a modest and retiring woman could have been hounded by publicity hunters as she was, after writing [*Gone with the Wind.*]

Even as a grown woman I was haunted always by homesickness. My family always took precedence over everything except my own work. Especially I missed my parents and I clung somewhat [limpet]-like to the family. When I was living in Brooklyn Heights there was a family feeling that was dear to me. Mother would come and visit me occasionally. She and W. H. Auden, a Southerner and an Englishman found it very hard to understand each other. Mother, bless her heart, would shout at [Wystan] as though there was something wrong with his hearing instead of the language barrier. [Wystan] is very kind and very understanding. I was once horrified though when he and George Davis took me to the Bowery. The debasement of those derelicts sent a shiver through my soul, so that I ran from the Bowery to Chinatown and got a taxi back to Brooklyn. There I sat on the steps, cold and miserable, until they came home. I remember this story because I just read in the papers that Dorothy Day,[46] who does social work in the Bowery, was surprised when a man came to her with a check. She thought, she said in the press, that it was some small donation from a former bum who was trying to repay her for her past kindnesses. As she rode on the subway she unfolded the check and, to her great surprise, it was from W. H. Auden with a note of congratulations for her notable contribution to social outcasts in the Bowery.

I had fled in the face of all that misery, but [Wystan] had stayed and done something about it.

I also missed very much my brother who is one of the most tender-hearted of all people. He has a great love for nature and the beautiful. I can remember when we had scarlet fever and he was forever escaping from our nurse so he could sit on his potty and look out at the beautiful trees. When we were older I used to follow him to "First Woods and Second Woods," a wooded place near our home. I also, when I was quite young, composed songs for him, and he would always dance to

45. Marshallville, Georgia, town near Massee's Landing where William Jordan Massee, Sr., was reared.
46. Dorothy Day (1897–1980), Catholic social activist, author.

them for me. Without self-consciousness he would just dance as I played the piano. I also wrote plays or imitations from movies when I was young. I remember especially copying [*Rasputin.*] The line that strikes my memory now is the line that Ethel Barrymore quoted, "You're a very cruel man, Igor."[47] My brother, sister and I put on this particular play together. My sister was supposed to faint, and since she was a chubby child, my mother always gasped when she fainted too realistically on the fragile chaise lounge.

When I was fourteen years old, the great love of my life, which influenced the whole family, was Isadora Duncan. I read [*My Life,*] not only read it but preached it. My daddy, who believed with my mother, that a child should read without censorship, could not help but be amazed by my preaching of "free love" to the family at large, and anyone else who would listen. One nosy neighbor criticized my parents for letting me speak so precociously about [Isadora] Duncan and her love life. I can only guess what the other neighbors thought. I begged my father to let me run away to Paris, and I told him I would dance there for the family's living. Running away to Paris—and worse still, me, awkward as I was, supporting the family by dancing—was beyond my father's wildest imagination.

But he only said mildly, "Honey, when you're older you'll understand better."

Although I was awkward, I was the best roller skater for all the blocks around. I was always coming home with scabbed knees or hurt arms.

My brother took the prize for being accident prone. He would climb out the window and BAM! break his arm. We were forever climbing trees and sometimes the fire department had to be called to get one of us back on the ground again. Brother's tenderness never left him as sometimes tenderness leaves a child when he grows up. I remember one time during the [Depression] when there were ten cent taxis. Our maid Lucille, who was one of the kindest and youngest of our nurses, she was only fourteen and a marvelous cook, had called a cab to go home. Brother and I were watching as she left, and the taxi refused to drive her.

"I'm not driving no damn nigger," he bawled.

Seeing Lucille's embarrassment, and feeling the ugliness of the whole injustice, [Lamar] ran under the house, (I must explain here that under the house is almost like a separate room that goes from the front door to the middle of the house. There's a special smell to under the

47. *Rasputin and the Empress,* 1932 MGM film, starring John, Ethel, and Lionel Barrymore.

"I also missed very much my brother who is one of the most tender-hearted of people." Lamar Smith, Jr. Used by permission of the Photography Collection, Harry Ransom Humanities Research Center, the University of Texas at Austin.

house. The dirt is blacker, and the smell is acrid and bitter.) Brother was weeping under the house, but I was torn with fury and I screamed to the taxi man, "You bad, bad man." Then I went to join my brother, and we held hands in order to comfort ourselves, because there was nothing, nothing else we could do. Lucille had to walk a good mile home.

Black and white people in those days rooting in garbage cans. People, kind, sweet people who had nursed us so tenderly, humiliated because of their color. I do not wonder now, as my father used to wonder, why I was a great believer of the Communist party when I was seventeen, although I never joined it, and eventually I became disenchanted with the workings of the Communists also.

We were exposed so much to the sight of humiliation and brutality, not physical brutality, but the brutal humiliation of human dignity which is even worse. Lucille comes back to me over and over; gay, charming Lucille. She would stand at the window and sing a current tune which went ["tip toe to the window."] Blues tunes were not her taste as she was much too gay for them. She was a great one for arranging little impromptu picnics of cocoa and dainties for my brother and me. It did not seem strange to her to fill up the basket that we would draw up to our tree house. All she would say and even this in a gay voice was, "Lord! Chillun! [You're] gonna break your necks one of these days."

Then in the middle of the depression, [Mother] thought she could do her own work and cooking, and so let Lucille go with every fine recommendation. She should have looked into the family Lucille was going to work for because they were abnormal, and accused Lucille of poisoning them. Lucille, with her good cooking! On their word she was sent to the penitentiary. There she was a cook and she also learned to sew and practice reading and writing. I think she got a pretty good liberal education there, and the experience did not harm her. Mother and [Daddy] testified as to her character and cooking ability, but the other people were so insistent and as he was an alderman, she had to remain there for almost a year. But she sewed and cooked and got on with her reading and writing. She wrote us several letters, and [Daddy] sent money for the prison canteen. When she was released she went to Chicago and met and married a fine, upstanding brick mason who made a good salary. Not too long ago Lucille visited me. She had found out my Nyack address. Although it was an August afternoon she had over her arm a beautiful fox fur, and was lavishly dressed. We embraced each other and talked about the old days and her new prosperity. I, too, had become a little prosperous, in that I was making a living with my writing which was a great pride to Lucille.

Since we were grown up I did not serve her cocoa, but gin and tonic, which she enjoyed.

When Lucille was fourteen she had one child, Johnny Mary, who was as big as a minute. This child had an illegitimate baby as a teen-ager, both of whom died at the birth.

I will never forget that funeral. The preacher was so awful, I could have hit him. He referred to Johnny Mary as the sinner, and the text for the funeral oration was apparently "the wages of sin is death." Lucille and her family were hysterical. The coffin was open so the preacher was gazing down into Johnny Mary's face, then we all filed passed the coffin with the little baby in [its] mother's arms, and Lucille got more hysterical.

She screamed, "God! you take care of her, I've done the best I could, and it's up to you now."

It was a hot July afternoon and the fanners had to work overtime. (Fanners are the people who fan the bereaved.) Then Lucille with a spurt of her own vigor screamed, "Lord God they are now yours."

Lucille went on with her life and finally met the brick mason in Chicago, who earned a fine and regular living, and is so good to her.

About once a month or perhaps less frequently [Daddy and Mother] took us children to visit Sis Laura, who had been our grand-mother's cook. Mother didn't like her too much because she'd been mean to her as a child, but we visited her anyway when she was feeble and old. She lived in her minister's backyard house, and before she was so feeble, she was a great prayer and shouter, and pillar of the [Methodist Church]. I dreaded those visits to Sis Laura. There was always an open chamber pot in the room with urine in it, which gave the room a bad smell. Daddy always brought money, peaches, pears or tangerines, and the old eyes would glitter greedily. Sis Laura was very old and she died one night in her sleep.

Vannie was Lucille's sister and she cooked for the people next door to us. Once, on my father's birthday I arranged a surprise for him. I arranged that at six o'clock in the morning, before [Daddy] went to work, he would have a fried chicken breakfast. Vannie cooked the chicken while Lucille made the biscuits. I gave my father what I knew he wanted most in the world; an ebony walking stick with a curved silver handle. The three of us wrapped it very carefully in tissue paper, and at six AM, which was my daddy's hour to leave for work, the fried chicken and birthday cake, which Lucille had cooked the night before, was served with great pomp to my daddy's complete surprise. We all sang happy birthday, and he was enchanted with his walking cane and tears came to his eyes.

He had completely forgotten it was his birthday. He had a small quickie and offered some to Lucille and Vannie before he tackled this great repast. He carried his walking stick all of his life, and when he died I gave it to his brother. Eventually it came back to me, and it is now in the umbrella stand in my hall.

When I was two to six years old I had a nurse called Nursey,[48] and she married and went to live on a farm with her husband. Mother was in tears. Called my father at his store for consolation and was so hysterical about this loss that [Daddy] closed shop and came home. After congratulating [Nursey] on her marriage he said something to mother that I will never forget.

"Nothing and nobody is indispensable."

Echoes of that come back to me when I remember Tolstoy's dying words to his daughter. "I just want to advise you to remember that there are in the world many people besides Lev Tolstoy, and you are looking only at this one Lev."

Nursey was replaced by Cleo[49] who was lovely, but a martinet. The back room was the play room and when brother would spit in his cocoa to make it more, as he explained, she would snatch him up and give him a good shake, "You're not fit to eat with Lula Carson and Helen Harvey, those two sweet [girls."] I was dainty if I was anything, my mother saw to that. She wanted me to be pretty and did her damndest to make me so. I wasn't downright homely, but I was no beauty no matter how [Mother] fussed over me. I would have to sit at the kitchen table and be primped. Since my hair was straight as a poker she tried to make little ringlets, and in so doing only mashed the hair of my head. Every morning before I went to school, she told me to say, "prunes or prisms," because she said it made my mouth be set in a nice sweet way. My grandmother told her that I was the most patient child that ever lived. I hated all this fussing over me, but I knew that in spite of my grandmother's protests Mother would have her way. I was sent to the oculist and [Mother], who dreaded the fact that I might have to wear glasses, whispered the letters to me until the doctor caught her and sent her out of the room. Thank goodness I have good eyesight, in spite of all the reading I have done. My librarian cousin once remarked that I didn't only read books, but libraries. It is true that my nose was in a book from the time I was ten until this day.

When I was about eleven my mother sent me to the grocery store and I carried a book, of course. It was by Katherine Mansfield. On the way I began reading and was so fascinated that I read under the street light and kept on reading as I asked for the supper groceries. We ate

48. The identity of Nursey is unknown.
49. The identity of Cleo is unknown.

extremely well in my family, the usual chicken on Sunday, leg of lamb in the middle of the week, but for some reason we never had desserts. Perhaps that was because mother knew that every morning I would go to King's grocery store and buy six bars of chocolate before I went to school. I would munch on these all during the day, and I cannot recall how many times I was sent out of the room for eating in class.

Thomas Wolfe is another author I love, partly because of his wonderful gusto in describing food.

The next and possibly one of the strongest influences in my reading life is [Dostoevsky]—Tolstoy, of course, is at the top.

As I grew older my love for Katherine Mansfield somehow was lost, and I seldom read her now, but I must add here that as a critic she is often dead right. I remember her criticism of [*The Idiot,*] especially her observations of [Nastasya Filippovna.] [Nastasya] has always been baffling to me also, and I wondered about such a strict person accepting jewels from a man she barely knew. There is a wonderful penny novelette quality of this work. One is just swept away from one incredible scene to another incredible scene. The scene when [Nastasya] lights a fire to burn up the bank notes in front of [Ganya] is almost like a [*True Story*] fiction, but in spite of it, the emotions of the scene make it so real.

Tolstoy is considered by almost everyone as the greatest novelist that ever lived, and I can only say, me too. From his first beautiful book on [war] and [Sebastopol,] all through his long and marvelously productive life he stands alone as a writer.

It is interesting to me to think of the seeds of his stories, "his illuminations." Anna Karenina was evolved because he had heard of a woman who had jumped in front of a moving train and died. The grandeur of [*War and Peace*], a historical novel, which must have brought Tolstoy almost daily illuminations. He was fastidious as Proust in his realism of the styles and fashions of the times, and like Proust he was working on an immense canvas. Great [canvases] are not my only criterion of works of art. I like books small and fastidious as Vermeer, and while we are on the subject of painting, I must say that I deplore my lack of understanding of works of visual art. I think I get along better with the moderns. Henry Varnum Poor, who by the way, is a neighbor of mine and has painted me several times, I get along with beautifully. Also I covet certain Epsteins[50] which I can't afford.

50. Sir Jacob Epstein (1880–1959), U.S.-born sculptor, later British subject, known for nude statues, religious figures, and bronze portraits.

Another author whom I read constantly is E. M. Forster. One of the most enjoyable times I've ever had was when Mary Mercer read aloud [*Where Angels Fear to Tread.*] We both went into fits of laughter. I must add here, that on the subject of E. M. Forster, Katherine Mansfield is completely blind, or for some reason she just didn't like him.

I am completely blind about Virginia Woolf. Try as I may I can't seem to be truly interested in her. This is strange because not only do many of my friends just adore Virginia [Woolf,] but personally I know many of the "Bloomsbury Set."

Elizabeth Bowen[51] is a dear friend of mine. I have admired her work for many years, and when we met in New York she asked me to visit her in Ireland. Bowen Court, her estate there, is not a beautiful house, but it is roomy and charming. Before her success in [*The Death of the Heart,*] she told me that she and her guests had to go to Jim Gates', a neighbor's house, for baths, but after the success of the [*Death of the Heart*] she was able to install bathrooms throughout her home. The bathtub I used had a little floating duck I remember in it. As well as Bowen Court, Elizabeth had a flat in London, and some years ago she sold Bowen Court because the upkeep with [its] very adequate staff had been too much for her.

I grieve over people who have had to sell their homes. Not only Elizabeth had to give up hers, but also my good friend Lillian Hellman had to sell her place, to say nothing of my L'Ancienne Presbytere which I loved so much, and which is now I hear, a dairy farm. Perhaps the most stunning loss of all these friends was the loss of Isak Dinesen's farm in Africa, which when the coffee prices took a nose dive, had to be sold. Afterwards [she] lived in Denmark in an L-shaped house that once belonged to the poet [Ewald].[52]

When I met the [Baroness] Blixen whose pen name is Isak Dinesen, I was a member of the American Academy of Arts and Letters, and I was invited to a luncheon party in her honor. I had admired her so much that I was hesitant of meeting her; I was afraid that the reality would not match my dream, so I waited a long time before accepting the invitation. When I finally went to the Academy lunch I asked Glenway Wescott[53] if I could be seated at the same table with her. Glenway said that she already made a request that she should be seated next to me. During lunch she said she would like to meet Marilyn Monroe, and since Arthur Miller was at the next table I said I thought it would

51. Elizabeth Dorothea Cole Bowen (1899–1973), Anglo-Irish novelist and short-story writer.
52. Johannes Ewald, 18th-century Danish Poet.
53. Glenway Wescott (1901–1987), Wisconsin author.

"That was how a lunch party between Marilyn Monroe, Isak Dinesen, Arthur Miller and I took place." Photograph courtesy of Jordan Massee.

be very simple. I asked the waiter to bring Arthur over and told him of the request. That was how a lunch party between Marilyn Monroe, Isak Dinesen, Arthur Miller and I took place. Marilyn was very timid and called me three or four times about the dress she was going to wear, and wanting to know if it should be low-cut or not. I said that anything [she] wore would be beautiful on her. She actually wore a dress cut very low so that it showed her lovely bosoms. Marilyn sat and listened while Karen talked, and Karen Blixen was a raconteur par excellence. She spoke of her times in Africa and [Denys Finch-Hatton].[54] Karen or ([Tanya] as her friends called her) had black jewel-like eyes. She used lots of [kohl] with bright lipstick on her mouth. Her appearance was more consciously artificial than I had expected, but I soon got used to this and I was left with the impression of unself-consciousness and absolute charm. Toward the end of her life she ate only oysters and drank only champagne. When Arthur asked her what doctor put her on such a diet, she shrugged, and just said scornfully, ["No] doctor, I put myself on this diet. It agrees with me, and I like it."

54. Denys Finch-Hatton, lover of Isak Dinesen, characterized in her novel *Out of Africa*.

When oysters were out of season she had to make do with asparagus. The rest of us had [soufflés]. Many of my friends were quite elderly. Karen at this time was about eighty. I received an invitation to Edith Sitwell's birthday party which was to be held in London. Since I was going to be in Europe at that time I accepted the invitation. I was placed next to my old friend Peter Pears who used to live in Brooklyn with me. Benjamin [Britten] and Edith had finished a beautiful song. She had entitled it "Still Falls [the] Rain," and Peter sang it before the luncheon. The luncheon was very fine indeed, and the list of people who were there to honor her was truly an international "Who's Who" in the world of art.

I had planned to go on from Europe to Denmark and visit [Tanya] but as I was preparing for the journey I learned that [Tanya] had died. Her dear friend and secretary, Clara Svendsen, wrote me of her death and added that she was buried under a [beautiful beech tree,] quite near the ocean.

In some subtle way, which I cannot describe, I think that her work influenced [*Reflections in a Golden Eye*]. Perhaps it was the beauty of her writing and a certain high-handedness that gives me such a connotation.

After two years of work on [*The Heart Is a Lonely Hunter,*] two years of contemplation of certain hideous aspects of the South, such as the white people's treatment of the [Negro,] I was gay as a bird to be writing just for the sake of words and images. It coincided with a visit that Reeves and I had made to visit our friends Edwin Peacock and John [Zeigler] in Charleston, South Carolina. They insisted that I read a book called [*Out of Africa,*] and since I thought it was about big game hunting, I insisted just as firmly I didn't want to read it. In the end they got their way, for when Reeves and I were in the car on our way to Fayetteville, they slipped two books in my lap; they were [*Out of Africa,*] and [*Seven Gothic Tales.*] I started [*Out of Africa*] in the car and read until sundown. Never had I felt such enchantment. After years of reading this book, and I have read it many times, I still have a sense of both solace and freedom whenever I start it again. I have naturally read all of her books, but these particular two are my favorites. I remember at the American Academy of Arts and Letters a friend said to me that [*Out of Africa*] was her touchstone book, and she judged new friends immediately on their reaction to it.

Another writer who was particularly dear to me is Richard Wright. Nothing could be more of a contrast than [Tanya] and Dick were. I met him in the house in Brooklyn when he moved in with his wife and baby. As usual there were no decent places for [Negroes] to live. Later,

"It coincided with a visit that Reeves and I had made to visit our friends Edwin Peacock and John Ziegler in Charleston, South Carolina. They insisted that I read a book called *Out of Africa*." Used by permission of the Photography Collection, Harry Ransom Humanities Research Center, the University of Texas at Austin.

we resumed our friendship in Paris where he lived until his sudden death. His death always gives me a sense of the great fragility of human life. Dick, apparently perfectly well, had just gone to the doctor for a routine check-up. The doctor saw nothing alarming, but that very afternoon he died of heart failure. Dick and I often discussed the South, and his book, [*Black Boy,*] is one of the finest books by a Southern [Negro.] He said of my work that I was the one Southern writer who was able to treat [Negroes] and white people with the same ease. I was so appalled by the humiliation that being a [Negro] in the South automatically entailed that I lost sight of the gradations of respectability and prestige within the [Negro] race.

When Reeves and I were living in a terribly run-down apartment in Paris, without a private toilet and no conveniences, Dick, who was moving from his own apartment and had paid for the [*clef*] of an elegant apartment also in Paris suggested that we move into his fine duplex. The woman who owned and lived in the other apartment was a dope addict, and he didn't want his child exposed to the sight of addiction even at second hand. Of [course] we moved in and the place was indeed charming; an open fireplace in the living room and the luxury of a complete dining room. There was a splendid garden with a fountain. When the toilets broke down, the landlord fixed the fountain first.

When I suffered the stroke that paralyzed me on the left side, Dick was in Nice and he chartered a plane to visit me at the American Hospital and to comfort me there. His mother, he told me, had suffered a similar stroke and brought up a number of children in spite of it.

Before our friendship in Brooklyn, Dick had become entangled with the Communist Party. A native [Negro,] intensely verbal, and an intellectual, was just their meat. They did not understand Dick's complete absorption in his art, nor his independence either, and when the Party started to dictate to him what to write, like school assignments, he was furious and quit the Party.

As everybody knows it is not easy to leave the Communist Party once you're involved, and Dick had many uneasy nights and fearful days; it is easier to join the Party than to get out.

I never had any inclination to join the Communists. For one thing, I'm just not a natural born joiner. The only club I belong to is [the] American Academy of Arts and Letters. Most of the people are older than I, but they are all extremely distinguished. There is not too much formality and when I'm able I enjoy going to their meetings. My sympathies at first were all with Marx and Engels, and when I think about the current riots I feel it's a pure application of Marxism. The Communists have learned very well to exploit, expose and socially enfeeble areas to their own ends. Personally, I would not be surprised if the riots were not communist inspired. Granted, the ghettos must be abolished and decent housing built in their stead. Adequate jobs, good jobs must be found for all who are capable of fulfilling them. This takes education & the [Negro] becomes more & more aware of this, but this unfortunately, will take years of effort and I along with millions of [Negroes] feel time is running out. My house is fully integrated & I try my best to live according to the teaching of Jesus Christ.

Among the great friends I always welcome are Janet Flanner and Natalia Murray, who is the head of an Italian firm that publishes my books. As a matter of fact, my books have been published all over the world.

Janet is "Genet" in the [*New Yorker* magazine,] and she is one of the most knowledgeable of all journalists, and Natalia, a voluble Italian is a good counterpart to Janet. I enjoy their visits and superb conversation whenever they come out to Nyack. Many visitors come to Nyack who have read my books in their own language; a Japanese professor came not long ago; a Swedish film director; English people, Finnish people, and people from wherever my books are published. I am always delighted to welcome them and Ida serves drinks and sandwiches. Newspaper people often come and I try to ask questions of them while they're trying to interview me. Tomorrow a man from the [*Atlanta Constitution*] is arriving, and I will question him about the riots which have troubled me so much. People come bringing their own paintings, and they write to me asking my opinions on all sorts of matters. Sometimes I wonder if they don't confuse me with Dorothy Dix. But most of the mail is intelligent and perceptive.

Tennessee Williams visits me whenever he is in New York City, and to my great delight I've found a real friend in John Huston, the director of the film of [*Reflections in a Golden Eye.*]

When Ray Stark, the producer of [*Reflections in a Golden Eye,*] called in Mr. Huston to direct it, John said "This film could be done in two ways; one, it could be a low budget art film; two, it could be a film using the best talent available. I'm not interested in a shoe-string art film, and I don't think Mrs. McCullers is either. I can only direct it with the finest [actors."] Ray Stark agreed and the contracts were drawn up. John meant what he said when he said the best talent available: Marlon Brando, Julie Harris, Elizabeth Taylor, Brian Keith, and [Zorro David.[55]] Then John came to see me, and immediately I felt his seriousness, and charm and wit. I gave him carte blanche and never felt the least hesitancy. He was in control and I was glad.

55. Zorro David, hairdresser at Saks Fifth Avenue in New York when cast in the role of Anacleto.

The more he discussed his conception of [*Reflections*] the surer I was that he was the right man for the job. He not only was the director; he, Gladys Hill[56] and [Chapman Mortimer][57] had written an excellent script in which they followed the novel very faithfully.

Also at our first meeting John said, "Why don't you come to Ireland to visit me?"

Since I've been in bed for three years, it seemed a little fantastic, [but I said,] "Are you serious?"

"As serious as I can get. You know there are always airplanes."

So at Christmas John sent Ida and me round trip first class tickets to Ireland, via Irish Airlines.

Before I was to be allowed to go to Ireland the doctor made the stipulation that I had to go someplace for a week-end to see how I might stand the trip. So Ida and I decided to go to the Plaza. This was quite a production. The community service ambulance had to be alerted and a stretcher readied for me for the trip. At first the freight elevator at the Plaza seemed to be a problem, but they eased the stretcher around and finally got me into the specially ordered hospital bed.

I saw old friends, arranged business deals, gave interviews and the Plaza food was up to [its] usual fine standards. I peruse menus like other people study a work of art. Anyway, I passed the Plaza test and had the doctor's permission to go to Ireland.

John lives in Galway. He loves hunting and is master of the local hunt. That is how he found his house when he was out fox hunting. (The farmers consider foxes as vermin and poison them, for they are very destructive.) Anyway, John saw this beautiful mansion which was just a shell of a country house. Eventually he bought it and began the work of building this shell into a magnificent country estate. There is plenty of livestock in the pastures. John's horses are magnificent, and he follows all the races. We bet together and he called me last week to say that our horse, "Busted," had come in first and we won fifty pounds.

There was a constant stream of visitors and John is a "Grande Senor." If a parlor maid is not in sight, John opens the door himself to welcome guests. It was in April of 1967 when we were there—still oyster season—and we ate oysters from the Irish channel only forty miles away. Mrs. Craigh served magnificent meals. Her bread is the most delicious I ever tasted.

Since my leg was jutting out, I had to stay in bed all the time, but

---

56. Gladys Hill, long-time assistant to John Huston.
57. Chapman Mortimer, British novelist.

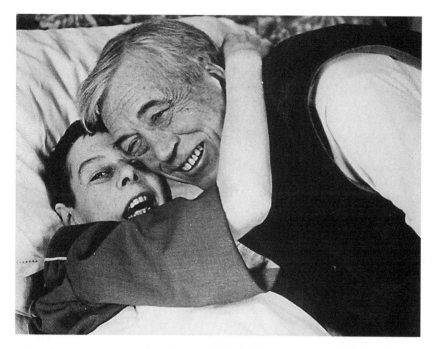

"Several newspapers interviewed me, and the *Irish Times* came out with a picture of John giving me a great big Irish hug." Photograph by Jack McManus courtesy of the *Irish Times*.

visitors came constantly to my room. There was another guest staying at the [house.] The weather was a bit chilly and in spite of a well heated room, the fireplace in my bedroom was kept burning all the time.

In the evening everyone would come in to have Brandy and coffee with me. There was talk of fox hunting, of art, of politics and of course, [*Reflections in a Golden Eye*.]

Several newspapers interviewed me, and the [*Irish Times*] came out with a picture of John giving me a great big Irish hug.

My bedroom had a beautiful head by Epstein. There was a view of the cattle grazing. Sometimes little lambs who looked almost too fragile to stand on their legs walked passed the window with their mother in charge.

There are beautiful moldings on the walls of John's house. When I wanted to have some fancy moldings for my bedroom at home, I was told by the local people that carved moldings were a lost art.

The bed I was in was a handsomely carved one that John had brought from Mexico. There also was in my room a lovely Japanese screen which he had brought back from Japan.

I will be glad when my operation is over and I can visit again John's house, and in my wheelchair go from room to room like folks. There are always plenty of men servants at John's estate, and he himself is very strong. Ida always pushes me in my chair and with the leg off she won't have to be so careful about hurting me.

I have thought many times about Bernhardt, and other people who have lost their legs, but a friend told me about a young man who in a fit of despair, jumped under a train. He lost a leg and an arm. I am not despairing, and don't like to dwell on that story, but rather think of Bernhardt who in World War One visited the trenches and encouraged the soldiers to such a point that the German High Command put an enormously high reward for her capture. Finally she was drawn back from points of danger by the Allied Command who also feared her capture.

Peter Freuchen[58] lost his leg and has lived a full life since. He wrote a beautiful book out of his vast knowledge of the Eskimos.

John Huston is a great authority on Aztec art, and he gave me a beautiful Aztec head as a going away gift.

Cole Porter lost a leg and kept on writing his charming music. I believe "Night and Day" was written in Harkness Pavilion where four times I was a patient, at least the nurses heard him singing it over & over.

Naturally, I expect to go on with my work as always, and look forward to being able to travel and move about with more ease.

I have not written enough about Marielle. She designs all my nightgowns and dressing robes, besides being one of my most cherished friends. She works half the year in Paris and half the year in New York. When she is working in Paris I miss her enormously. She also works in the cotton mill factories in the South, where her designs are [printed.

New York] is about thirty miles from Nyack and the only way of transportation to the city is by bus. It was on the bus that I met Marielle. She is one of my most charming and enduring friends, French, born of Rumanian parents who went to France after their marriage. She combines the wild extravagance of the Rumanians with the good sense and good cooking of the French. But she was too shy to meet me head on. She sat in the back of the bus and only after I was trying to leave the bus did she offer to help me, as I was lame. Then we asked each other where we were [going.] It was in the old [*Square Root*] days and I was going to Saint Subbers. She was going further downtown in

58. Lorene Peter Elfred Freuchen (1886–1957), Danish explorer.

"It was on the bus that I met Marielle. She is one of my most charming and enduring friends." Marielle Bancou. Used by permission of the Photography Collection, Harry Ransom Humanities Research Center, the University of Texas at Austin.

the heart of the garment district. She told me we lived next door and I invited her to drink or whatever the next afternoon. Some inspiration told me she drank only wine, and fortunately there was a bottle of [rosé] in the refrigerator. Our friendship flourished and there was hardly a day that we didn't visit each other.

Then there was a terrible night. I was sleeping when Marielle came in and jerked me awake. Still half asleep I looked down and she was in her bare feet which were cut by the sharp ice.

"Wake up and [look,"] she said.

I looked out of the window and the Gray Court apartments were in flames. We went to the kitchen window to have a clearer view and

I tried to make her go in the living room to get away from the sight. Meanwhile the refugees from the fire were coming in my house and Marielle made them coffee and sandwiches. Then the policemen came calling out all the names. There were three names called over and over but there was no response. Three people had perished in the fire. I pleaded with Marielle to lie down on the studio couch and I would lie down near her and hold her in my arms, but she had seen her house burn, her house with the beautiful paintings, the art collection of books. I had just returned a five hundred dollar copy of [Baudelaire] that very day, and I had also returned the diamond cross she had lent me. Little things like that kept going over and over in my mind. If I had not returned the book and the cross they would have been saved. Meanwhile the firemen were wetting down my house so it wouldn't catch fire, and we were ordered into the dining room. What caused the fire nobody ever knew but everything was lost. Marielle stayed with me until she was able to find a house of her own.

I've never known people so generous about clothing as were the people in this town. Everybody brought clothes down to pocket books with handkerchiefs in them. But plainly, Marielle was thinking about the paintings and her lovely limited editions of Verlaine [Baudelaire] and her poets that she had lost. Since [André] Girard had illustrated them they were in a sense, irreplaceable.

Marielle was stoical, but even so at times she wept. The two of us hunted through the cinders of the fire hoping to find her diamond cross, but nothing, nothing remained, just ashes.

In the early spring she found an apartment in New York. When she moved away I missed her terribly, but she still managed to come for Sunday supper. Nobody could put together left-overs better than she, or serve them with such elan. She would tell me all about her work as a fabric designer and show me her lovely prints.

Marielle was soon the president of her company which operates both in America and France. The fire didn't finish her or even slow her down very much. Gracious, and with the beauty of spirit I've seldom encountered, funny, witty and profound, she's my oldest and along with Mary Mercer my best friend.

Edwin Peacock and John Ziegler remain two of my closest friends, and they go to Europe every summer, and always stop off at Nyack coming and going.

I used to visit Charleston often when I was well. Edwin and John have "The Book Basement," a wonderful store where almost every book can be found. They give beautiful parties, and once at a garden party, (garden parties are very fashionable in Charleston), I met Robert and Hilda Marks. For me, the first of that party was a disaster. My shoes felt queer, and standing in line to greet the guests they felt queerer and hurt. It was at that time, with my feet hurting very badly, that I met the [Markses]. My face was all screwed up with pain, and my graciousness at that moment was quite false. Hilda had a very bad impression of me. Then when that endless party was over, and I could lie down in a long chair, John suddenly said, "Oh! my dear! [Your] shoes are on backwards."

Later I met the [Markses] at another party with my shoes on the right feet, and it was a very happy occasion. Hilda, Robert and I have been friends ever since.

In Charleston, Edwin and John also took me to the Swamp sections with the eerie swamp birds hovering overhead, and to the magnificent azalea gardens.

I met many friends with Edwin and John. One of whom, the adopted son of [Isabel] Whitney,[59] gave me one of her robes, a beautiful Japanese garment which I wear often. I love Japanese and Chinese robes and wear them on all state occasions. I have one, given to me by my cousin [Jordan Massee,] which is 2000 years old. It was worn in the old days only on protocol visits to the dowager empress, and handed down from one generation to the next. It eventually wound up in San Francisco where [Jordan] bought it. John Huston has extremely handsome ancient robes bought on his travels throughout the world.

It irks me terribly to know that I can no longer travel with anonymity and ease. When you have to get from one place to another by ambulance and stretcher, it takes a lot of doing. My friends usually have to come and see me, but after the amputation I hope I will be more mobile.

This week I've been rereading [*Dubliners.*] How such a spasm of poetry could have come out of the grimy Dublin streets of that time is miraculous to me.

[*A Portrait of the Artist as a Young Man,*] I also read every year or so.

[*Ulysses,*] is tougher going, and not my meat, although he has influenced so many writers.

59. Gordon Langley Hall (a.k.a. Dawn Langley Simmons).

[*Finnegans Wake,*] is way beyond me, and I only enjoy the ["Anna Livia Plurabelle"] section, for [its] rhythm and strange poetry.

James Joyce had a psychotic child, and they spoke the same language when they were together. Joyce, who had been partially blind during most of his life, died on the operating table. At the funeral his daughter watched narrowly while her father was lowered into the grave and covered up.

Then she said, "There he is all covered up in the ground, and listening to what everybody is saying. Cunning, isn't he?"

Whenever I think of artists having a hard time I think of James Joyce. He had one hell of a time to earn a living for himself and his family. [*Dubliners*] was suppressed, and at one time burnt, I believe. [*Ulysses*] was suppressed and pirated all over the world, and of course, James Joyce did not receive any of the pirated money. He earned only the fame and the grandeur of a noble spirit.

A friend of my [sister,] who is a Catholic priest,[60] came to see me and, noticing that I was reading Joyce, said that the ban against his work had been lifted by the [Church.] Since he was my guest, I couldn't observe the johnny-come-lately feeling that was in my heart.

Sylvia Beach[61] of Paris, published Joyce, and softened his hard life. He and his children were able to live in comfort.

I wish I could say the same for another lesser writer who is also dear to me. Scott Fitzgerald, always in debt to his agent; with a wife that was mad and confined to institutions. Scott, extravagant, [lovable,] playful and impossible. His genius flourished, and he wrote [*Tender Is the Night,*] in the most appalling psychological situation.

I have been reading [*Papa Hemingway.*] I turn from one book to another. The build-up of Hemingway's psychological problems was indeed complicated, but lucidly analyzed by A. E. Hotchner. I'm not a Hemingway admirer, but for the first time I really realize him as a man, as an alive and suffering person. Fundamentally, he had been joyful, fun-loving, generous and a precious friend. I want to go over Hemingway again now after the Hotchner book. He also was a language path-finder. His short, terse sentences are a heritage to the American prose writer. But what I deplore is his sentimentality, and fake toughness.

I read everything; books on house decorations; catalogues on

60. Perhaps Peter O'Brien, S. J., who visited McCullers during the final years of her life.

61. Sylvia Beach (1887–1962), expatriate American whose bookshop in Paris, Shakespeare and Company, was a center for expatriate writers.

flowers; cook books, which I especially enjoy, and like the [*New York Times*,] everything that's fit to print.

Ida Reeder is the backbone of my house. She was my mother's house-keeper, and she is among my most faithful and beautiful friends. She does everything almost to perfection—even flower arrangements which my mother taught her to do. Since I have tenants in the house, the job is one that demands a great deal of tact, judgement and diplo-macy. Thanks to Ida I've never had a bad tenant in all these years. She is a superb cook, and John Huston just called all the way from Ireland, to say that he wanted her fried chicken and potato salad the day he arrives.

She and John get along marvelously, and when we left Ireland ev-erybody wept: John, Ida, the whole staff. She endeared herself com-pletely to the Irish at St. Clerans, as she does to everybody else.

Since my mother's death, she has taken her place for me, and calls me her foster child.

She concerns herself about me and among her other duties she is my social secretary. She alone remembers the comings and goings of people. She is the one who regulates my daily habits, such as reading and working. Other people come and go, but Ida always remains, and I thank the good Lord for her.

She is less a housekeeper than a beloved friend, although of course, she's a marvelous housekeeper too. I know that at any time, where ever she may be, day or night, if I need her she will come.

I went professionally to Mary Mercer because I was despondent. My mother had died, my dear friend John La Touche had died and I was ill, badly crippled. Several psychiatrists who are social friends of mine, Ernst [Hammerschlag][62] and Hilda Bruck and others had suggested strongly that I go to see Mary Mercer. I resisted just as strongly; not only was the horror of Payne Whitney Hospital still fresh to me, (to this day I sometimes think in times of distress, at least I'm not in Payne Whitney,) but I resisted psychiatry itself, as I did not accept it as a

62. Dr. Ernst Hammerschlag, New York psychiatrist and amateur photographer.

medical science. The last thing left me, I argued, was my mind, and I was not going to let anyone fiddle with it.

Dr. Mercer lived in the county and was a specialist for children I was told. That seemed to let me out. Ida was a firm ally with me. She knew that my sister had been more than a dozen years in psychiatry. Tennessee was in psychiatry and he was all for it. So between Ida and Tennessee I did not sleep very well or many nights.

I had expected that Dr. Mercer would be ugly, bossy and try to invade my soul's particular territories. I would have to call her to make an appointment Hilda and Ernst had said. That was one telephone call I delayed and suffered over. Walking with my crutch to the living room, picking up the receiver, putting it down, and going through all the motions except actually calling. Finally, I did call, and in a low, pleasant voice Dr. Mercer made an appointment for me.

The day before I went to see her I was awake at three o'clock in the morning, and was getting dressed by nine for an eleven o'clock appointment. Ida had tears in her eyes, "Why you're not crazy, Sister, you're just depressed because so many awful things have happened these days."

So, well before the appointed hour, I was waiting at Dr. Mercer's office. The screen door was hard for me to manage and almost knocked me down. I was breathless by the time I actually faced Dr. Mercer. She was and is the most beautiful woman I've ever seen. Her hair is dark, her eyes gray-blue and her skin very fair. She is always impeccably dressed and her slim figure radiates health and grace. She always wears one strand of pearls. Most of all, her face reflects the inner beauty of her noble and dedicated mind.

I not only liked Dr. Mercer immediately, I loved her, and just as important, I knew I could trust her with my very soul. There was no difficulty in talking to her. All the rebellion and frustration of my life I handed over to her, for I knew that she knew what she was touching. When the fifty minute session was over, she asked me what I was going to do then.

"Go home and think things over."

"It's my lunch time," she said, and to my great surprise and unbounded delight, she asked, "Would you like to join me for lunch?"

We never mentioned psychiatry at lunch time. We talked of books, but mostly we ate in silence. She had said in our first fifty minute session, "I love words, but I tell you Mrs. McCullers, I'm not going to be seduced by your words. I've seen your play [*Member of the Wedding,*] but I've not read any of your books. I want it to stay that way, and will not read them until our therapy is finished." Thereafter after every

"I went professionally to Mary Mercer because I was despondent." Photograph courtesy of Dr. Mary Mercer.

session we had lunch together, and that was the solace and high point of my day.

Therapy went marvelously well, and in less than a year, she discharged me as a patient. We have become devoted friends, and I cannot imagine life without our love and friendship.

There was nothing we did not discuss, even silly things, like the time Herman tried to bite the top of my head. Herman was Gypsy Rose Lee's monkey. Gypsy had told me she was going to give me a monkey, and I was delighted. I was staying with her for the week-end and I said, "Where's the monkey?"

"He's with his keeper," she said.

That should have warned me; a monkey with a keeper was not like the cute monkey I'd expected.

I began to dry my hair in front of the fireplace, and suddenly this big, tailless ape came into the room. He took one look at my drying hair, and swung on to it.

"Gypsy!" I [hollered. "Take] this beast off me."

She called the keeper who brought in some bananas. The monkey was still slavering over my head, and I expected the skull bones to crunch at any moment. Finally, he was lured by the goodies and eating them he let me go. For me, that was the end of Herman, and in the fall I bought a boxer pup.

It was more difficult to discuss Reeves; he was hard to live with and harder to describe.

Mary, of course, had no way of seeing the shine and beauty of his young days, only I could remember, and then when his beauty passed into a corruption that I clearly had to realize, I could only describe it, helpless to do anything except advise he go to a psychiatrist. From being a man of glory, he descended little by little to forgery, theft and attempted murder.

Mary understood. She did not think it was romantic when he sneaked onto the Queen Mary and threatened to jump overboard if I wouldn't take him back. She sensed, as I knew, that we were dealing with a potential murderer as well as a thoroughly dishonest man.

[Hervey Cleckley][63] has written a masterful book called [*The Mask of Sanity*,] and in that book I could see Reeves mirrored. Psychopathic people are very often charming. They live on their charm, their good looks and the weaknesses of wives or mothers.

In psychiatry, I realized the first time I discovered him in a theft. I repeated to Dr. Mercer the episodes of when we had left Fayetteville

---

63. Dr. Hervey Cleckley, psychiatrist, author of *The Three Faces of Eve*, and professor of medicine at the University of Georgia Medical School.

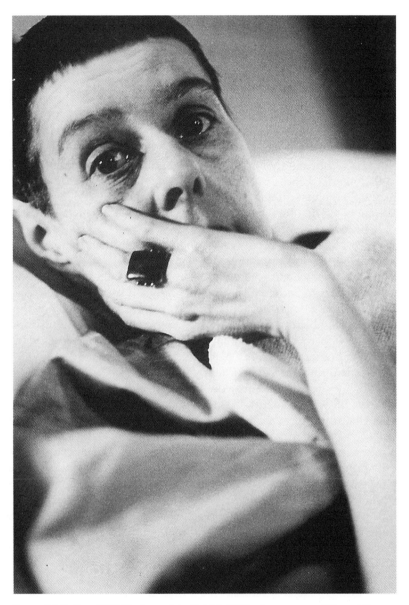

Carson McCullers, 1967. Photograph by Patrick O'Higgins courtesy of *Harper's Bazaar.*

and moved to a room in New York City, because of the imminent publication of my books, [*Heart,*] and then later, the already written [*Reflections in a Golden Eye.*] The world should have felt good to me. I had struggled very hard, and at last my work was finished and I could look forward to a month of rest.

Reeves sold the car which we had no further use for, as he planned to get a job in New York. The morning after, I asked him about the money from the sale and he said he had put it on the dresser table, and that was the last he saw of it. I looked all over the dresser and all the drawers but the money was not to be found. I even went to the landlady and asked if her maids were strictly honest, and she bawled me out. So the first publication of my books was tarnished by Reeves's dishonesty. At that time we'd been married for four years and I could not believe that he would do evil.

I had to believe it a few weeks later. As I told her, I had gone to Yaddo to write, and my father called me to ask if I had noticed any irregularity in my bank account. Puzzled, I said no. Then [Daddy] said a substantial number of checks had been signed by me, and knowing my strict punctiliousness about money the bank wondered if they could possibly be forged. Even though Reeves was dead at this time I felt that I had to describe them to Dr. Mercer to give her a clearer understanding of me and my relations with Reeves.

"But you must [have] had happy times," she said.

"Yes," I said, "I remember one night we climbed up on the mansard roof of our house just to see the moon. We had good times, and that's what made it so difficult. If he had been all bad, it would have been such a relief because I would have been able to leave him without so much struggle. And don't forget, he was of enormous value to me at the time I wrote [*Heart*] and [*Reflections.*] I was completely absorbed in my work, and if the food burned up he never chided me. More important, he read and criticized each chapter as it was being done. Once I asked him if he thought [*Heart*] was any good. He reflected for a long time, and then he said, 'No, it's not good, it's great.'"

World War II Correspondence
of Carson and Reeves McCullers

World War II Correspondence of Carson and Reeves McCullers

INTRODUCTION

Between passages in which she detailed Reeves's departure for Europe in 1943 and recalled her father's death during World War II, Carson indicated, with the words "Insert War Letters," where she intended to include in "Illumination and Night Glare" the letters she exchanged with Reeves during the war. Like "Illumination and Night Glare," these war letters are part of the Carson McCullers Collection at the Harry Ransom Humanities Research Center at the University of Texas at Austin. There are sixty letters and one telegram from Reeves to Carson written between February 1943 and November 1945 and thirty-five letters and four cablegrams from Carson to Reeves written between mid-November 1944 and early May 1945. There are also two cablegrams from the United States Army to Carson (one from June 1944 and one from December 1944) apprising Carson of Reeves's condition after two battlefield injuries. Carson's letters to Reeves before November 1944 did not survive his war service, primarily because as a U.S. Army Ranger infantry soldier he was not allowed to carry any personal items on his missions. As he wrote shortly before his embarkation for Europe, "Tonight there was a sad little ceremony when I burned your letters of the last nine months (we must not take anything that will identify us as a separate unit)." With the exception of a few letters written from Yaddo Arts Colony to Reeves in Nyack following his return from Europe, all of Carson's letters and cablegrams were written from Nyack.

Although Reeves's letters to Carson primarily chronicle his training for and service in World War II, they are also a powerful testament to the strength of the couple's mutually supportive and yet ultimately destructive relationship. Particularly revealing in Reeves's reconciliatory letters is the couple's consideration of remarriage. These letters reveal the complexity of their continuing emotional interdependence despite the fact that they had divorced two years earlier.

The reconciliation that would lead to their eventual remarriage in March of 1945 began with a February 1943 letter from Reeves at Camp Forrest, Tennessee, to Carson at her parent's home in Columbus, Georgia.

Although I am hesitant to write again and don't know just what to say, I must write to you again, I have to. Even though the letter be returned unopened as I never know if you receive it, having put a few thoughts on paper and mailed them to you will help some.

Almost two years have gone by since that rainy, dismal, horrible afternoon when I last saw you. Many things have happened to both of us and each of us has probably changed some but there has not been one day during which your image has not appeared in my mind. You have always been first with me and I know now that no one else could ever mean what you did. That sort of talk may make you uncomfortable so I shall say no more.

I have not talked with or heard from any one in several months who had news of you. I don't know where you are or what you are doing but I concentrate on you and wish you well and hope you have been able to make some adjustment to the times we live in. . . .

If I come out of the war in one piece I should like to live in Europe for several years if I can get a job. . . . I have a feeling the States will be depressing, but then to breathe clean, free air again will probably be good in any country. It would be good to sit with you then and have drinks and talk. If we ever meet again can't we talk together?

This letter does not beg an answer and one isn't expected but I do ask this of you. Somewhere way back in a little corner of your mind I want you to wish me well. I am not religious but that may help.

One other thing I will mention before closing. I wonder how you are fixed for money. I make more than I need and I agree with my Colonel who says it is amazing how few things there are to buy on a battlefield. If you can use any money I would be glad to repay some I owe you by having some sent from Washington each month. There are no strings attached to that offer and if you have all you need well and good . . . .

The debt Reeves mentions in the final paragraph is perhaps the money he took from Carson by forging checks on her account, which Carson mentions as the primary reason for her initiation of divorce proceedings against him in the fall of 1941.

Carson obviously responded positively to Reeves' appeal for reconciliation, for he wrote her on April 2, 1943, without hesitancy, declaring his continued affection and thanking her for her generosity in responding to his letter.

Carson, dear, you cannot imagine what it means to me to know what is going on in your world. How good you are to write me! Our life together in the past was in general so mixed, hectic and insecure and as we both know now transitory in the then relationship. We have come a long way since then and I feel that I have finally grown up. We seem to be much closer and more understanding of each other than in any of the days before. I will never let anything mar or affect the love and friendship that have survived our unhappy times. I hope we will write openly and freely whenever we wish and bring our troubles to each other. I can be an X quantity in your life and I can also be your brass serpent. I am strong and I can be depended upon.

Reeves apologized for his past mistakes and emphasized the mutually supportive and positive aspects of the couple's young married life in a letter from late April 1943.

The main reason I wrote was that I felt that I had changed and that time and expiation had made a better person of me. Inwardly I have changed and I am sure of myself and know that I am a person you would like. Unless *you* are sure of that we shouldn't see each other.

Reeves continued to write Carson as he was transferred for further training in Tennessee, Florida, and New Jersey. As his embarkation for Europe neared, in the fall of 1943, Carson and Reeves discussed remarriage.

Our marriage would indeed give a certain "rightness" to our situation, and I can say this for myself it would tie together lots of powerful drives, ambitions and plans which after the war would make the difference between disenchantment and working hard at what I want most to do. Even if there will not be enough time for us to be married seeing you and the personal vows would nearly mean the same thing—but not quite.

After a brief visit by Carson to Fort Dix, New Jersey, in late October 1943, the couple finally decided not to remarry. Reeves wrote Carson of his final thoughts on their decision in November of 1943.

I remember talking a long time explaining just why I thought our ultimate choice the wisest. What you say in your last letter about our hard-won individual wholeness, our acceptance of a certain dull loneliness (but that loneliness should be piercing for either of us now) and the absolute necessity for each of us maintaining a definite separate freedom for our own different types of expression—in our personal loves as well as in our individual work— . . . all that I know to be true. I have talked and written about this before. A domestic or marital tie isn't for us. It simply isn't necessary and I want you to always realize that I know that it is not. In the important ways I am closer to you than any man has ever been to a wife. You must never have any doubt about us, and, please, always remember how I feel about and I believe I understand you more than any one has.

Since you left the days have been sullen and dark and there has been quite a bit of rain. Today has been colder and the skies have cleared. Occasionally there was the rumble of artillery from the impact area. We have been having marches almost every day but the training has been light and the men are getting fat and sassy.

Reeves once again mentioned the couple's decision not to remarry in a February 19, 1944, letter from England.

I answered your two long letters about us and marriage but apparently you didn't get my letters. It seems you misunderstood me about our relationship and marriage. My proposed plans did not entail any possession for each of us is alike in the sense that neither would tolerate possession. That is one reason why I shall never find the "mate" you so fondly wish for me. Although our marriage was a disaster I don't think it was in any way wrong that we ever knew each and were close to each other. I still feel close to you. Each day I feel your warmth and great spirit and tenderness. I know that you love me. I wish you would understand that I love you in the way that is most important— the great and enduring love of one human being for another. Let's not ever misunderstand each other again on that. You are first in my thoughts about everything and you are my dearest and most beloved friend.

Unfortunately, it is not clear which of the more than three hundred pages of war letters Carson intended to include in her autobiography. The letters included below are those for which both sides of the correspondence have survived and begin with a letter from Reeves to Carson written October 10, 1944, from Luxembourg.

To preserve the unique styles and idiosyncracies of composition of these personal letters, very few editorial changes have been made. To assist the reader, however, descriptive notes are included in brackets in the text and a few footnotes provide further information. All text included in brackets is that of the current editor. Some errors have been noted with [sic]. No effort has been made to regularize punctuation or correct mechanical errors.

The first group of Reeves's letters was written between 23 February 1943 and 1 September 1943, while Reeves was stationed at Camp Forrest, Tennessee. One letter, dated 8 September 1943, was written while Reeves was training in Fort Pierce, Florida. Another group of letters, written between 5 October 1943 and 12 November 1943, was written while Reeves was stationed at Fort Dix, New Jersey. A letter of 13 November 1943 is identified as being written from the "Eastern U.S." and Reeves's location when writing the 15 November 1943 letter and an undated letter while on training is unknown. He wrote a letter dated 5 December 1943 while stationed in London. A group of photo-reproduced "V-mail" letters were written between 19 February 1944 and 19 March 1944.

Reeves wrote Carson two letters just before and after the D-day invasion. One dated "Early June, 1944," was written aboard ship awaiting the June 6 invasion, and another, dated 10 June 1944 (which appears to be a form letter with blanks left after "Dear" and "Your" for salutations), was written aboard the U.S.S. Texas following the Normandy invasion. Reeves also wrote a message in longhand on the back of the typed form letter. Three more "V-mail" letters dated 20 June, 27 June, and 10 July 1944 were written while Reeves was in France serving "on the line."

Another group of handwritten and typed letters was written by Reeves in France between 9 July and 13 September 1944. A letter from Reeves to Carson written in France on 14 July 1944 includes a newspaper clipping titled "No Stalling Features Crazy Ranger Gang," written by Weldon James and distributed by the Associated Press and features a quotation from Reeves regarding his experiences following the Normandy invasion. Two letters both dated 5 October 1944 were written "somewhere in Europe." Five letters written between 10 October 1944 and 8 November 1944 were written from Luxembourg. One letter dated 22 November 1944 was written in Germany. Three letters written in Belgium are dated 3 December (two letters with same date) and 4 December 1944. One letter dated 8 December 1944 was written in Germany. A "V-mail" letter is dated 12 December 1944 and was written in Paris. Reeves wrote Carson two letters, dated 17 December 1944 and 26 December 1944, on American Red Cross stationery from his hospital bed where he was recovering from an injury suffered in Germany. A Western Union cable from Reeves to Carson, dated 24 January 1945, asks her to send him one hundred dollars and relates that he "may be home soon." The remaining letters from Reeves to Carson were written after Reeves returned from England to the U.S. Their postmarks range from 16 July 1945 to November 1945. Of these nine letters, three were written while Reeves was back in New York and six were written while Reeves was stationed at Camp Wheeler, Georgia, awaiting discharge from the army.

[Reeves to Carson]
10 October 1944
Luxembourg

My Dearest Carson—
It is late afternoon and the fog is rolling in thickly from the north. The towns and country around here are so like descriptions we have read of Germany and always wanted to visit. When times are different life is so pleasant and uncomplicated here. The people are about the same as they have been for years and years.

Even if I am dead in twenty four hours from now I have had a very happy afternoon. We rode for a while on business then stopped at a cozy inn in a border town. It was one like Kay [Boyle] described in "Avalanche" on the French border. Clean, fresh, with white table cloths. The people were old Germans but transposed to this country. It was so good to sit quietly drinking Schnapps and beer not having to talk to anyone and look out over the mountains. There was a quiet homey efficiency and hospitality about the place. How I longed for you to be there.

This war treats one strongly. Suddenly in a flash there is an afternoon like this one that makes bearable all the times of drudgery and terror and horror. What a pleasure it is to be alone an hour or two and have our own free thought. It is one of the terrors of combat that impressions are forced on one and there is no freedom of mind and thought or time for the willing acceptance of impressions. Nights are the most horrible of all times—even if there is no firing.

But just an hour or so freshens one and now I am good for another week or two.

I suppose the war is changing me and will make other changes but I won't grow too old. As you do, so do I hope to keep a freshness and expectancy of life. It is all there for us to find and experience. We must never bow to the philosophy of despair.

There are some things I must do before dark so I will close.
Your,
Reeves

[Reeves to Carson]
17 October 1944
Luxembourg

My Darling—
What a beautiful day here! I would give anything I possess if you were here with me. I am sitting in a cozy little cafe in a small Luxembourg town drinking mulled wine and looking out over the mountains toward Germany. The only thing missing to have it nearly perfect is you.

We *will* see each other again, won't we Dearest? It was so long, long ago that we were last together. There are so many long pleasant hours we have to spend talking, there are so many things for us to see and do together. Cross your fingers for us and say that we will.

Although the weather here has been rainy cold and misty there are occasional bright cheerful days. Today the hills are so beautiful with all the autumn colors. Germany across the valley looks the same. The wine of the country is good and warms one's belly.

You will love parts of Europe. I think you would like the little country I am in now. The people are good and very industrious. I haven't come across a poor family here. They are robust and healthy, a surprising number speak English; in some sections the children go to school twelve months of the year. They are bright and sharp and don't beg and whine—but then French and English children didn't use to beg and whine.

At the home where I have a room there is an adorable little Italian boy. He is a refugee whose mother works in Paris. He is the beautiful precocious Cameo type like the boy in "Death in Venice." He is thirteen years old and speaks four languages well. He follows me everywhere and has about extracted all the knowledge I have of America. I wish I could bring him home for us to keep.

At this time my unit is resting and we hold our breath for it to last as long as possible. I am afraid it won't be very long. I feel that there are more horrendous battles ahead than Europe has yet seen. The general prescience is that the enemy will not formally surrender and that we will have to hack them to pieces. Then Japan.

At a table near me four fat burghers are playing cards and drinking beer. A little girl is sitting near the stove preparing her lessons. An old couple in the corner are drinking hot wine and talking about money.

It is too bad that America doesn't allow herself any institutions like the English pub or the Continental Cafe.

Life is good to us here for the time being. The thing missed most is Cigarettes—American. They just aren't to be had. We smoke that stuff the natives remove from the rear of horses, dry out, roll up in paper and call cigarettes. But I hear there is also a shortage in the States. I haven't had a cup of coffee in five days but that's ok—in fact it's fine. I'll undergo any privation in preference to the crump of 88's and the ripping of MG 42's or burp guns. There is nothing so pleasant and intriguing as to sit quietly and reassemble the remnants of one's mentality. Life is good, and sweet. We don't need nearly so many things as we think we do.

Every day I wonder how you are, whether you got settled with Bebe [Carson's mother] in Nyack. I am completely blank of what has happened during the past two months. It has been that long since I have heard from you. I know you have written and probably cabled—but word just hasn't gotten through to me yet.

Write to me when you get this.

My love for you,

Reeves

[Reeves to Carson]
8th November 1944
Luxembourg

My Own Darling Carson—

Yesterday was one of the biggest events for me since D-day. I received a total of 18 letters—this being the first correspondence I had gotten from the States since August 20th. Most of the letters were from you, of course,—the last one was dated October 22. There were several from mother, one from Tom, [John] Vincent [Adams], Kanto [Alfred Kantorowicz], a dun from The Infantry Journal and a request to subscribe to Common Sense. I enjoyed reading each one.

I went into a room by myself to read them and opened my flask of Scotch, saved for extreme emergencies. (The flask is an exquisite thing given to me by a Luxembourger at whose home we stayed some time ago. The first chance I have I want to mail it to you to keep for us.)

Oh, Precious Carson, your letters were so good, good. I have read them all over starting from the first. I was becoming quietly frantic at not hearing from you—although I knew exactly why since I am in another unit and we have been on the move so much. I knew that all during that bleak, silent period you had been writing to me.

I haven't written as often as I should or as I wanted. We have been busy. For a short time now we have been in a quieter sector. Today is really the first time I have got to any reasonable quietness and write. However, artillery is whistling and crashing outside. I won't tell you there isn't any danger for danger is very much present and death is a daily visitor. For some mathematical reason my luck has held good and as of the afternoon of November 8 I am still among the living.

Carson, because of the tone of some of your last letters—your extreme anxiety and frantic worrying—I must say this again. You *must* accustom your mind to the possibility of something happening to me. You must realize that within 100 square miles of part of Europe is located the very center of hell—then you must consider the possibilities of survival. I hate to say all this but I must be entirely honest with you. I know that you love me and *how* you love me and my feeling for you could never change. Believe me, the closer I have been to death, the closer I get to it, the more I love life. When I am able to think of myself my thoughts jump immediately to the beautiful times we shall share and the great future experiences we will have. That is the only important thought in all this madness, the only *idea* I can grasp and cling to. But, Carson, my position is different from yours right now. You have other things to hold on to and you must not lose them.

There are interruptions to this all along but I will write as much and as long as I can. I am only half-hearted about your coming to Europe. It is very sad to realize that if you do get to Europe the chances of our meeting until after the Hitler war are very remote. You see, I'm in the unenviable classification of "combat officer" and they just don't get any time off and loved ones just don't visit them at the front. It isn't in the books, Darling. But seeing you again would be the miracle to return my sanity.

Of your other motive I am not so clear. Down in the slough, mud, grime, and blood one sees Europe now as complete revolutionary insanity. I know I have written several little purple letters about the people in this garden spot. This country suffered less under the Nazis than any other and what I said was true. But, Good God! The chaos in the other countries. The bitter nihilism is incredible. I know you do not have in mind a haven of peace and security for creative writing but when you come here and look down deep you will only see an ugliness left out by Dante and Goya. Most people feel that this war isn't nearly over and that excepting part of France it can swing in any direction destroying everything in its path. In truth, lots of people in

Europe feel that, and only a general complete surrender will convince them death isn't looking for them. When the nervous system anticipates danger and death the body and mind aren't normal or rational.

But if you do manage to get an assignment (and if you wish it, so do I) I hope you are able to go where you have planned and do what you have in mind—*including* our meeting somewhere. If you do come you will probably stop in London. Cable me. Also give me names and addresses of any intermediaries in London or Paris and if the war has ended by then we will find our way to each other somehow.

I have heard nothing from A.M.G. and I fear my papers are bogged down in some branch office file. In the past two months I haven't even had time or opportunity to trace them. When this is over here and if I am not considered as "essential" to the Pacific theatre my nose will stay pointed towards the Statue of Liberty. Then to debark and buy a ticket to Nyack or meet you wherever you say. If I could see you again I know that any problem life could present would be easily solved.

Precious, if you come over you must be careful of your health. Be especially careful to keep warm. Your gut isn't the same as mine so you must mind what you eat and drink. Actually, I hope you get a job to come to Europe for I know it is something you want and feel necessary. I have always trusted your decisions. We both know what seeing each other again means. There is so much we have to tell.

I received Kanto's letter and was glad to hear from him. I want to answer right away. He had some interesting things to say and some pertinent questions to ask about this war in Europe which I will try to answer.

Vincent is living in Orlando, he has three children and is a major in the Air Corps! He can f____ and talk himself into more things than things than [sic] anyone I know. However, I am not jealous of him on any count and feel rather happy about being a line lieutenant. The only children I would want would be one or two I could pick out myself and adopt. It was good to hear from V. If you wish to drop him a line his address is A. A. F. Board, Orlando, Florida.

Tom is about set in California now and ready for school. He has a job in a brewery and says he works hard. He never got close enough to the goddamn Infantry.

All the friends we know in N. Y. seem to be getting along fine and settled except you, me and possibly Kay. Our day will come.

There's no use my trying to say anything about the war. You get news there that reaches me days later. We sometimes go for a week here without any outside news. What happens 1200 yards down the line is a great deal more important at the time for us miserable dogs than happenings 1200 miles away.

I have no conception of when the war will be over. We just sweat out each day and look for the day when word gets around that "It's Over!" But if you explain unconditional surrender to a farm boy from Virginia or a steel hand from Penna. and ask him if he would want anything else—no matter how much action he has seen or what the present action is—he will say "s____t no, let's finish the bastards off." Even the few intellectuals in the company will say words to that effect. That great political innocent, the American Soldier is learning the hard way things he should have been taught in school and college.

I have been with the men I have now for over two months and we have been through a little part of west hell together. They are good men and I am proud of them. Their sense of humor sustains me. There are times when I think my nervous system will split wide open but I only have to look at them and realize they are under the same if not a greater strain and I am able to do what we are called on for and just a little more. Their love and concern for each other is still to me one of the miracles of life.

I must close now, my dearest. You are always in my heart.

As always,

Reeves

Later—

There may be time for a short note. Don't worry about the Christmas boxes being sent to my old unit—they will get to me. Thank you for thinking of me. I shall enjoy your gifts so much. I sent the socks and sweaters because I was well supplied at the time. Since then almost everything I have is worn out and your gifts will be needed and welcome. Do you remember the beautiful blue sweater you gave me the last time we were together in Columbus? It has kept me warm since the afternoon I left England and I wear it all the time. The original color is gone but the wool is still good. It has become something of a talisman.

Give my warmest love to our Bebe. So many times I think of us sharing joys together. The teas and meetings you have with the [Henry Varnum] Poors, Kay, and other people sound so remote and civilized. How I long to be with real people again. Although some are killed or missing I have some friends in England I hope we can find some day. In France and other places I have been on the continent there hasn't been time for other than fleeting acquaint[ance]ships.

Young Armando, the Italian refugee, I believe I mentioned in another letter captured my interest. I saw him again ten days ago and he is more charming than ever. Some time ago I met a Luxembourg school teacher who had escaped after being many months in a concentration camp beyond Berlin. He had some pretty stories to tell. He was very down and out but will get over it, I believe. We shared a bottle of cognac and talked for hours. I convinced him how lucky he was—after all, he is home again.

I must close now and go check on the men. The first snow has fallen and it has covered the ground and trees. It is nearly dark and time for the dirty work to start. There are those who would call the landscape beautiful but it isn't. There is no beauty for the time being—anywhere.

I am sorry to close on a sour note. There *is* hope and there *is* love left.

R[eeves]

[Carson to Reeves]
Nyack, N.Y.
November 12 [1944]

Reeves precious:

Yesterday the postman finally brought a letter from you; it was dated Oct 10—I think you must have written twice on that date. But think of it, darling, a whole month getting here! It distresses me to know that my letters to you are not reaching you. Oh I hope so much that by now you are hearing regularly from me.

Now the communiques occasionally identify the various infantry units. The 29 is mentioned in the fighting around Aachen, and six divisions were named in Patton's assault around Metz. I read every line hoping to come on some news of the 28th—or rather I fear, rather than hope, to read such a mention, for it would mean you are in combat.

It's a cold, bright Sunday here. Kathleen is spending the week end with us, and last night we all went over to the Poors. Bessie [Breuer] had a tremendous roast veal, and some "Southern" dishes—collards and sweet potatoes. We sat around by the fire and drank whiskey and talked. Then, at about midnight, we went over to the Anderson's house, as they were having a party. Henry drove us home about two o'clock. And this morning I feel completely crushed. You know that ghastly feeling that comes after too much drinking, the guilty and hopeless penitence. The againbit of inwit, as Joyce calls it.——If only we could be together for an hour and walk in the woods and have maybe a few beers then these ugly feelings would go away, I know.

Darling, I think that surely the mail situation will get better now. I am hoping to get another letter tomorrow—one written much more recently and telling me that my letters are coming through.

We have had quite a stir of excitement here in the house. There is a young school teacher who lived just over our apartment. Wednesday, the day after the election, she suddenly disappeared. There was absolutely no clue—she had few friends in Nyack, as she moved here only in September. The house has been blue with policemen, and everyone very much disturbed. Her family came down, and it was particularly sad as their oldest son has recently been lost in action. Anyway, the girl was missing for three days—but now this morning the word comes that she has been found, although we don't know any more of the details.

Dearest Reeves, please take care of yourself. I will go out for a little walk now. The trees have a wintry, brittle look and the river is very gray and cold. I'll be thinking of you, as always—

Your,

Carson

[Carson to Reeves]
Nyack, N.Y.
November 21 [1944]

Reeves angel:

This morning the first snow of the year has come. The whirling light wild flakes are at the window; the river is veiled and only a deserted brown little house with two red chimneys is there by the river's edge, looking more lonely than ever. I have been out in the streets—but the snow doesn't stick, and the alley ashpits and wet sidewalks are very desolate. These are the times we loved together. Do you remember, darling, that first snow at the MacKethan's—the way it piled up soft and blue on the porch outside—and how we walked around the cemetery, and later went out in the automobile and drank beer. We always made a festival of our first snows. It is so lonely without you this First Snow.

I still have no letter. I am grown sickeningly anxious. I wait and there's no word. The radio tell[s] of the new offensive—and I hunt for some news of the 28th in all the newspapers. Perhaps there will be a letter in the afternoon mail.

I spent the weekend in town, and came out late Sunday and Aunt Tieh [Carson's maternal aunt, Mrs. Martha Elba "Mattie" Waters Johnson] was still here. I stayed the night with the Morrisses, but we all had a great party over at Kay's. Karen Michaelis was there, and Kanto and Louise Ra[i]ner (you remember her in The Good Earth) and James Laughlin of New Directions and altogether quite a gathering. Edita Morris brought the food over to Kay's, as she was in the middle of moving to a new house. We had lobster and Swedish food and quantities of some strong drink that was kept on the table in big pitchers. We sat down to the table at six and stayed there, except for changes of seats, until about two or three o'clock. I hadn't been to such a party for years—and I must say it was fun for a change. But I kept missing you and wishing for you. I think you would have liked it. The next morning I went back over to Kay's and she was alone in the hollow house with the three babies. I felt sad when I left her.

But it's not very good for me to go into town often—it breaks the thread of work. And you know I am not much of one for parties, except rarely and when I know that work has been done.

The snow is getting thinner, finer. It's cold and the sky has cold blue tones in it. The snow melts to water on the windowpane and the wind rattles the casements. If you were here we would have a cozy drink together and play a game of chess. The next First Snow, I feel that we can be together. This one I'll just try to ignore. I am worried and too sad.

Take care of yourself, darling.

always your,

Carson

[Reeves to Carson]
22 November 1944
Germany

My Dearest one,

It is a cold, rainy, bitter Thanksgiving Eve where I am. Yesterday there was snow but it has turned to slush. What a happy time Thanksgiving weekend used to be! Do you remember? When I was a child there was not just the mountains and surfeit of good food but there were special games, and then one could be gone all Friday and Saturday by oneself in the woods roaming and exploring. The weather seemed to have been different in those days—clear and cold and bright.

There is not much we poor miserable remnants of humanity here have to be thankful for—except the mere fact that we are still alive. But even that has reached proportions of gruesome humor—it is a joke on German artillery to be alive. It is a little strange and funny to be doing something as normal as writing a letter for in the next instant [one's] brains and bones may be scattered by a delayed action shell all over the cellar in which we are staying today. This is the most hellish any of us have seen—even the old soldiers. The din outside is unimaginable—small arms fire crackles like raindrops. The dead of both armies and all nations are scattered all about. You can't see any place where there isn't a shell hole; in what was a fair sized town there is one building left with walls. For two days there has been right outside the door a dead German from whose flank a cat eats two or three times a day. Then it strolls down the steps sedately to be petted. This irritates the men and one will pick it up by its tail and throw it squalling back out where the hell is flying. Once the cat went over and curled up under the German's arm to sleep. It has a charmed life and will probably live longer than any who has watched its actions the past 48 hours.

Suddenly there is an unearthly silence for five, ten, twenty minutes. Then a jeep is seen or someone down the line moves or sticks his head out and the whole goddamn German army opens up. Then our artillery and fire opens up and the 4th of July is on again.

This is the phase of war which statesmen say "takes the cream of manhood of a nation." All the men from a county, commune or burger can be wiped out in ten minutes. This is the war that gets directly to everyone—you see dead civilians scattered in fields, along roads along with soldiers. A house with a roof is a rare thing. It reminds one of Goya's paintings and drawings of the Spanish Wars.

For all there is dirt, mud, cold and extreme fatigue. With all there is extreme fear. For the weaker ones death is a release. The stronger ones fight and hold on until the mind no longer communicates with the body.

A few days ago General Eisenhower released a heartening statement. From it one can hope the war will be over by the first of the year. The German army is almost beaten and will collapse when it gets beyond the Rhine and has to give up Prague. Even here where are supposed to be the remaining crack troops the morale of the individual soldier in the army is poor. Our average soldier would not think of surrendering unless it meant sacrificing his and others' lives; they even dread capture. But the average German looks for the opportunity of giving up. They creep through the lines every night to surrender. However, that doesn't mean that there are not those who will fight to the death. The pitchfork civilians and ten and twelve year old kids operating mortars do not give us concern—that is strictly bullshit propaganda.

It was good to see my old outfit the other day. Many of the men are still living. They miss me and talk of me. It's rather ironical that since Brest they have seen no action while we have been continually busy.

The men I have are good and tried soldiers—and brave. During the night most of us are out in foxholes but during the day we can pull back into the cellar of what was a house. Right now some are sleeping and resting and rubbing each other's feet. (There is such a danger here of freezing and losing [one's] hands or feet.) Others are sitting at the table around a feeble light with me writing home or eating K rations, bitching, wisecracking and gossiping. Now and then one comes out with a terribly funny story, everyone stops, looks around suspiciously and laughs—then the shelling and hell outside doesn't matter tinker's damn.

Darling, Carson, I have written only about things that go on here for that's all I can think about—that's all there is for me right now.

I am not one to write a "last letter" to be mailed to you if I am killed. In the first place I have said all the last things to you; in the second place there is no one here to leave such a letter with—for if I get it he will probably also get it. I am sure that "last letter" business occurs only in World War I novels and concerns only young British officers and privates.

Any last words would be simply: I have known you and loved you dearly. Knowing and being with you and loved by you is the greatest and most beautiful thing in life. I don't think there has ever been another person like you. I would want to spend all the days of my life near and with you. It may be that many more of our days will be spent together.

But, we are both strong and can live within ourselves. It may be the secret of our relationship that we can do this; we would miss each other terribly for some time to come but there would also come recovery. Others with great love lose each other and are brave about it. If it comes to us we will be the same.

Be kind and gentle as you always are. Try to see and cause all the beauty in life that is possible.

A pleasant Christmas and a peaceful year in 1945 for all of us. As ever,

Reeves

(over)

P.S. There are others we know I would like to write but there just isn't time right now and besides you are the one in my mind at this time. Give them my love and say we will have some long talks in the future if God wills it.

R[eeves]

[Carson to Reeves]
Nyack, N.Y.
Thanksgiving [November 22, 1944]

Little darling Reeves!

How happy I am today! The cable came yesterday, just as I was mailing that sad little letter about the first snow. And now *two* letters, the last written only November 8. My God, what a relief! But I almost cried when I read that for two months there had been no letters from me—and if you only got 18 letters, including those from others—then all my mail is *not* reaching you. It's the most maddening dreary feeling to suspect that my letters are lost or thrown away before they reach you.

I love all that you write about Luxembourg. But I think of that Hell of front line combat. No I won't and can't "accustom" myself to the thought that something might happen to you. My mind just can't work that way. You should not ask that. I have to *believe* in life—especially in your life.

Henry has a theory, derived from his experiences in the last world war, that a man's chances are proportionate to his love of life and hope in the future. He has told me of some of the men from his outfit—many of them boys from the worst and poorest sections of the south, with a tinge of the Caldwell–Faulkner fatalism and poverty of spirit; Henry says that the casualties among them were noticeably high. So, Reeves, going a little by that, I *know* you will survive—you have ahead of you so much richness, so many varied promises for the future. But, though I talk like this, I live always under this tension. God knows when this war will end now. No, I don't think the Germans will surrender all in a piece, either.

Reeves, you *must* promise me, that when this European war is over

and they begin shipping men to the Pacific you will take advantage of
all your combat credits etc.——Yet I know I should not put it like this,
as a personal demand. I never want to influence you in any vital decisions you might make. I want you to be on your own; we've talked
about that before. Oh but it would be something to hold on to if I could
believe that you can come home before summer.——I won't whine
any more.

Today is bright and clear. The sun is out, but the air is cold. Kanto
and Friedel [Kantorowicz] are coming out to share Thanksgiving dinner with us, and Louise Rainer is coming with them. I know, precious,
that these gatherings and our little "teas with the Poors and Kay" that
you mentioned are very remote to you. They are remote from me, too,
Reeves. I write you about them because I want you to know everything
that we do—and I know you are fond of Kanto and Kay and the Poors.
But, back to the Thanksgiving, we have read that every soldier is having turkey today—although I won't be too sure of it until you write
me. We've having a big hen with oyster stuffing, country captain (the
new dish I wrote you about), stuffed eggplant, and mother is making
a pumpkin pie. She and Rita [Carson's sister, Margarita Gachet Smith]
are busy in the kitchen now. We have all said over and over that you
would like this dinner. But we are having a much better one the day
you come home. It will really be turkey, perhaps, or a grand roast beef.

I am so anxious to hear from you about Kay's poem. She thinks
that J. is due for another assignment soon.

I will be relieved when this week-end is done and I can get back
to work *every* day. Somehow, as you know, organized pleasure never
has appealed very much to me.

It seems as though my chances for getting to France this winter
are very unlikely. I'm sorry I wrote you about this.

It's almost twelve o'clock and I must write Jessie [Reeves's mother,
Jessie Lorane Winn McCullers] a note and then go help mother and
Rita in the kitchen. Darling—the same little refrain—take care of yourself. You can't realized [sic] what the cable and the two letters have
done for me! Bless you darling.

Carson

[Carson to Reeves]
Nyack, N.Y.
December 3 [1944]

Reeves darling,

This has been a scrambled, unproductive week. First I wasn't well for four or five days—a touch of fever etc. Then Martha Johnson came out and spent Friday and Saturday here—and you know how restless it makes me having visitors in the house. Now though that wretched fever is over and I am altogether well again. And everything is clear again for work.

It's late Sunday afternoon. The sky is a lovely faded rose along the horizon and the air is bitter cold. We have storm windows now, and need them. I worry about you constantly, wondering what miserable conditions you may be enduring now. I've still not heard from you, but tomorrow is Monday and I hope so desperately to get a letter.

I have had quite a disappointment about the cigarettes I wanted to send to you. For some reason one is not allowed to send packages now that Oct. 15 is over. It seems that one is supposed to have a written request from the receiver in order to send packages now to France. It seems queer—I don't understand it. However, I read in the paper that overseas troops are now getting five packages per week. And surely there are some non smokers in your company who can give you a pack or so in addition.

This afternoon I read Evelyn Waugh's "A Handful of Dust"—a brilliant book. I wonder that I'd never read it before.

Annie Poor hopes to go to China soon. Sometimes I feel so restless and isolated. I long to be in France or—almost anywhere. But I'll try to be better and work hard. Maybe later someone will give me a correspondent's job.

I have missed you especially today—as I always do on Sundays. I think of all the things we could do together—the books we could read, the walks in the late afternoon together, the cozy feeling of a winter Sunday night.

Take care of yourself, dearest. Please write me soon. I worry so when there are gaps between your letters.

It's time now for the six o'clock news and I go into the other room now. Goodbye for the time being, Reeves. Remember how tenderly I love you.

Carson

[Reeves to Carson]
3 December 1944
Belgium

My Darling Carson,

Three days ago (and it seems that many years) I got your letters of 30th Oct, 5th and 7th Nov. Right in the middle of a thirty minute artillery barrage the mail orderly crawled by my hole and threw them in to me. I was dazed and absorbed by the business at hand and it was only today that I could read them and understand that someone had written me. They weren't long letters but I was nourished by every word and line in them.

For twelve days I had been smack on the front, cold and wet all the time. Rheumatism or something began to lack my hips so the old man sent me back for a day or two of rest. I feel much better now after a night of warmth and rest and will go back up where I belong tomorrow or the next day. It was nothing serious about the hips and I feel o. k. now. I'll be all right if I can just keep German shrapnel and bullets out of my system.

It was something ironical last night (I got here yesterday afternoon) to be told I would have to stay in bed and couldn't go to the hospital movie—sorry. Ha! Brer Rabbit in the briar patch. Today the doctor said not to walk around much but stay near the stove or in bed. The treatment and manner here is wonderful. I am in a hospital just inside Belgium. They seem to understand just how a man feels coming out of battle and that it takes only a few simple, normal things to put the light of life back in his eyes and expression.

It is pitiful and heartbreaking to watch the men brought in. The battle fatigue cases seem worse than the seriously wounded. They are more like zombies than men, dazed, reflexes numbed, just out of their graves with very little will to live. But they recover quickly under treatment and rest—I was like that last night. My nerves are steady and I am all straight in my mind about returning to the hell from where I came.

What I have found back here the most horrible and nightmarish are the surgical wards. Everyone who considers himself an active part of the United States Government should make that visit. If they did and *remembered* then there might never be another war. It is too much to ask that they fully understand what an active battlefield is like at day or night but the contents of those wards might penetrate their comprehension. It seems to me that at this time America is in such a powerful position to lock world politics and enforce peace after the war. But it isn't velvet gloves business—a few political heads have to be bashed. If Russia and America don't seal and enforce the peace actively then our world of the next thirty years will hardly be worth living in. For the foundation of our house will be the bubbling tension, coils and springs of World War III.

Darling, I am sorry I can't write oftener—I do write every chance I get. Yesterday when I got here I tried to cable but there is no service up here yet. I remember writing about a week ago from the cellar of a house we pulled back to. It is snatch and grab, touch and go with us all these days. You are in my mind always, Dear One. Your image is part of me and you are always with me wherever I go and in whatever I do. If you don't hear from me as often as you should please realize it isn't my fault.

You write asking for more information but I tell you all that is allowable, Dear. While the senior officer was gone I was in command of a Company but he is due back soon. Then I will take over my old platoon—that is, what is left of it. The Company is a good one, one of the best in the Regiment—there are some old soldiers left in it and some good fighters.

As far as the fighting in Germany goes—well, you read the papers. Most of them devote at least one column to the war these days. For some reason inconceivable to the editors the war in Europe is still going on. Actually the fighting here is the bitterest yet. I have had men who have fought in the Pacific tell me that. It is the hardest of any European phase of this war and ground is as bitterly contested as some of the knock down and drag out affairs of World War I.

Later

Have just finished supper and what a wonderful meal it was! Plain GI Army "B" ration, unimaginative but nourishing *and* hot. Pork chops, baked potatoes, corn[,] beet salad, *white* bread and coffee. A Red Cross skirt was by earlier with a ration of cigarettes and chocolate. Later I will shave my chocolate in a can and have a hot cup of cocoa before turning in.

There is no point in writing you all the incidental and cumulative miseries and hardships here—misery and suffering is the same in one town as another. After the war, if you like, I will talk of whatever you wish to hear. However, I feel you know and understand pretty well what it is like here.

There is one thing I will mention that piques and interests me— the mental processes of the average German we capture here. I have varied pictures in my mind of the different types of Germans. I have met and talked with hundreds and I thought I knew him pretty well.

These S.O.B's will murder Americans to the *very* last minute, then at just the right time (for him) he will surrender and come out with his hands up. Five minutes later he will be smiling, smoking, pleased as punch. Life and death to them is a business, an item of trade in their shop. This shocks the sense of fairness of the American (the German could easily have given up in the first place) but he does nothing about it. Death, to the American—as with the Russian—is more traumatic. If given the opportunity and proper setting he goes out grandly. With a great bellow, fighting to the last as a good soldier should.

I am so happy to know that your work progresses. It will be about Christmas when you read this and the "novel" you mentioned may be finished. I hope so, and that you are satisfied with it. How I long to sit and have you read some chapters to me—to see how far you have gone and how you have developed.

My Dear, don't feel too badly if the overseas assignment does fall through. I know of your restlessness and that this is what you want most at this time and I want it for you too, but failing that, if you are able to do your chosen work that will be best in the end. I promise you that when this is over we will travel where we wish and we will come back to Europe. Part of our life is tied in Europe. There is much about Europe that I want to understand. There may even be a little fun and happiness here after the war. Those two commodities aren't at all expensive and it is only in America that their manufacture requires intricate machinery. So try to work, Darling. The future will be waiting for us.

I must close now as it is nearly bedtime. Perhaps I will be able to write another note tomorrow before I leave.

I adore you,
Reeves

[Reeves to Carson]
3 December 1944
Belgium

Dearest,
I have your letters of Oct 30, Nov 5 and 7 and have read them over and over. It is heartening to know that you are working again. I hope your plan to finish the work by Christmas is accomplished. It will be after Christmas when this reaches you, I suppose.

Try as much as possible, Dear Heart, to continue work during these times. Work is of such enduring importance. I long to read what you have been doing and to talk with you. That time will come, my Darling. Believe me, it will.

I am writing you another type letter today also so that one will reach you through the fastest medium. It is not possible to cable from here. I am spending a couple of days in the rear but will soon be back on the line where I belong. It seems I am getting old and have a touch of rheumatism in my hips—had been lying in water and mud for twelve days. The fighting where I have been is the most bitter of all I have seen. The cold, terror and hardships are almost incredible but old Johnny Doughboy sticks it out and we will continue to do so until the last Boche[2] gives up.

Keep faith with us and be of strong heart.

My love and devotion for you,

Reeves

[Reeves to Carson]
4th December 1944
Belgium

My Darling—

The medics have kept me here a day longer to treat my sinuses. Being dry and warm for forty-eight hours has taken care of my hips and knee. The sinuses have been drained and I feel better today than in weeks. Tomorrow I will be on my way back up front.

Last night's Stars and Stripes and men coming in from the front hear good news. We are slowly but gradually shoving the bastards on back to the Rhine and thus far we have stopped dead every counterattack.

Since my letter of December 2nd I have been resting, lolling, reading and writing a few letters to people I hadn't written since leaving the States. You are the only person I have been able to write all along.

There is no one to talk with here and I have been lonely. I should hate to be in a hospital long—there is nothing so boring as the endless talk of war, war, war. Anyone with whom one strikes up acquaintance starts immediately relating how many narrow escapes he has had. Then he begins talk of mother, wife, or sweetheart then of all the things

2. Derogatory French slang word used for German soldiers. From French *caboche* meaning "noggin."

he is going to do when it is over and how drunk he is going to get and that is a bit sad because there are so many in the room who will never do those things. Some realize that, others are happily ignorant of that fact.

Last night I dreamed that the war had ended. We were walking along a wide path through a linden grove. It had been raining and water was dripping from the leaves. You had on a pink frilly dress which I didn't like and you had a flashlight in one hand which I kept asking you to put out. We had been talking about death which I insisted I knew all about. You stopped and said, "No, you don't, Reeves, but I do." I was terrified at the way you said it. I asked you to tell me and you said, "No, I can't. It would hurt you." Then you turned left, went into a little house and closed the door. I stood in the lane a moment and realized I would have to go on in the dark. I left the path and went toward a thick group of trees and finally got lost.

I don't believe too much in dreams but if you do find out what that one means and let me know later.

I haven't been outside today so I don't know what sort of day it is—we are in a huge tent inside a factory where there are no windows. I am interested most in a little stove near me going merrily and cooking me cocoa whenever I want it.

It is getting on toward late afternoon. You are probably closing up your typewriter and will go into the living room for drinks and probably play some or listen to music. Perhaps you will take a walk before dinner. Maybe there will be visitors later and a talk fest. I carry with me the pictures you send in your letters and long so much to be part of them.

Life with me is only half lived and enjoyed unless you figure in it somewhere.

Supper call is due soon so I will close.

Give my love to Bebe and Rita. I am so glad Frank was able to get by to see Rita.

Your,
Reeves

[Carson to Reeves]
December 5 [1944]

Reeves Precious:

It is late afternoon and I have been working and studying all day. First, I worked on my book all morning until about one thirty. Then this afternoon I plugged away with French idioms. Now in a little while I want to go out for a long walk. It's a bit warmer today, with masses of softly tinted clouds the color of mother-of-pearl. Mother keeps hoping it will snow, but I think it is too warm.

The situation in the occupied countries seems to get more disturbing every day. Especially the Greek trouble is alarming. Why can't Winston Churchill keep his reactionary nose out of the internal affairs of other nations. The EAM is certainly more representative of the Greek people than that feeble King George and all the rest of his gang. Why should the British Empire impose its will on nations who want and need a democratic government[?] Everywhere there is the sorry story of British (and American—*sic* Darlan, Badogglio etc.) meddling. Sometimes I feel that peace, when it comes, will last no longer this time than before—if as long. And the distrust that Britain is creating among her own allies, is bound to create by such behavior, is just what the Nazis have been waiting for.——I won't go on in this tack. But it's a bitter and tragic situation.

There is a jangling, eerie sounding piano out in the front hall and sometimes, late in the afternoon, I go out and play. The Bach preludes and fugues have an uncanny sound on the untuned piano in the empty hall. I miss my piano so much.

I went in town to see Annie Poor's new exhibition, and it was stunning. When in town for that afternoon I also went by to see Kay—then came back to Nyack on an early bus. Kay has a chance to go to Europe on a special trip, traveling by air, that will last six weeks. (This is rather a secret). But she is terrified of leaving her babies and can't decide what to do. I think she ought to go, as such chances are extremely rare and she has been trying to go a long time. I'll let you know what she decides.

My last letter from you is still the one dated November 8. This strain of waiting is so hard to bear.

Take care of yourself, darling, always. Remember who loves you.
Tenderly,
Carson

[Reeves to Carson]
8th December 1944
Germany

My Dear, My Dear,
    I am back again. The earth trembles, thunders and roars, the scenes and setting are about the same. Many old faces are missing and new ones have taken their places—a week is a long time to be away from one's unit in battle. I am used to this business now and there is no longer any extreme fear and the nervous strain is less. There is only a cold contempt for death and a hatred for the German beyond any passion. But that does not mean I am not careful or that I take unnecessary chances.
    When I returned I had a windfall in letters from you. The last one was dated 29th November! Nine days since you wrote it—I do hope my letters reach you in nearly that time.
    The best news is that you are busily at work again. When I feel that you are at work and reasonably calm my battles seem easier. Then there is some reason to all this horror and seeming chaos. Try not to let *anything* deter you in what you want to do—in what you *must* do.
    I was so touched to read of your sacrifice in sending me a whole carton of cigarettes. That was so sweet and thoughtful. But you shouldn't have done it—the cigarette shortage for the time being isn't acute here. However, if it becomes bad again I will have a spare tire. Hereafter, Darling, you must keep the few cigs you can get for yourself and Bebe. When we are at the front we get first priority.
    Through you I will thank Dear Bebe for her package I got yesterday. Each thing in it was carefully thought out and much needed. When I divided the Coke among the men you should have seen their eyes roll. Such a luxury is almost incredible—they had had nothing but K and C rations for days & days. Give Bebe a hug and kisses for me, and thanks from the men.
    There are the usual number of wild rumors flying around but all day I have felt that there is something big in the air. I can't describe the feeling, I can't put my finger on it but something is doing. However, there is no good, general news up where we are. The P.B.I. is usually last to get exciting news—except the unwelcomed news and orders that we will attack at such and such a time. Will the good Lord continue to forget the poor Infantry of life? Something was said thousands of years ago about the meek and humble but I cannot observe that much has been done about them. Never has life been more miserable

or less desirable than the existence of the poor wretches with whom I live—and whom I fight.

There is not much time tonight so this will only be a note. There is the matter of a patrol and some information of enemy positions to get. I prefer this nastiest job of war at night for daylight is usually full of death.

There is a great deal of speculation but I believe the Boche will give up when we reach the Rhine. Eisenhower has inferred that and I believe he is right. Although I know the Nazi party is still in absolute control and something way back in my head says they won't release control of Germany until her field armies are destroyed. The German field armies are not nearly destroyed. If the General Staff could only swing a coup.

My Dearest one, have faith in my return, in me, in us, and the future. I will come back to you and we shall have many happy hours together.

Thank you for sending Kay's poem. I will not be able to read it for a few days. I don't want to spoil its first impression in all this hell and thunder and muck. I have it in my pocket next to personal papers and long for the day of quiet when I can read it.

Will not seal this until I get back tonight.

Always,

Reeves

P.S.

Next morning. Mission accomplished, everything ok, nobody hurt. It is very cold here, snowed all night. There is a cup of coffee waiting for me so goodbye until later.

Love,

R[eeves]

[Reeves to Carson]
12th December 1944
Paris

Dear Carson,

I will be here in Paris a few days and then be sent on to England. Three days ago I was wounded and smashed my hand in a barrage. It is not serious and I will not lose any limbs. The doctors say I will be

hospitalized from six weeks to three months. Don't worry about me—
I am all right.

Have used this means of writing because it is said to be faster
than cable. Will write at length later—am very tired and battered up a
little—every bone and muscle in me aches.

But it is good to be alive this morning. It is a clear, sunny day and
Paris is very beautiful. We must explore it together after the war. The
air is purer here than at the front and it is good to be surrounded
by life.

Please wire or telephone Mother—I don't feel up to writing any
more and want to rest.

Love,
Reeves

[Carson to Reeves]
December 13 [1944]

Reeves Precious,

This has been a long weary day. There was no letter, and I can't
help being anxious. I tried to work, but this particular section I'm now
on seemed so cumbersome and heavy when I read it today that I realized it will have to be done again—but first I'll finish it and then see
what needs to be done.——I have been wondering if the letters I wrote
when you first went into the 28th Infantry have reached you. For about
a month I wrote only to the 28th Infantry, for you had not sent me the
number of your company. Could it be that the Company I was essential
and my letters never arrived?

Yesterday Mother and I went to the movie a few blocks up the
street. It was a windy biting afternoon and I wore the knitted G. I. cap
down over the ears. When we left the movie Mama handed me my
cap, but somehow, in the confusion of putting on wraps and leaving
the theater the cap was dropped. I discovered this in the lobby and the
usher went over every inch of the aisle with a flashlight; we hunted
everywhere, but someone must have picked it up and stolen it. Any-
how, I burst out crying like a child. I have always been so careful of
the cap you gave me, and it seemed somehow a dreadful thing that I
should lose it. I cried all the way home and Mama was miserable. *But*
when we got home we found that the lost cap was Rita's (I'd taken it
by mistake) one that Frank gave her when he found she liked mine.

And Rita very generously said I could keep my own, the one you gave me, and she would write Frank to send her another.

Today for some reason I can hardly see. I think I must have caught cold in my eye, for the right one is almost blind. Or maybe it is the very finely printed copy of Vanity Fair I've been reading. Anyway I'm trying to rest my eyes as much as I can today.

There is no news here. The international situation seems to grow worse and worse; it's so disheartening. This capitalistic division of spheres of power can only end in another war.

Darling, do you need any warm socks or sweaters or anything I can send you? If so, write me a formal letter to show at the post office (for some reason that is necessary) requesting what you need. I am so anxious about you this cold weather. I need a letter from you so badly.

Take care of yourself, and remember who loves you.

Tenderly

Carson

[Reeves to Carson]
17th December 1944
England

Darling—

It has been a rather pleasant Sunday here. It has been raining and windy most of the day but inside the ward it is warm and cozy and one can toast by the fire, read or lie back and smoke and just think and not hear rifles and machine guns chattering and artillery coming in.

My last letter from Paris should have reached you about a week before this. I have tried all the angles to get a cable to you but have had no success.

I was evacuated by plane from Paris to England day before yesterday and am finally settled and suppose I will stay here until I am fit again. It is pleasant enough—the usual type General Hospital. I had hoped to be nearer places where I had friends though. However, I'm not complaining about *anything*. I am quite satisfied to be alive.

I am not completely adjusted to the great change from the front to safety. It is still strange to sleep on a bed between sheets, to be near a stove, to have hot food three times a day.

It seems I was banged up more than I felt at first. The way it happened was quite usual: a barrage had lifted and I was outside trying to round up some replacements that had just come in. I heard a bastard round coming and dived for a dugout. Several bones in my left hand and wrist were smashed and I got some shrapnel in my rear which didn't follow me quickly enough into the hole. I was evacuated the next day and learned later that I had trench foot and that my right big toe was frozen. Sounds pretty bad but it isn't. My feet will be all right and feeling will gradually return to the toe. The shrapnel has been removed and my arm is in a comfortable cast. I find though that I am in a generally run down condition even after the few days previous rest. I had been going at a pretty good pace since "D" day. Under high nervous strain the body itself after a time feels the pressure. However, I am comfortably settled here now and in a reasonably quiet state of mind.

A new major looked at my x-rays today and said the hand would be from two to three months healing up. So if it relieves your mind any I won't do any fighting until at least March 15th. (After 60 days hospitalization they give one 3–4 weeks rehabilitation). I am not at all bashful about a long rest, although I know I will get restless before they turn me loose. However, I have been taking care of some of Uncle Sam's men for quite some time so I am going to lie back and let him take care of me for a while.

Thus far I have been getting everything here I need. Patients get a package of cigarettes each day. There are enough books around, such as they are, to last two months.

After a few weeks I hope to get a sick leave to visit friends in Southampton and on the Isle of Wight. If Kay's Joseph is still in England send me his A.P.O. and we can arrange a meeting. I plan to write Kay this week when I feel better. I also will write Mother later. I honestly am not up to writing anyone except you right now. If you haven't done so already please let Jessie know that I am all right.

The news the past two days has been depressing. It has just been announced over the radio that the Boche has effected a salient right in the area where I came from in the forest where my little group fought so hard and died. The 7th Army gains balance things up a bit but it is all such painfully slow progress.

Dearest, you must not worry about me—I will be right here in England until March 15th. Try to stay settled and finish the work you are doing. I hope to be home by late spring to read some thick manuscript of yours.

Take care of your precious self, Carson.

All my love,

Reeves

Write c/o this address:
Detachment of Patients
U.S. Hospital Plant #4109
A.P.O. #316
c/o P. M., N.Y.C.

[Carson to Reeves]
December 18 [1944]

Reeves, little heart, the V. mail letter of December 3 has come! It has meant everything to me, and I still have the other one you were writing that day to look forward to.

The new German counter offensive has terrified me. I think you must be there where the worst of it goes on. I hang over the radio and walk the floor and wait and dread.

Reeves precious, *please* don't go back to the line if you have hip rheumatism. You can't fight properly when you are ailing like that. Won't the doctor send you back for a time long enough for you to get over it entirely? To think of you lying out in the water and mud makes me despondent.

You must excuse this odd, abrupt note. For the last days I have had some severe eye trouble, and am forbidden to look at a typewriter or to read a headline. It seems only to be a case of acute eyestrain, and I'm taking care of it—wearing dark glasses and using poultices. But it's so annoying; I can't work, of course. I'm writing this with my eyes closed now. Don't worry about this little trouble. If it doesn't clear up promptly I'll go to the best oculist in N. Y. You can trust me there.

I can't get my mind off the German offensive. If there were only some way you could cable or let me know that you are all right! But I know there are no cable facilities where you are, and will just have to wait as patiently as I can.

Try to take care of yourself. You know how I love you. Goodbye for the time being, Sweet.
    Your,
    Carson

[Carson to Reeves]
December 19 [1944]

Oh Reeves darling,

If only I could have some word from you today—but I don't mean a letter written two weeks ago, but word about you now. This new German offensive has me in the same state I was on D day. You see I *know* you are there where the most bitter fighting is. I can't seem to think about this offensive with any strategic perspective; over and over I am haunted by a picture of you, there in a ditch at the front line, when the German blitz attack came. You may even be taken prisoner now as I write this. It's almost more than I can stand—these next few days until more details come through.

For security reasons they are not giving us many details. We only know it is a desperate last ditch maneuver and the Nazis are putting everything into it. And I know you are there. Always before, you know darling, I have been able to think to myself that you are at some other part of the front, other than the place of the fiercest battles.

The only little thread of comfort I have is the faint hope that the hip rheumatism you wrote me about has grown worse and you were not directly on the front line when the attack came. I'm such a coward about you; I hang onto the most fantastic hopes.

Offensive fighting is so different from defensive war. In a retreat I am haunted by the thought of the wounded, and the probability that many may have to be left behind.

Write me, Reeves, the instant you get this letter.

I can't get my mind on anything else except these battles going on now. I keep the radio on, as on D. day.

My eyes are better—absolutely no disease; just a severe strain. We had the first real snowfall last night, but I can't enjoy it.

I'm writing a V-mail letter in the hopes it will reach you sooner than this. So I'll get busy with that one now.

Goodbye, darling Reeves. You know that my heart and mind is with you every moment.

Carson

[Carson to Reeves]
December 19 [1944]

Oh my Precious Reeves,
   I have just written another kind of letter, but am sending this also in the hopes it may reach you sooner. This new German attack has me so terrified. You see I *know* you are there. Day and night I am haunted by dread for you. I have not felt such fear since D day. I keep the radio going all the time but for security reasons we are getting very few details.
   If I could just see you this instant and know you are well. I hang onto a little thread of hope that, because of the hip rheumatism, you were not directly on the front lines when the Blitz came. But I can't really take any comfort from this; for on December 3 you expected to return to the front in a couple of days.
   This dread and uncertainty is anguish. Write me the <u>instant</u> you get this. I know cabling is impossible. But write <u>immediately</u> the quickest way.
   Remember that I am always with you in my heart and mind.
   always your
   Carson

[U.S. Army to Carson]
20 December 1944

Telegram

To: Carson McCullers
From: U.S. Army

Regret to inform you first lieutenant James R. McCullers Jr was slightly injured in action nine December in Germany. You will be advised as reports of condition are received.

[Carson to Reeves]
December 21 [1944]

Reeves dearest,
    After those days of suspense and anguish the telegram from the
War Dept has just come. Knowing that if you were slightly injured
Dec. 9, it is not likely that you were again in combat when the German
attack came. These last days, since Sunday, have been the worst I've
ever known. I can't help but be relieved. Yet I remember that the last
time you were "slightly injured" on June 6, you were back in combat
almost immediately. Write me immediately.
    I have the dreadful feeling my letters are not reaching you. For a
long time I wrote only to the 28th Infantry, as you had not given a more
complete address.
    Be sure to have the doctors look into that hip rheumatism while
you are under treatment. I don't want you to go back into combat too
soon.
    The news is terrifying, but we must be brave and hopeful. My
darling, I'm writing another kind of letter today, but am sending this
on the chance it will reach you sooner. Write me at once when you get
this. Remember always how tenderly I love you. Oh how I long to be
near you!
    Carson

[Carson to Reeves]
December 21 [1944]

Reeves angel,
    I've just written one of the v mail letters, on the chance it might
reach you sooner. I have been so worried for fear my letters are not
reaching you. The War Dept. telegram has just come. After these last
dreadful days it was an unspeakable relief to know you were "slightly
injured" December 9. At the same time I remember how promptly you
returned to combat the last time you were slightly wounded. I am so
anxious to hear more. Surely you will write to me in the hospital—
long letters. I tried to call Jessie, but was unable to reach her—so I sent
a telegram.
    I am so agitated I can hardly write. When the telegram came my
eyes went blind and for a moment after We Regret I could not read at

all. Then when I knew what it was I burst out crying and laughing at the same time.

I try to picture you lying between clean warm sheets, with a good book and good meals brought on a tray, and with a wound in the foot that is not painful, not serious at all, but will take some little time to heal.

I am a little worried for fear the German Blitz might have caught up with your hospital. So don't fail to write me the moment you get this.

Reeves, listen to me carefully. While you are in the hospital be sure to consult the doctors about your rheumatism and the sinus trouble that has been plaguing you. This is very important.

The news that leaks through the security blackout is frightening. But somehow I believe we (We!) will be able to smash the Nazis, and turn this piece of desperation to our own advantage. I can't help but believe that Eisenhower and the other generals know what they are doing. And foresaw the possibility of this attack all along. It is like the chess games we used to play—remember, Darling—when you would lay a little trap to catch my queen and I would wail her out only to have you pounce on her with a knight I'd never noticed before.—— But then I know it isn't exactly like that. This is a grim, hazardous business. If we can't cope with it the war may go on and on.

I can't tell you too many times to write immediately. And Reeves, when you go back to the battles try to tell me somehow where you are and give me some indication of the danger. I hope they won't send you back to the front line at all.

My eyes are much better—I wrote you that it was only a bad case of eyestrain. But today I have a cold and sorethroat that is going the rounds. So I'm drinking hot tea and not doing much. In fact, I haven't worked in about ten days, *and* the book is far from finished. I am discouraged sometimes. But it will be so much easier to work these next weeks knowing you were not the first shock of the German attack.

Goodbye for the time being, Reeves. Remember how much I love you.

Carson

[Carson to Reeves]
Christmas

Reeves Angel,
You have been with us all through this day. We burned a special barberry candle for you that blazed on the central table and lasted all day. Your health was drunk so many times. Oh, Reeves, I missed you so! But I believe next Christmas you can actually be here. We had many guests all through the day. Bessie was ill so the Poors couldn't come; but they sent so many beautiful gifts—a painting by Henry, (an exquisite still life), perfume, a handsome lustre candlestick (that was the one that held your candle), table mats, rare jellies and other gifts. In the early afternoon Kanto and [Friedel] came out bringing the Lehman album of Schumann's Dichterliebe. I was so touched. And Rita's school friends came out together and brought so many beautiful things. And, a crowning touch, the Morrises with their sweet handsome 16 year old son who is an Ensign in the navy and here on a five-day pass—they came out with Louise Rainer. *And* they brought a thirty-pound turkey already cooked, and good bottles of whiskey, and a beautiful Sweedish [sic] brandy glass Mama had admired in their apartment. Oh Reeves darling, you would have liked it today. I missed you so and couldn't help crying from time to time. Everyone felt as I do—that it is a good thing you were slightly wounded. Kanto feels that you couldn't have been in this German attack. We brought out pictures of you and everyone remarked how handsome you are (even in those Ranger battalion photographs). Your ears sure must have burned.
It has been a very full day. It touches me to realize how kind people are and to realize how our friends love us. Oh Reeves, little heart, knowing that you are perhaps in a hospital (even <u>hoping</u> so) is so strange and bitter. Surely next Christmas you will be with us and we can have drinks and turkey and music and we can be together.
I am waiting so anxiously for a letter. This suspense is so hard to stand. If I hadn't got the war dept. cable saying you were slightly injured I doubt if I could have stood the suspense—knowing we have had a bad setback. I wonder if your regiment has suffered many loses. Oh, darling, I am waiting to know just how and where you are injured. I long to be near you. Is there <u>anything</u> I can send? I can't mail any packages unless I have a written request from you for specific articles. Blessed Reeves, goodnight for the time being.
always your,
Carson

[Reeves to Carson]
26 December 1944
England

Carson, Dear,

By now you know where and how I am and I feel relieved about that. My status is about the same except that I have improved some. I feel much better than I did the last time I wrote. My feet and the shrapnel wounds are o. k. now and my ailments are reduced to the bad hand. For several days the doctors were undecided about sending me back to the States or keeping me in England. All that time I held my breath and had my fingers crossed but it did no good. It was decided that I would heal up here in time. However, if the bones do not knit properly an operation will be necessary and *that* will most likely preclude a trip back to the States. But that won't be known for some time—at least two months from now. In any event it seems my fighting is suspended until the spring offensives.

The news of the past two weeks has been just about as black and gloomy as it could be. It may be a daring gamble on their part but even if they lose the gamble all I can see out of it is a prolongation of the war until late spring or early summer. I don't think history will show that the counteroffensive did us any good.

On top of all this I received news that my old outfit was almost completely annihilated near the area where I came from. They had been near us all along and I hadn't known it.

That hit me pretty hard. It is especially hard to take the death of my old Sergeant, a Pole from Rochester, who had sort of looked after me for nearly three years. When I was in bad trouble and looked around somehow he was always there. Coming in "D" day my foot got caught under a vehicle and with bullets flying all over the place he plowed in without any regard for himself and saved me from drowning. At Brest he pulled me out of another spot when three others and I were hopelessly pinned down by machine gun fire in a field. He sneaked around and got the whole crew of krauts by himself. It was a habit of his to see that J[ames] R[eeves] M[cCullers] stayed alive. When I left he insisted on transferring with me but I persuaded him not to because he had an important job where he was. How I wish I had not done that.

We get very little news here except the garbled stuff over the radio.

The weather has been clear here for several days. That is always thought of in terms of the Air Corps:—is it clear over there? Will they be able to stay up and help the Infantry?

It is quiet and peaceful where I am but there is no peace or rest for me until it is all over. Thoughts of what is going on up front run through one like a current of electricity all day.

I eat, walk a little, try to rest, and my nerves are steadying down some. I am all right.

None of your letters have reached me since December 8th but I know you have written and word from you will catch up with me soon.

Take care of yourself, Dearest.

Love,

Reeves

[Carson to Reeves]
December 27 [1944]

Reeves Blessed,

The V mail letter written in Paris has just come. Oh my darling! After this dreadful suspense it's such balm to know you are safe and cared for and warm in a hospital. Your note was rather ambiguous, and I shall be very anxious until I learn more precisely what is wrong. You say you "were wounded and your hand smashed in a barrage"— the and seems to imply that there are other injuries besides the hand. I long with all my soul to be with you now. And I am haunted by the fear that my letters are not reaching you; somehow the address does not look proper to me. I'm hoping you will send the English hospital address so I can send mail directly there. I don't know how I'm going to wait until I hear more. My heart is so full of tenderness and you are so far away. Oh, how I wish they would send you home! Is there a chance of this? Or if there were some way I could get to England! From six weeks to three months is a long time to be in hospital. Poor little lamb! Does your hand pain you, darling? Write me everything. I can't bear to think of you suffering. Yet Reeves it is not as agonizing as the constant thought of the grisly miseries of a battlefield—the nightmarish dread for your very life. I know now that you are warm.

next sheet [indicates this letter will continue on another V mail page]

[Carson to Reeves]
December 28 [1944]

Continued—
Today I'm still in bed with this cold. I keep wishing you could be lying here close beside me. It's a clear bitter day outside. The sky is the palest blue, with a cold wintry yellow along the horizon. The river is iron gray and frozen on the shores. But here in the house it's cozy and there is the usual litter on the bed—a couple of volumes of Proust, several of your letters, <u>two</u> handsome boxes of Christmas candy, etc. It's just the time in the late afternoon when the lamps are being turned on. Mama and Rita listening to the radio in the living room and I have the card table with the legs folded up on the bed with me as a base for the typewriter. I lie here and wonder how you are, if you are comfortable, if you have whisky and plenty of cigarettes. I look for a letter any day now. Be sure and make a list of the things I should send. You will want plenty of good books to keep you occupied as well as all sorts of other things. Do you need any money? Are you allowed to wear your own pajamas etc.? I am so anxious to hear from you.

Mama has just come in to put a mustard plaster on my chest, and I'll be smelling like a ham sandwich all night. Goodbye for just now, my little darling.

always your,
Carson

[Carson to Reeves]
December 28 [1944]

My dearest one,
Your letter written on Thanksgiving Eve, during the time of the ghastly fighting in Germany, came just after I had written you this afternoon. Never have I read a more terrible and moving letter. There is nothing for me to say. Thank God it comes to me only now, when I know you are out of battle—otherwise I wonder how I could have stood it. Reeves, my love, if ever anything happened to you the harmony of my life would be destroyed forever. I won't write any more about this now; you know how I love you.

I realize that the letters I write you now will have to go all the way to Belgium or Germany and then back to you in England. I'm so anxious to get the hospital address. Soon I should have the medical report that will be sent from the hospital. And I should have my precious letters from you. I read and read them and they are all quite ragged. Kanto telephoned a while ago to say he has a letter from you—the one written in the rest camp on Dec. 4.

The news seems better today and yesterday. Patton's tanks seem to be slicing us through the German salient. But they say the losses have been very great. I think of all the wives whose husbands have been killed. God knows how long this will go on.

[no closing]

[Carson to Reeves]
December 28 [1944]

My Angel Reeves,
The letter written in Belgium on Dec. 4th, before you were wounded, came this morning. Oh my little one! You say that you would hate to be in hospital long—and I'm afraid that now you are fretting. But Reeves, I can't feel that way. Knowing that your injuries will not be permanent, I can only feel only feel [sic] the most heavenly relief. I think of you in England safe and warm. Or I have a small drink, and then immediately wild marvelous fantasies come—I imagine that you will be sent home to me. I think of a sudden wire sent from a hospital here—you have been flown over. I picture the scramble of packing a bag and getting the next train (or bus to N. Y. and then the train.) Oh my darling, it hurts me to think of your being in pain, or even being bored—but I have been in such cruel dread for you so long. You can't imagine what it has been like!

I'm waiting so anxiously for the hospital address. <u>Captain</u> Kay Boyle will be in England for about a week after the first. I <u>must</u> have the address so she can see you. She says she will do her damnedest to find you—but it will be hard to do, I'm afraid, without an address. Oh how I wish I were Kay!

Little darling, that was a sad dream that night in Belgium. You must know I would never go in a house and close a door, leaving you alone out in the rain under the linden trees. You ought to know how I love you.

always your,
Carson

[Carson to Reeves]
[late December 1944]

My Beloved Reeves,
   This morning both Mrs. Clay and the postman knocked on our door and handed me a letter. It's the first time in many weeks I'd not been waiting for the mail in the hall, and they were so happy to hand me the letter. Then, when it was opened it was the beautiful letter written Dec. 3 at the rest camp behind the lines. I have been reading it all during the day. But still I know no more about where you are now. Sometimes I picture you in an English hospital, without letters, with no boxes from me—and I weep when I think that the letter will have to go all the way to Belgium or Germany and then be forwarded to you. Surely I will know soon where you are. I am still possessed, really possessed, with the fancy that you may be on the way home. Every time the telephone rings I tremble all over and expect to hear your precious voice. I try not to be this way, for I am probably letting myself in for the cruelest kind of disappointment. There is no way of saying how much I long for you.——I won't go on in this tack, because I know there is nothing we can do about it. But surely soon I will hear from you. Soon you will be able to answer all the questions I have been writing you these past weeks since you were wounded.
   Reeves, my own darling, I have read many war books, letters, and stories. But your letters to me are the most powerful, suggestive, pieces of writing about war I have ever read. I have showed a few of the letters, parts of them, to other people—and it has been suggested that they ought to be published. Bessie (to whom I read certain parts) is especially insistent about this. Write me what you think. Of course I know they were written with no such intention—they were written only to me, and they are the dearest treasure I possess. You may not like it that I read parts of the letters to anyone else, but I don't think you will be angry with me. These days it seems I cannot open my mouth without talking about you, without shaping the conversation so that it turns constantly on you.
   I know my letters to you fail sometimes even to make sense. They are only the letters of a desperate woman, a little unbalanced sometimes by fear.
   My darling heart, it is a bright cold day again. I am quite well again, and yesterday for the first time I went out with Mama for a

walk. The river is frozen hard along the shore. The sunrises are especially lovely now, and we are up to see them almost every day. Sometimes the sky is a pure geranium color, and the sun is fiery gold across the ice.

This morning I worked for four hours. There is none of that inner composure, the first essential with me for work, the fruitful tranquillity of the old days when I lived with you and worked and we were happy. There is none of that now, but I believe that there will be other times like those for us in the future. And in the meantime, in spite of crying nerves, I will try to work. I failed to finish the story by Christmas but maybe by the middle of March it will be done.

Reeves dearest, everything I see and feel is connected so closely with you. The music I hear and the books I read. For a Christmas present I was given a beautiful pair of velvet slippers, lined with a soft lambswool and very warm and beautiful. I think you might be able to wear them, for they are so soft that even if they are a little tight they wouldn't hurt you. I long for you to have them as I know how you feel about stepping on a cold floor. I long to look after you and spoil you— and be spoiled a little by you too. Oh Reeves, I love you so deeply and tenderly, and I feel that we, each of us, has so much to make up for to the other.

It is late afternoon, four thirty. I have been here at the typewriter, dreaming and writing, for about two hours. Now I shall go in to Mama, and start one of our endless conversations about you. I adore you.

Your,
Carson

[Carson to Reeves]
January 1, 1945

My Beloved,
These days of limbo—until your hospital address reaches me— are almost unbearable. I know my letters of the past few days will have to go all the way to Belgium or Germany and then be forwarded to you, they may take months. And you, my darling heart, might think I have not written. True, there are no words that I can say to tell you of my love. I ache with tenderness. To hold you close, to feel my arms about you—there are no words for my longing. My loved one, my husband and everlasting friend, I need you so. After the suffering of

these last ghastly months, I know that no tenderness could be lavish enough; I feel that we must always be so gentle with each other. Always.

There are some things I must know as soon as possible. William [Mayer] came out to be with us and he seemed almost sure that you would be sent home. You can imagine my burning excitement. I can't rest a minute. Tomorrow there will be several days accumulation of mail and I hope to get a more direct address. So I won't mail this letter until one comes. Meanwhile I have to regret questions I have been writing to you all week. Listen carefully. First, do you think you will be medically discharged? Second, will you be sent home to me? Third, you *don't* think you will be sent back to combat, do you? Until I have answers to these questions I cannot rest.

[Handwritten in margin:] Now Jan 8, the Hospital address has just come! Writing again this morning. Oh my Angel!

William says that a smashed hand can take a long, long time to heal and often the nerves and muscles are stiff or do not function. You can imagine my state of mind when he told me he thought you would be sent home. I have been like a crazy girl. The relief, after these last unspeakable months, is beyond my powers of description. But oh, if only you would be sent home!

Little Darling, I don't know what to write. I need your address in order to send boxes of things you will need. And then there is this dazzling chance that you may be sent home. I am afraid to let myself think of this—but still can't think of anything else. I imagine a sudden telegram comes from a hospital in this country—you have been flown over. I picture myself washing my hair, packing the suitcase, dashing to make the next bus to N. Y. and the train from there. I know I ought not to set my heart on it too much but I can't seem to help it. Meanwhile it is now twenty two days since you were wounded. And still I have had only the War Dept wire and your little v mail letter from Paris. But I feel it in my bones that tomorrow more news of you will come.

This is the first day of the New Year. Mother is cooking black-eyed peas—but she was unable to find any hog jowl; they seem never to have heard of it up here. But we will have the peas and white meat for the New Year's luck dinner. And I will be thinking of my darling with every pea.

It's a ghostly, foggy morning. There is some sad looking porous snow on the ground and housetops. Beginning tomorrow I will make a great effort to work. As long as I can feel you are in hospital I am not so paralyzed with fear and dread. I must write some stories that will make you proud of me. I even must try to make some money—or at least finish what I have to do and then see if it won't bring me something. I feel I owe you a lot of money. But the main thing is to do work that I know is good. I believe that I can. I don't ever want you to be disappointed in me.

Now Reeves, remember that you are to write or cable <u>immediately</u>. You know how I love you.

always your,

Carson

[Carson to Reeves]
January 4 [1945]

Reeves, my dearest one:

I am still in this queer purgatory, waiting and waiting for more news of you. I haunt the hall, waiting for the postman or for a sudden telegram. At times I am seized with the feeling you are <u>on the way home</u>. It is now 26 days since you have been wounded, and still I have only that short v mail note from Paris. It distresses me to know that my letters have to go all the way across France and then sent on to you to England—so I have one long letter already written, but held until I can send it to a more direct address. Surely I will hear soon.

Today is pale and icy again, and it is late afternoon. Rita gave Mama a collection of seven short novels by Henry James, and I have been reading them. I have been much too restless to settle to work, but the James is damn well worth while. One in particular I long to share with you. But, good as they are, the instant the telephone rings or there is a knock on the door my heart nearly jumps out of my throat. I have a notion, fantastic perhaps but unexpungable, that suddenly I shall open the door and you will be there, or that from the hall I shall suddenly hear your voice. It keeps me keyed to such a pitch. Surely soon I will hear or something *will* happen.

You know always how I love you. your,

Carson

[Carson to Reeves]
January 6 [1945]

My dearest one
 Now, on Jan. 6, your first letter, written Dec. 17, from the English hospital has just come! At last, oh my darling! I have just posted three v mail letters I had saved until the address would reach me. Yesterday I wrote many pages, but sent them to the old address. You see, little darling, all the frantic letters I have been pouring out to you since the War Dept. cable came will have been sent all the way to Belgium and will very likely take months to reach you. But I had to write them and send them out, just as Noah sent out his doves. (Or was it ravens?) But now, at last, I know where you are.
 I don't want to run you wild, with my insisting questions. But I must know the answers as soon as possible. (1) Is there any chance that you will be sent home to me? (2) Is it at all likely that you will be medically discharged? From what I understand it often happens that certain nerves or muscles are more or less permanently damaged so that, while not seriously incapacitated otherwise, a man is unfit for the army. (3) You mention that you do not expect to be in action again before March 15. But are you sure you will be returned to action? If a man's hand is stiff or weak it seems to me he would be unable to handle a rifle properly, and so would not be sent to the front. Tell me, my Reeves, isn't it likely that when your hand is well you will be transferred to some other unit other than as a combat infantryman? My darling heart, answer these questions immediately. These last weeks, since the War. Dept. cable came, have been so unreal. I lived with the fabulous thought that you would be sent home, that any instant I would hear your voice out in the hall. Or you would call from an American hospital—and I would be with you that very day. I have lived like a crazy girl. And now, with your letter that has come at last, I can't help feeling a little dashed. I know, my precious, I ought to be down on my knees this very minute and stay there all the time you are in hospital. I am grateful to God: the blissful relief of knowing you are safe in a hospital is more than I could ever write you. But at the same time this fantastic notion—that you were on your way home to me— dies hard this morning. Why is it that in all concerning you I make such monstrous demands? From you and God I'm always asking more, and never satisfied. Why is that, darling?
 Kay will probably already have been to see you when this reaches you. As I've written so many times before Captain Boyle will be vis-

iting you in the hospital sometime after the middle of the month. Oh how I envy her! She is bringing the great and lovely poem dedicated to us.[3] I have sent you two copies already, but I have the dreadful feeling that my letters never get to you.

This morning I'm going out to see if I can't manage to get a cable off to you. Then I'll send off some boxes to you. Make a list of everything you need so I can send them to you. The trouble is I'm afraid my boxes won't get there until you are almost ready to leave the hospital. I weep when I think that you have been there over three weeks now—with no boxes, no letters, nothing.

It's a fair, radiant day. Mama and Rita have gone into the city to buy Rita a coat, and I had intended to go along with them—but of course when your letter came all thoughts of anything except cables and boxes and letters to you went out of my mind.

Oliver Smith has produced a show called On the Town, which is the most successful comedy in many years. The critics agree that it is the best thing of its kind in ages, and now suddenly he is wallowing in wealth. Two weeks ago he couldn't pay George [Davis] the rent. He expects to come out to see us this week end. But he is ill with his old ear trouble and sounded very tired over the telephone.

My dearest one, I believe that sometimes, rarely, there are those who were meant for each other; I believe that about us. Our love for each other is like a sort of natural law, independent of our separate wills, inalterable by circumstances. Goodbye for this morning, Reeves. I'll go now to see about the cable and the boxes.

always your,
Carson

[Carson to Reeves]
Nyack, N.Y.
January 7 [1945]

My darling,
It's a quiet, snowy Sunday morning. We got up very late for us (at nine o'clock) and had pancakes and sausage and hot good coffee. Then we heard a Mozart recital on the radio, and Bach. Later we sat

---

3. Perhaps Kay Boyle's poem, "American citizen naturalized in Headville, Colorado."

around talking and drank beer. This morning, in short, has only lacked you.

Yesterday I spent a furious afternoon, after writing you most of the morning,—an afternoon of looking through the Nyack shops, making enquiries, getting off a cable to you. To my great disappointment the post office wouldn't take my box to you. It seems they only accept boxes of 8 ounces, unless accompanied by a written request from the person overseas. So, little darling, you must write me out a formal list of what you need—so I can show it at the postoffice.

I read your letters over and over; I carry them with me wherever I go. So often I have brooded and suffered at the thought of women who receive that letter after a War Dept cable saying their loved one has been killed—the letters, you know, keep on coming a month or more after the casualty cable. How do they stand it? Or does a sister or mother sometimes intercept the postman and keep the letters until some later time when she is more able to bear it? Will this war, these tensions and miseries, ever ever end!

Now that I know you are safe and warm, after these unspeakable months, I can tell you I have nearly gone out of my mind with worry. If I could know that at the moment, the very instant, you were wounded or killed, I would be wounded or killed also—if that could be possible, then I could be brave. But as things are—I can't. These last months I have felt as though every nerve in me had been picked out and torn up and put back in by a madman. But now I can get myself in order again during these next two months. And, of course, it is my secret dearest hope that you will [not] be be [sic] in combat again.

I want to know everything about the hospital—the routine, the treatment, etc. Do you have any whiskey? Can you get beer, darling? Does your hand pain you? I would give all that I have if I could be near you.

Some lovely Bach has just come on the radio. Mama is cooking a little hen, and I shall go in and "help her" and pick around. Yesterday they came in rather late from the city, and Rita had bought a handsome coat. She bought it with the money she made from the story she sold.[4] It's black wool with soft lambswool lining, warm and becoming.

I hope soon some of my letters will begin to reach you. To think of you lying in a hospital with no letters, no boxes, nothing—I cry when I think about it. But you know, it is not my fault. Still I am filled with a sort of helpless exasperation.

4. Perhaps Rita Smith's short story, "White for the Living," which appeared in *Mademoiselle* in 1942 and won an O. Henry Memorial Award in 1943.

Mother and Rita have been talking this morning about buying a house here in Nyack. They have heard of a place for sale near here and we are all going out into the snow this afternoon to have a look at it. But somehow I don't actually want to "buy" a place until we have your advice. None of us know anything about "foundations" and that sort of thing. They have been planning the curtains and what each person will have in her room—and still they've never laid eyes on the house.

Kay will be seeing you very soon. I imagine your meeting and nearly faint away with envy for her. Reeves, the poem is so very beautiful. I wish I could see your face while you read it.

My dear one, I'll go in now to the Mozart and the sitting room. You know how I love you. always your,
Carson

[Carson to Reeves]
January 7, 1945

Western Union Cablegram
James Reeves McCullers
London
Beloved Reeves first English hospital letter here at last. My letters on the way. Kay will visit you around middle of January.
I adore you.
Carson McCullers.

[Carson to Reeves]
January 8 [1945]

My Darling,
It's a bleak white January day, and I've been drinking cup after cup of hot tea and reading Henry James. I'd never realized how really good he is. One is quite willing to stumble through pages of ambiguities for those sudden, exquisite lines, those almost unexpected revelations. I'd never realized how deeply he has influenced the present poets—Eliot, Auden, etc. I want us to read the Beast in the Jungle together.

I'm still arguing with the Post Office about getting a box to you. As it stands they won't take my things. You have to send a written request that I can show them. I had counted so much on sending books that I know you are needing and other little things. By the way, do you need money? Be sure to write me immediately what I should send. Also, dearest, we read in the papers that a million Christmas boxes were lost in the mail—most of them when the Germans broke through in Belgium. It seems that a great shipment had just arrived and the Nazis captured them. Did the boxes we sent ever reach you, darling. I can't bear to think of a Nazi wearing that special combat hood that, (it occurred to me) will also come in handy on bitter winter days, after the war, when you will go out in the snow to chop wood for our supper stove or work around a farm we might have some day. I had particularly seen you wearing that little hood. Also I don't like to think of the Nazis having your pipe and other presents, so write me if the boxes ever reached you.

[Harwick Mosely] is coming out to see us today. I expect him on the twelve o'clock bus, and he will spend the afternoon with us. We're having salmon souffle and beet salad for lunch. Then in the afternoon I imagine we'll go out for a walk. As a rule I don't much like to have week day visitors out here; but I haven't seen Harwick in such a long time, and I'm very fond of him. I do hope, though, he won't be too curious about my work, for I have a great feeling of guilt. But Reeves, now that for two months you will be safe in the hospital, I think these desperate anxieties will go away and I can find the composure for work.

Little darling, I think of you every moment. I expect that by now you are more rested and your nerves are better. How do you weigh? Be sure to answer this, as well as all my questions. You must get built up and strong—but I hope that hand is permanently damaged. It's a queer world when a woman can have no peace of mind unless she knows her loved one is in a hospital.

I must hurry and get dressed, as it's already twelve. Goodbye for today, my Reeves.

always your,
Carson

[Carson to Reeves]
January 9 [1945]

Reeves dearest,
Your cable came last night, and it is just as I had feared; my letters have not yet begun to reach you. I imagine that mail service must have

been acutely disrupted by the German December attack—especially that part of the front where you were. I'm also afraid our Christmas boxes never arrived. As I cabled you last night, it makes me sick at heart to think of your lying there without letters, although I have been writing every day since the War Dept cable came. By now though you should at least have a cable I sent a week ago. It's exactly a month now since you were wounded. And there are few waking instants during this month when you have not been in my mind.

Today is the coldest day of the year so far. The thermometer is down to two degrees. But the sun is out, but there is a pale lemon yellow sun and the sky is a clear, cold blue. Yesterday I bought a pot roast, which we had for supper—and we'll have it again tonight. So we won't have to get out of the house today. The sidewalks are dangerously icy.

I keep thinking of the men fighting in Belgium, in those snowstorms. There are times when, out of unconscious self protection, the imagination grows numb and fails to function. I was in that state during those terrible days, after the German breakthrough, when I thought you were there. We heard on the radio how the Germans shot prisoners—oh Reeves, it was ghastly—I told myself that you might be one of those prisoners; but I couldn't _realize_ anything. I suffer for those women who haven't yet heard. It must be unbearable.——But I won't write on and on about this. For me, for the time being, it's over.

I'm making a pact with myself to finish this monstrous story by March 15. This morning I worked several hours. But it's one of those works that the least slip can ruin. Some parts I have worked over and over as many as twenty times. I must finish it soon and get it out of my system—but at the same time it must be beautifully done. For, like a poem, there's not much excuse for it otherwise.

The Henry James could be very discouraging at this point. Some of the nouvelles are among the best I have ever read. I gawk over them like a child watching the trapeze lady at the fair. They are really supreme achievements.

Mama has just come in and suggested we open a can of shrimp we had been saving in the cupboard. So we'll have a treat for lunch today. Shrimp and soup and perhaps a tasty salad. These days I can eat without the sickening thought that you are hungry.

There is not much news. I live so quietly, that there isn't much to write. The _real_ things that happen to me concern you—or, to a lesser degree, this book. When I write "you" that includes the war in general.

I've still not been able to free myself entirely from the old delusion you are on the way home. My brain tells me better, but certain reflexes still go on. Yesterday I heard a cough out in the hall that sounded like yours—and instantly my whole heart lighted. But I didn't rush to open the door, as I would have done a week ago.

Since I'm not going out today, I'll give this to the postman to mail.

This afternoon, after lunch, I'll read a hour or so, then try to work in the afternoon. Then about sunset I'll shut up shop and go in to mother. We'll talk a while and I shall have a drink. The conversations we have together always turn around you. [Then] later we'll have some music perhaps, and Rita will come in from the city. She always brings with us echoes of the big doings in town. We'll go to bed quite early, about nine thirty.

Darling, will you write me just what you do?

It's time for the postman to come, so I must stop.

My love, you know you are always in my heart.

your,

Carson

[Carson to Reeves]
January 10, 1945

Western Union Cablegram
James Reeves McCullers
London
My Angel
Physically well but frantic my letters don't come through.
Have written daily.
You know how I love you.
Always your,
Carson McCullers.

[Carson to Reeves]
January 10 [1945]

My darling,

It's late afternoon, very lovely and still. There's a milky glow in the sky and the ice on the river is snow covered. This afternoon I read more Henry James, but otherwise the day was very unsatisfactory. Last night I was awake almost the whole night, and was so deadly tired today I couldn't work.

But for an hour or so last night I did sleep, and there was a dream. I dreamed that I waked up and you were lying there beside me. That was all—I didn't see or touch you in the dream, but I knew that you were there; the dream had no sense of war, and there was not the least surprise about your being there, it was all so beautifully natural. In the dream I felt only a contentment, knowing you were there, and (in the dream) turned over and went back to sleep again.——This morning, of course, I made a point of telling this before breakfast. Tomorrow I'm supposed to go in to New York. But I have become such a hermit that the thought of going into the city, and being with people (even friends I am fond of) can disturb me for days in advance. So I'm going to call it off.

There was no letter from you today, but soon surely mail from me will begin to reach you. And I may hear again from you tomorrow. I wonder endlessly, and with the tenderest anxiety, about you. But I don't worry in the old unbearable way I worried when you were in action.

It's six o'clock and now I'm going to take a shower, have a simple supper, and go straight to bed. Maybe for a half an hour we can hear some Schubert.

This is the stupidest sort of note. But I don't think I have ever been so exhausted, and can hardly keep from falling out of the chair. So goodbye for today, my darling. You know how I love you.

always your,
Carson

[Carson to Reeves]
Nyack, N.Y.
January 11 [1945]

Darling Reeves,

It's late afternoon and snow is falling. This morning I worked, but not hard enough, and somehow the afternoon has slipped away. For a long while I've just been sitting at the window, watching the snow; the flakes are thick and whirling, coming in on an east wind. A part of me longs to be out in it, and if you were here I think we would wrap up and go for a long walk together. Then, after dark, we'd come in and have some strong warming drinks. But, as it is, I don't feel much like walking by myself, so I just sit here by the window dreaming and drinking tea. A few days ago a package came addressed to me and marked in the left hand corner Santa Claus, The North Pole. It was a carton of Camels from Edwin. He has a San Francisco A.P.O. number, but I'm not sure where he is. The Camels were quite a prize, as we have been smoking the strangest concoctions. I'm so glad to feel that you have plenty of cigarettes in the hospital. I wonder if you are able to get whiskey and beer.

I still have had only that first letter you wrote just after getting to England. I wait every day to hear more, and to have the answers to my questions. By now I imagine you are able to walk around, but I hope the cast will be on for quite a long time. The news today was better than it has been, but it looks as though the Germans will be able to make it back behind their Siegfried line without too many losses. If only the weather would clear up and let the fighters give tactical support! But it seems that we are to be eternally cursed with foul weather.

Mother has just come in with an immense bag of groceries and wine and even whiskey. She had a chance to go shopping with Mrs. Clay, in her car, and took the chance to stock up on all sorts of good things. We put away the things together and now she has settled down to play some records. We depend on music so much these days.

I didn't go into the city this afternoon, as I had planned, because I knew I'd stay up late and not be in good trim tomorrow. For I <u>must</u> work. When you come home, (this spring as you wrote it might be) I must have this book ready to give to you.

Constantly I think of the day you will come. Take care of yourself, my precious. You know how you are loved by me.

always your,
Carson

[Carson to Reeves]
Nyack, New York
January 14, 1945

My darling,
Another Sunday has come round again. And for some reason I seem to long for you with a special intensity on Sundays. All day long I have been haunted by the sense of absence, of your not being here, and have been unable to settle to anything. I try to imagine what you are doing, what you had for lunch today, what you are reading. Surely

by now my letters are coming through. I'm hoping to get a letter in the Monday morning post.

Yesterday I was very excited by the news that the Russian offensive had opened at last. It snowed nearly all day yesterday and I worked until around four in the afternoon. Rita was at home, as she doesn't have to work on Saturday. So when I had finished work we all walked over to visit our French friends, the Mions. We sat around a beautiful big fire and drank some sourish good white wine. The children dragged out all their Christmas to show to us. I wish you could have seen little Pauline (aged four) dressed in a very real looking little soldier's uniform, complete with stripes and the little gold U.S. on the shoulder, making machine gun noises and shooting with a crutch from behind a barricade of chairs. We stayed rather late, then walked home in the snow. There was more news about the Russian offensive on the radio when we got home.

This morning it was still snowing, and has not stopped all day. The thin fine flakes are blown in gusts and the drifts are deepening. Mother, of course, adores it, and could hardly wait to get out in it again this morning. We had a late Sunday breakfast, and then tuned in on WQXR. We heard the Mendelssohn E minor concerto, and it carried me back to that Sunday afternoon, so long ago, when we heard Yehudi Menuhin playing the same concerto in Charlotte on the Sell's radio— do you remember?

Kay has left, and soon I trust that she will be seeing you. Of course it may turn out to be impossible; she is on a conducted "tour," and to a certain extent her freedom is restricted. I mean she has to arrive and leave with the others etc. But if you are within possible traveling distance I feel sure she will come to you. And finally you will read the poem. Already I've sent you two copies (they were sent ages ago) but it seems my mail just doesn't reach you.

I am now entirely over that little spell of grippe—altogether well. And, as I wrote you, I have made a little pact between us, you and me, to finish this book in March—I hope by the fifteenth, but in any case before the first of April. I must have something to show you when you come home.

This morning I saw in the Times that 1,300 combat soldiers had been sent back to the states for a thirty day furlough. Do you think anything like that might happen to you? I sat at the breakfast table reading every word of the newspaper story, imagining how their families must have felt—to suddenly get the telephone from Camp Shanks or the sudden wire that they were on the way home.

Reeves, do you know whether you will be sent to the Pacific after the war in Europe is over[?] Somehow I feel you won't. You have been wounded twice and have seen so much combat, and you are over thirty years old. If they would send you to the Pacific I don't think I could stand it. Tell me, precious, if you have any way of knowing. Of course the war in Europe is far from finished—but you know how I always, when anything concerns you, look anxious ahead.

I still have no answer to all the other questions I have been writing you. It is even possible that you will be discharged, if your hand and wrist doesn't work properly. Or you may be sent home.

It's getting dark, and I don't have a lamp for this desk. In fact we have no good reading lamps in this apartment. If you were here you would rig up something.

My dearest one, take care of yourself. I adore you.

your,

Carson

[Carson to Reeves]
Nyack, N.Y.
January 15 [1945]

Dearest,

I had resolved not to write you in the mornings, but to make myself wait until the day's work was done. But today again I've broken down; after sitting at the typewriter for three hours, unable to tear my thoughts away from you for more than two seconds at a time, I've taken the story out of the typewriter and now am writing you. This morning, Monday, a letter came. It had the old A.P.O. address in the corner and when I opened it the first lines I read said "mission accomplished." For one dreadful moment I had the thought that you were already back in combat; my heart gave a jump like a shot rabbit, and seeing my face Mother took the letter from me. Then when I read the date—December 8, the day before you were wounded—everything was all right again. But all this morning I have been unable to think of anything but you. My darling heart, I know all your letters by heart and always carry one or two around with me (two hearts in one sentence, but that doesn't matter).

Reeves, it is only when I am living close to you that I feel natural. When we are not together I feel insecure, exposed; it's as though I lived in a room without walls. Do you understand? There is a sense of terror about the simplest things. Sometimes I'm afraid to cross the streets, or again when I am riding on a bus I suddenly <u>know</u> the back wheels are coming off. William would call it an "anxiety neurosis." But you know, darling, it's not like the old Carson who used to live with you. When Mama goes to the grocery store I am uneasy until she gets back. I suppose the central terror of this war, the worry about you being too immense to be coped with, my mind transposes the essential fear and divides it among a hundred minor possibilities. But now, with you in the hospital, I feel nearer to my old state of mind than I have felt for a long time. For the first time in many months I sleep without nightmares. And twice, Reeves, I have even dreamed that you were sleeping by my side.

I suppose I shouldn't write you about these neurotic little quirks—and I wouldn't if they were not disappearing. I look ahead to the day when we can be together. <u>Then</u> I know that all this funny business will be over forever—and we can live and work in simplicity and even with some of the old joy.

Since you have been in England, I imagine you must have looked ahead and made some tentative plans about what you will do after the war. I'd like to hear about them.

Dearest, I don't want you to get the impression that I am not well. That <u>absolutely</u> is not the case. It's just that ten years ago you started spoiling me, and I have not learned to manage this life without you since. I don't have to feel that we are living in the same house, necessarily, (although it's what I would want). But I <u>have</u> to know that you are somewhere in the world and that we can always reach each other.

It's almost one o'clock. I have this work that must be done. I'm to finish a chapter, but it seems somehow to have "wandered", and needs such a lot more work. After this chapter I think the book is fairly plain sailing, but this chapter must be exactly right.

Mother has called me to lunch. We're having asparagus soup and chicken salad sandwiches. Since you have been in the hospital I'm always hungry.

Please God I'll get a letter from England on the afternoon post. I want the written requests for things that will enable me to send you boxes. Among other things I had some very fine French chocolates from a place in New York—but the other day, being so disappointed, I opened them and passed them around to Rita and Mother. But as soon as I have your written request I can send anything. But you have to list what you want.

I must go now, darling. I am kissing this letter.

Your,

Carson

[Carson to Reeves]
January 17 [1945]

My dear one, your letter of December 26 came this morning, twenty four long days it took. The worst of it is that, if my letters take as long to reach you, you have <u>not yet</u> heard from me. When I think of this (and I can't get it out of my mind) I want to cry and walk the floor. I wonder if you have the two cables.

It's morning, and I've broken my promise again. But when I hear from you, especially now that I am doubtful if my mail is reaching you, I can't settle to work until I've written.

You can imagine what I felt when you said the doctors were undecided for several days about sending you back to the States. I've told you how, during this past month, I have been absolutely possessed by the feeling you were on the way home. Even now I can't rid myself of this feeling of expectancy. Whenever I see a bus pass, I follow it up to the corner and watch the passengers get off. Now you say that if the bones don't knit properly an operation would be necessary, and in that case you would probably be sent back. You say it will be two months until we know about this—that is, counting from December 26, sometime in the latter part of February. So until then I will be busy trying to put a spell on your poor bones. Don't knit, don't knit, don't knit, bones. Darling, be sure to cable me just as soon as you know anything more about this. I shall be waking up each morning with the thought it is still possible you will be sent home to me.

Yesterday there was a blizzard here. I had a dental appointment over at Sparkill, and so was out in it quite a while. There was a sort of [Brueghel] heartiness about the streets after the storm cleared. The cheeks of the children in their snowsuits were bright scarlet. Workmen were busy clearing the roads, and there were little fires in ashcans on some corners. This morning I was out again, [very] early as soon as the stores opened, hunting for cigarettes. The storm is quite over, and the sky is a delicate silvery blue. These Northern skies in the winter time—somehow they are lovelier than the skies of the South.

Speaking of cigarettes, I bought a little hand roller and some Bull Durham this morning. Also, I got a pipe—and it promptly made me sick. So I'll stick to Bull Durham if nothing else is to be found. Usually, though, we have had very little trouble getting cigarettes of one kind or another. In fact I feel constantly the guilt of living in a country that has not suffered in this war—excepting always, of course, the dreadful

anxieties of those (and that means most of us) who have loved ones
overseas. Sometimes I think it would be easier to stand this war if we
had a bit more of the sense of deprivation.

Dearest, I'll stop now and try to work. Soon, surely soon, you will
be hearing from me. God bless you.

Always your,
Carson

[Carson to Reeves]
January 18 [1945]

Precious Reeves,

It is late afternoon and for a change I've been a hard working girl
today. Only a page or so was done, but I have been sticking steadily
on the job.

Now that the Russian offensive has started, I have a constant feeling of expectancy. Yesterday there was the fall of Moscow, a Lublin
report of the capture of Krakow, a Stalin bulletin announcing the fall
of Chestakkowa. I listened to the radio on and off all day. Now the
Russians are reported at the Silesian border. It is very possible this
immense campaign will end the war, if an attack can be coordinated
from the West.

I wish we could have been together yesterday. I went out for a long
walk around two o'clock, and I have never seen such a radiant afternoon. The sky was flawless azure and the snow, dazzling in sunlight,
was like spun sugar. I tramped for a long time on the road along the
river. The Hudson, too, was blue—but much darker than the sky, a
deep kobalt. When I came indoors the hall and our apartment looked
pitch black for a minute or two, after the brilliance out of doors.

There was a letter from Jessie yesterday. She writes that Tom seems
to be working hard, seems to be happy. The longer I know Jessie, the
more I admire and love her. She, too, was hoping you would be sent
home, of course.

I wonder if Kay has visited you yet. Over and over I've imagined
the meeting between you. I'm so glad the shrapnel wounds have
healed and that you can walk about. Is the hand very painful? I loathe
the thought of anything hurting you, but I dread the day when it will
heal. Since your letter came I've fixed my mind on my spell—don't
knit, don't knit, don't knit, Bones. Be sure to let me know the minute
you find out whether or not an operation will be necessary.

I wish I would get a cable tonight saying my letters are beginning to come.

Dark has come on, and it's time to listen to the evening news. I've been at this desk almost continually since this morning at eight o'clock, and so I'm dead tired. Rest, read, and relax, my darling. Write me your present weight, and take care of yourself. You know I love you.

always your,
Carson

[Carson to Reeves]
January 24 [1945]
Nyack, N.Y.

Reeves dearest,

This morning there was a cable from Kay saying that she had been with you, and that all was well. If I can't feel that my letters are reaching you, then a visit from her is the next best thing—so I am relieved.

It's been four days since I have written—the longest time in many weeks. But one thing and another, quite out of my control, has kept me on the run. Saturday I went into the city and had drinks and a talk with Oliver (we hadn't seen each other for months). Then I took him with me to see Louise Ra[i]ner, whom I had promised to visit that afternoon. I had hoped they would like each other and some sort of mutual benefit would come about, since she is an actress and Oliver now is a producer—but as it turned out they argued a great deal and I was busy placating both of them. After that I went to the Morrises for dinner, and stayed the night. Then Sunday morning I went over to Kay's to see the children, and spent the morning with them. They are all beautifully healthy and Bobby manages extraordinarily well—as I cabled Kay. George was ill, so in the afternoon I went over to Brooklyn. That was the first time I've been to 7 Middagh street since we came up here. I spent part of the afternoon with him, and then came home utterly exhausted. That's the account of the first two days that I didn't write you.

When I got home I found Mama sick with the flu—and she seems to be having a harder time of it than I did. Rita was not feeling well either, and the apartment was in a squalid state. The combination of dreary disorder and illness is something I can't bear. So after making Mama comfortable, I rolled up my sleeves and set to work. I took out every rug and beat and swept them out on the porch. Then mopped all the floors, dusted, cleaned, and made the place orderly. That took me almost the whole day and when I was finished, and had made a little supper, I was too tired to write.

Now this morning everything is in better shape. Mother is still ill, of course, but it seems to be only a ordinary case of flu. I had it in December, and am just now getting over it. So don't worry; she will be quite all right. I shall take good care of her. The doctor has left some capsules for her, and a tonic for me. So we should all be strapping soon. Until she is better, though, I doubt if I can do much work. Mother is very little trouble, but you know how nursing is: there's always something to be done.

I long to get a letter from you. The last one is still the letter dated December 26—during those anxious days when it looked almost as though the Germans would break through. Now the picture is so changed. Today there is fighting in Silesia, in Poznan, and East Prussia is all but surrounded. There is a great elation here over the Russian successes; but professional commentators are rather cautious about making predictions, after the spoilt hopes of last August.

In a few minutes I must go and make Mama some milk toast. Then I'll begin waiting for the postman. Somehow I feel almost sure there will be a letter this afternoon. I long to know more about how it is there in the hospital. I long to know the answers to those three questions I have been asking in every letter.

After the postman comes this afternoon I'll read Proust. Today I was thinking of the immense debt I owe to Proust. It's not a matter of his "influencing my style" or anything like that—it's the rare good fortune of having always something to turn to, a great book that never tarnishes, never become[s] dull from familiarity. Or course, part of this everlasting quality is due to sheer length; but only a part. This morning I was reading the parts about Swann and those early lovely Cambray scenes.——The copies, of course, are those you gave me years ago. It was books like these I wanted to send you to have while in the hospital.

My dear one, I think about you constantly. You know that. It's a strange day. For an hour the sun shines, then suddenly the sky will darken and a heavy snow will blot the world from the windowpanes, then suddenly the snow stops and there is quite, sunny fairness again.

I must go make the milk toast. So goodby for now.

always your,

Carson

[Reeves to Carson]
24 January 1945

Western Union Cablegram
[Carson McCullers]
[Nyack, N.Y.]
If not done so already cable me one hundred dollars care of APO 316[.]
May be home soon[.]
Love
Reeves McCullers

[Carson to Reeves]
24 January 1945

Western Union Cablegram
[James McCullers]
[London]
Sent money[.]
Need anything [more?]
Watching and waiting for you every moment.
Love[,]
Carson McCullers

[Carson to Reeves]
January 27 [1945]

Precious Reeves:
    MAY BE HOME SOON! Those words have sung in my head con-
stantly since the cable came. The days, from now on until I see you,
are dedicated to suspense. How soon does SOON mean? Has my spell
worked? Are the bones not knitting? The MAY is what bothers me—if
only it could have been WILL! How likely are the chances of your
coming? What change has taken place in your condition? And when
and if you do come home will it be only on furlough or for good? If
possible cable me more definitely.
    Did I send enough money? Let me know if you need more.
    Oh darling, I'm so excited. Mother and Skeet [family nickname for
Carson's sister, Margarita Gachet Smith] and I can talk of nothing else.

I hold the cable and read it over and over. You know that all along I've been haunted by the notion that you will be here soon.

Today I'm in bed; it's only a cold, but I want to be sure to be in tip-top shape when you get here. I wonder if you will be flown over or will come by ship. I can do nothing but plan how it will be the first few days. I see myself cutting up your meat for you—or just gazing at you, and touching you lightly to see if you are real.—Reeves, let me know <u>immediately</u>, as soon as it's more settled. Until I know more I feel like somebody floating around in air. Excuse this crazy letter; under the circumstances it's the best I can do.

Always your,
Carson

[Carson to Reeves]
[February 4, 1945]

Western Union Cablegram
[Nyack, N.Y.]
[James Reeves McCullers]
[London]
Are my letters coming[?]
Do you need money[?]
Will you be home soon[?]
Cable me[.]
Love[,]
Carson McCullers

[Carson to Reeves]
February 8 [1945]

Reeves dearest,
There's still no word from you since the PROBABLY cable. I watch for the mail twice a day, and surely soon there will be a letter. I watch for you every day—but somehow I think it will be nearer the end of the month when you come. Please, Reeves, if it is to be later—please, darling, sit down and write me a complete letter about it all. Answer those three questions I bombarded you with so long [ago].

It's about six, and I have been at this typewriter since nine this morning, except for a lunch and a walk to the store. The snow has been coming down all day. It's piled up on the fence outside and in the crotches of the trees. The sky is dark.

There's nothing for me to write. I work, and spend the rest of the time wondering when you will come. Every evening when I go into the sitting room Mother and I play a little game—supposing how it will be when you knock on the door, or telephone, or wire.

God Bless you, Reeves. Remember, if you believe you will be later than February please write me a thorough letter. But maybe you will be here in a week or so or even tonight—who knows? This is the slowest month I've ever known.

Goodbye for now.

Always your,

Carson

[Carson to Reeves]
Nyack, N.Y.
February 19 [1945]

Reeves precious:

I have not written this last week because I was almost certain you are on the way. I hope we shall read this letter together. Every time I go out on the street I expect to see you, every knock on the door means for a moment that you've come.

Today Jinny [Virginia Standard Smith, wife of Carson's brother] wired us that Brother [Lamar Smith, Jr., Carson's brother] is in San Francisco and will be home in two weeks. Mother cried with happiness, and is now writing Jinny.

Today I expect you even more faithfully than usual—perhaps because it's my birthday. Also, I have heard that a big shipment of wounded men is expected at a camp near here. I can hardly keep myself away from the telephone—I sit and *stare* at it, trying to will it to ring.

Our laundress came in the other day almost overcome. Her boy, who was wounded about the same time you were, had walked in the door two days before. Of course I questioned her endlessly.

There is not much to write. This suspense leaves me no peace of mind for anything else. I haven't heard (except the two cables) from you since that letter written December 26. Surely, if you are not on the way, I would have heard more from you. If anything has happened, if you are not coming, you *must* write me and let me know in detail what has happened and what your status is now. You must answer those questions I have harassed you with in so many letters.

It's a clear, marvelous day. Yesterday I went out walking and noticed that the first reddish buds are on the trees. The river is ultramarine and the sunlight so yellow and springlike. It would be a fine day for us to go out walking.

I try without much success to work, but I read a great deal. I sit before the typewriter for hours, making pretense of working, but my mind wanders and hunts for you.

Dearest, I hope and expect that this note will be forwarded to you here. But I shall send it just in case something has happened to disturb, or put off, your plans for homecoming.

Remember always how I love you.

always your,

Carson

[Carson to Reeves]
April 2 [1945]

My adored one,

I woke up at dawn this morning, wondering what sort of trip you had back. I'm afraid you were dreadfully tired. All day I have been with you. My Reeves, do you know my love? I want you to feel my tenderness for you every instant—I want you to feel it in each nerve and muscle and bone. I feel your love for me in that way. My love and safety in you—that is what keeps me going. We want to live and work, quietly and with some measure of serenity. We have so much ahead of us, so much to do.

I just wrote a letter to Elizabeth [Ames], and shall probably hear from her soon.

Henry just telephoned to say that he was going over to read parts of his book to a blind friend, and wanting to know if I want to come too. I don't, not a smidgen. But that's the kind of invitation it's impossible to refuse. He is coming by, and will have supper with us.

Mother is still obsessed by the notion of the house. Henry said he wants to look it over with us.

My blessed Reeves. There are no words tender enough for me to call you. Take care of yourself. Drink very little, as I mean to do; too much drinking is very bad for both of us. Study and work. Our future, the chances of our being together these next few years, may depend on how much German and French you can learn these next months.

This is just a love letter. Goodbye for now.

Your,

Carson

[Carson to Reeves]
May 8, 1945

Reeves dearest,

This is just a note written after the morning work. Have done about two pages, and intend to work harder and more this afternoon.

You are with me always. Yesterday, after listening to the victory programs, I longed for us to have a quiet glass of wine. I can't understand those who were able to mill around Times square and blow horns and carry on. I kept thinking of all those men who can never come back. But you are back, and I can never thank God enough.

I'm glad you wrote to [John] Vincent [Adams] about UNRA. When you write again give him my love. But I rather wonder if the medical requirements for UNRA are not about the same as AMG. I also am greatly anxious to know about your chances of being released from the army. You will let me know at once—just as soon as anything happens. And I am waiting for the telephone call about your wrist. Dear darling, I'm being very good. Only two jiggers of whiskey a day. Work. And I'll get out for a walk every day.

The town seems to be totally stripped of cigarettes. If you are able to, and have any left over, can you send us a few packs? My precious husband, I miss you so. You know how I love you. I won't write any more, because my back is tired.

Goodbye for now,

always your,

Carson

[Reeves to Carson]
[July 1945]
Tuesday Night

My Dearest One,

It was so good to have your letter today and also to talk with you again Sunday and Monday. Weekdays are bad enough in this penitentiary but week-ends are particularly hellish. However, my "stretch" here will soon be over.

I am sorry I have to repeat that the situation is exactly the same as when I last saw you. But my papers are due back from Washington any day. I have learned this: it will be one of two things—a desk or administrative job with the army wherever they may need me, or retirement. Officers with any degree of disability incurred in line of duty are not put on inactive duty. A lawyer here tells me that they either work or are retired.

I will let you know the minute I get something definite, Darling. In the meantime, please, please don't be tense or worried but carry on there with your book which is almost done.

All of our difficult times are behind us. Believe me. We have paid for some peace and happiness and I intend to see that we have it.

If we can't travel for some time or do just <u>exactly</u> as we want to we can at least be settled and enjoy each other's warmth, gaiety and company. There's plenty we have to do right here at home.

I have never felt closer to you or loved and yearned more for you than I do right this moment. I have imaginary conversations and think of you all during the day. I shall never get enough of you. Oh, my Darling Girl, how tenderly and deeply I love you.

With the war nearly over and all the big trouble behind us our life is just opening into its full growth and beauty. You believe that, don't you? *You have to!*

When I am able to squat in a quiet place I read and study French and am brushing up on some math. After I read some more Henry James I should like to talk with you. He is very fascinating. Also read lately a sad but strong little book—Alan Seeger's Diary and Letters. This war isn't much different than the last one except that I was in it.

For some reason I made an agreement with myself last week to not have another drink until I see you next. Well, it does ease the sinus pressure which has been terrific these past two weeks—and also saves money.

If anything comes up I will call you but if not I will telephone Saturday evening at 7:30.

I will see you soon my Precious.
All my love,
R[eeves]

[Reeves in Nyack, New York, to Carson at Yaddo Arts Colony in Saratoga Springs, New York]
Late Sunday Night

My Darling,
It has been raining here all day but has just stopped and it is cool
and pleasant. I have just been out in the garden for a cigarette. It is a
pitch black, still night and a dog is baying in the distance. The nights
and days are much better than the ones we were spending this time
last year.
Today has been a busy one. Rita, Moe and I have been in the basement painting, cleaning, etc. It will be very cozy there when all the
work is done. I am hesitant about going ahead with the attic since we
could never definitely decide on a color. If I am back here soon for any
length of time I will send you a color chart to choose from. Then I will
go ahead. If not, by the time you get back here the book will be finished
and we can have fun doing it together and you bossing me.
When Moe came out yesterday she brought a big roast of beef and
Bebe fixed it for dinner today. Everyone wished you had been here to
partake with us. I do hope you are getting enough to eat there. Please
write me in detail what your trouble was and if you are all right again.
Last week I called Utica and as my papers had not returned for
Washington I asked for an extension on my leave and will return there
the 21st unless they wire for me sooner. I shall probably go to Washington Wednesday and I will let you know immediately if there are favorable results. The hospital sent me a *routine* form to fill out stating all
my service and military history. I have learned that this is something
they do on all cases of permanent limited service and does not necessarily mean retirement. The very minute anything breaks I will let you
know, Precious. 131 isn't the same without you. Nothing is the same
for me when I am away from you. You are always in my thoughts and
sometimes just walking along the street I imagine meeting you. If we
live to be a hundred years old I will never get enough being with you.
You are as much a part of me as my own brain and heart.
I have no further word to give of my immediate destiny until I get
back to Utica. I hate this feeling of suspension but it can't be helped,

Darling. We will soon know. In any event, it won't be like any horrors of the past.

I am well, healthy and take care of myself. I am being a good boy and will continue to be one. I know that you are taking care of yourself. Bebe and Rita are both well and miss you. Rita up and planned to go to New Orleans next week but after a telephone call decided to wait as New Orleans said he would be here in 2–3 weeks. The same old run-a-round. She took a few days off from the office but is going back Monday.

If I am still at Utica when you finish the book and are ready to leave Yaddo I will come there and bring you back to Nyack until our plans are all complete.

I couldn't say it over the telephone since other people were there but you know always, always that I love you more than it is possible to comprehend in the realms of all mathematical conception.

Reeves.

[Reeves in Nyack, New York, to Carson at Yaddo Arts Colony in Sara-
toga Springs, New York]
Tuesday Night
Nyack

My Darling,

Although I was glad to hear your voice tonight you sounded a bit tired, hollow and disappointed. I cannot blame you. I, also, feel let down. At the moment I am so goddamn mad with the United States Army I could spit tacks.

When I called you Monday night I only had orders to report to Fort Dix for reassignment. This morning War Department orders straight from Washington came through assigning me to Camp Wheeler, Ga. The interpretation of that means that I will only go there for reassignment. If they can think of any worse place than Wheeler (which is in Macon Georgia) I will probably be sent there. Although I have had quite a bit of amphibious landing and training experience I am sure they wouldn't dare send me to Florida where we could be near the beach. No, we might find that happy and pleasant.

There is the other side of the fly paper, Carson. I am an experienced infantryman. Down South they are trying to make fighting doughboys out of shoe clerks and ribbon salesmen and they say I am badly needed there. OK. I have told you about replacements I got in the Hurtgen

Forrest—shivering, demoralized kids who didn't know the first thing about war, the enemy, fighting—they didn't even know about death. I hated and cursed the officers who had pretended to train those men. As you know the Infantry is my first love, that is, as regards the army, and I am not really too unhappy about getting back in the saddle. I don't like to boss men but in such a serious thing as war I like to talk, be with and direct them in something I know about. If they need me for Infantry training OK, but I think I would be of more value in the AMG in Europe, so I am resubmitting my papers to them next week. Most likely I will be given 10 more days leave and I will see the people in Washington again. Also I am taking Helena up on her offer . . . about Sen. Wagner and Rep. Meade. Mrs. Flood, who is from Charlottesville is a personal friend of General Cabe (head of the AMG school at the University there), says she will call him to put in a plug for me from that end. *If* AMG is taking on any more officers for the ETO then JRM will make it. I will keep you posted.

In the meantime I will spruce up the attic and on the 9th of August I will go on down South. After I get assigned to a permanent station there I will get quarters for us if you still want to come down. I would like for us to be together but it is only reluctantly that I drag you down South again. Perhaps it won't be for long.

I got in from Utica about the time Bebe's call to you came through. The place is the same, or, more pleasant and comfortable than ever. There is the feeling of <u>Home</u> about every corner of the place. Bebe looked very good. Your letter had terrified her in to smoking only eight cigarettes during the day. She swears she hasn't had a beer in two weeks and I can't find any empty beer bottles around the kitchen. We had fried chicken, grits and biscuits after waiting until nine o'clock for Rita. We played some records, talked to the Floods for a while and R[ita] came in at about nine. Every one is in bed now and after finishing this I will read for a while.

My beloved, my own darling Carson, I miss you, I think of you every hour of the day. Someday soon, we will really be together and be able to sit and look and contemplate each other for hours on end. I don't think we need a vacation, we just need to live together about five years straight without interruption. It will be good if we can do that in Europe but it will be all right in the states too. Do you think so?

I called Bessie tonight and she and Henry are well. She is coming over in a few days to see us. Annie is still in California sweating out a B-29 to the Pacific. She met Muriel [Rukeyser] in Los Angeles who sent her love to us. Bebe has, I suppose written you all the family news. All is well. Lamar is still in California.

I am glad that the typing goes well and I hope it will soon be over. I wish I were there to help you.

I will be here for the next ten days. Write to me now and then. ILYMTIPTCIAMC

Reeves

[Reeves to Carson]
Friday Night
3 August 1945

My Darling Carson,

Finally I am settled here—that is, I have been assigned to a unit and my work for the next 4–5 months is outlined. I am assigned for an indefinite period to this station.

I remember the first line in "Reflections"—all army Posts in peace time are alike. They are alike in war-time too. The only difference is how far distant you are from the people or the one you want to be near. It was damn bad to have to return south; it is harder still to be cut off from you.

First of all I want to protect you and me: us. I want to describe this place adjectively, how life will be like for us in Macon in the months to come; and then you must decide whether it will be harmful to you and us.

Prologue: you know how much I love you, so much that I can bear our being apart if I think it is better for each of us at the time. And you must never forget you are the only one for whom I have ever had any affection and with whom I feel deeply identified in life. But I don't have to say all those things—you already know them. Tonight I wired I hoped we could be together in September but must consider all the things I am going to say.

I. Duty here for junior officers is a bit hellish. The discipline for men and officers is more severe than in any army I have known. The physical strain what with the heat and intense training program is terrific. The mental strain is less than in combat because death is not imminent. Gerald may have been in I.R.T.C's but I'm damned if there's been anything like this outside of the French Foreign Legion. They aren't all alike, I have learned that. There is something else in the atmosphere here which I can't very well put in a letter but if I see you soon I can tell you. But, Hell! I can take anything the U.S. Army can dish out; in fact, I can dish it out myself. I can sweat it out here for months, and months and months *if* I know you are all right—if you are able to work and be at reasonable peace with yourself.

II. We will be lonely here. Both of us. You more than I because during the long days I will be identified with work that is to some of concern and importance, although not interesting. We won't meet or know any people to be with at night. They just aren't here—on the Post or in town. I don't know if you are familiar with the wartime army officers and wives or not. I have met all the officers and there isn't one that would interest us beyond the second drink. They are good chaps and all right during the day because they are doing something that is important and necessary, but after 5:00 p.m—Nein!

I will be able to be with you at the most only four nights a week, only 2 or 3 week-ends in the month and on occasion I will have to be in the field a week at a time. That is no exaggeration—<u>that</u> is the schedule. It will be terribly lonely—and, my Darling, there may not be a piano or even music.

Macon is a crowded army war time town with thousands of men and hundreds of officers due for overseas duty soon trying to snatch a few last days or weeks with their wives and families. I have started enquiries today but have no idea what sort of apartment I will be able to get. With luck one may get something that is livable.

III. Life here for single officers is quite monkish. I have lived a monk's life and if I am not with you such is my life. It is hard but not intolerable. If I know that you can settle in Nyack for the winter, work and not be too lonely, then I will get along all right here. After all, Carson, I missed you last June '44 with blood squirting out of me—fear in my guts; behind hedgerows at Brest, in cold, muddy fox holes in other parts of Europe—missing you here won't be quite so bad.

IV. I have finally gotten around to what I am trying to say. We know that we love each other. You should know now that I am absolutely devoted to you. There has never been and never will be any one else in my life. I don't mean that to sound of an ultimatum to you. I have presented mostly the unfavorable side of the picture. You know that we will have times of bliss, and peace, and happiness together no matter where life may cast us—but here in the months to come you will be alone as you may have never been before—that is, just you in a room in a little apartment in the south by yourself a great deal of the time—with me on the Post here not able to get to you.

This is it: <u>The great fear</u> (the only fear left in my soul; the others I have destroyed, or they have been destroyed for me) <u>that the imaginary friend would come between us to the extent that I would be destroyed that time.</u>

To forestall that I can bear our being apart for a long, long time.

So the decision is with you, Dearest. I am not weak but I can neither say yes or no about this.

I hope all goes well with the typing and I wish I were there to help. Pack it off to Ann, go back to Nyack and take your time before making up your mind if you wish.

You are my own Precious Carson and I don't believe any one has ever been loved as much as I love you.

Reeves
4th Battalion, I.R.T.C.,
Camp Wheeler, Ga.
Telephone # 288.

<u>over</u>

After reading over this letter I beg of you caution and consideration and that you make what you believe to be the right decision. I will abide by it.

I love you,
R[eeves]

[Reeves to Carson]
Sunday Night
5th August [1945]
3 miles SE of West Hell

My Darling Girl,

To anyone listening to us I am sure we sounded like the damned and condemned on the telephone last night. We are both pretty well fed up and browned off but we will just have to hold on. Remember, Darling, that we are old sweats and have been through much worse than this. It won't last for long. The war may be over sooner than we expect.

I was afraid my other letter may have sounded a little cockeyed and to tell the truth I was deadly tired and I had a few drinks. However, after reading the letter over the next morning I went ahead and mailed it. I hope I didn't say anything wrong or that would upset you. I would never knowingly say or do anything that would hurt you. You know that.

It is hot and hellish here, the same old fierce, diabolical fascist

South that I spent over twenty years trying to get away from. I stay right in the post and will do my work the best I can.

I still think it would be wiser for you to stay in Nyack or Yaddo this winter. By that time perhaps I can have wangled somehow to get away from here. I will repeat I will be all right here. I can stick it out and will not drink but will work and work hard. The harder I work the better off I will be. Also it is likely that I can get a leave during Christmas to be with you there. I can hold on here, Precious.

In the event you feel that you must come down I have tried several angles on getting a place to live with little or no results so far. I telephoned Bessie Dunwoody today and she was not optimistic. She only has a furnished room in a friend's home. However, I will keep trying.

I am so depressed but it will wear off after a while. Next week the new men come in and I will be very busy all the time. Days and most of the nights.

Some of the chaps here are nice and I have made friends with two or three. The Colonel seems to be OK. His home is in Utica. That's the army for you.

Don't fret, Carson, and try to keep steady. For our sake and our future happiness I beg of you not to drink too much. You will make your decision as to what you think best and we will stick by that decision.

My own precious Darling, I adore you,

Your,

Reeves

X X X X X X X X X X X X

[Reeves to Carson]
Tuesday Night
7th August [1945]

My Darling—

I am very tired but want to get a note off to you before turning in. It is nearly ten o'clock. We get up here at five-thirty and training begins one hour later. Chaps who live in town have to get up at <u>four-thirty</u> in order to get here in time. If they are late they are restricted to the Post for a week and fined half-a-month's pay—<u>that</u> particularly includes officers.

I put that nasty bit of information in to let you know that husbands and wives here don't have too good a life.

There was a shower this afternoon and it is a bit cooler tonight. There is even a little breeze. It won't make tomorrow or tomorrow any pleasanter though.

There is nothing new here with me. I work eleven hours each day with the troops and occasionally have night duty. I am usually so tired I flop right into bed. What few minutes I have free are devoted to reading and studying math.

Sometimes I am almost too tired to be lonely. I give strict attention to duty but otherwise there is a shocked, fuming indignation of what has happened to me. I'm afraid I seem anti-social to my *Confrères*— and that isn't my real nature. But I will get used to it soon and into a nice little rut like everyone else here.

Who knows? What with the atomic bombings the war may be over in another year.

I have 88 points but it takes 100 for Infantry officers to get out.

[John] Vincent [Adams] is keeping in touch with AMG and is to let me know the minute an European quota comes in. But I don't want Europe if Mister Truman won't let you go along, and I am afraid civilian passenger traffic won't open for over a year.

At the moment our immediate future isn't too cheering, is it. But, believe me, Darling, this time last year our future was almost non-existent.

Let's get the lemon juice out of our system and try not to be glum, my angel. We have gone through much harder things than 5–6 months separation here in the States. We can take it.

Bebe needs you this winter and, after all, you have thirty or forty more years together.

The training cycle we are on now ends the second week in December and I know of no reason why I shan't get two weeks leave to be with you in Nyack at Christmas. That will be fun, won't it?

It seems so long since I heard from or saw you. Write when you have time. Let me know when you get the book off and I will give a couple of hurrahs.

Take care of your precious self.

You are my own adorable Carson, and I am crazy about you.

R[eeves]

Give my love to Elizabeth [Ames] there.

[Reeves to Carson]
Thursday Night
9th August [1945]

Dear One,
Your letter came this morning—the first I had heard from you in a week, except the telephone call.

When you get too tired of the book, that is, finishing it up, just remember others who are tired of things they have been with for years also. I am so sick and tired of this goddamn army and everything about it that I have the dry heaves. It is like a bubbling cancer in my side.

I wish I could be there with you to help—I feel it would go much better. Together we can always surmount any trouble as tedium. But our attempting a pleasant existence together here in the South in the summer calls for too high a price.

Since Monday I have looked at two "apartments" and one furnished room. They were all terrible and depressing and within a week we should be miserable—what with the weather like it is and the Gestapo conditions the Commanding General imposes on officers here. It's not worth it, Carson.

From the tone of the note to your letter I feel you may be reconciled to staying there this winter—either at Yaddo or Nyack. I believe that that would be best—after carefully thinking the whole thing over many times. I am reluctant to take a chance on anything happening to us now after what we have both been through. I won't allow you to be exposed to the different kinds of starvation you would undergo here.

So let me know how you feel about this tentative decision. Stay on there until early spring, but if an emergency comes up and either of us becomes desperate you can join me here right away. I am reasonably sure I will be able to be with you Christmas. Let me know how this strikes you, Dearest.

A major in headquarters told me yesterday he would bet a bottle of whiskey that most limited service men and *all* permanent limited service people would be out of the army by the first of the year. I could only say "Bull S___ Major," but I hope to heaven he is right.

The time has changed a bit here due to the atomic bomb and Russia's declaration. When we announced the news through the loud speakers yesterday afternoon the men nearly tore the barracks down. Within the past twenty-four hours they have begun to feel that it will be over before they are sent to the Philippines. That just couldn't happen to them! Usually in the air here there is a pervading gloom and inner trembling fear among the draftees and also the bright, fresh lieutenants from Benning who are all scheduled to go over soon. None of them want any part of it. It is bad enough to be in the army at the end of nowhere like this, but it isn't pleasant to be working with people who feel that way. Not that I blame them for the way they feel. But if I were in their position I should take my lot more philosophically.

There is nothing interesting to write about what I do here. A bunch of live bodies come in dressed in civvies. We put army duds on them, issue equipment and a rifle and in seventeen weeks try to make infantry soldiers of them. The instruction is by rote—basic individual and squad training. Damn boring.

Today hasn't been so bad. It is late afternoon and I have been sitting in my room looking out the window and sipping a drink of Scotch. Quarters are in a large pecan grove. Along the road across the way are some Crepe-myrtles. Two Negro men, whistling together, trudge along the road going somewhere.

Don't worry about me, Precious. I will be all right soon. After I get used to the routine of this rat race here I will be able to make use of what spare time I get. I have lots of reading and studying to do. The time will pass quickly for both of us. The few months left will go by and we will be together again. When that time comes I know I won't want to let you out of my sight for at least five years.

I wonder whether you will stay at Nyack or Yaddo. You know which will be the best for you and I want you to stay wherever you feel you can work better—that is, if you have any plans for work in mind. I would say you are entitled to a vacation if you want one.

I lead a very quiet life here. One can't drink much and do his job well here so I drink very little. My expenses are slight—$30 a month for mess, about $30–40 for laundry, cleaning, drinks and incidentals. I can more than get along on the pay I get. Use what you need of the check coming to you, and after paying Bebe put the rest in the bank. Hard times are around the corner and we must save. I expect you will have quite a few expenses in August so if you need any additional money be sure to let me know and I will send it to you.

Take care of yourself, My Darling Girl, and I will do the same.

You are very busy just now so don't feel that you have to write too often—but write *some*.

You are always in my heart.

Your,

Reeves

In about a week I will send the fatigues I promised. They were the nearest your size I could get.

R[eeves]

X X X X X X X X X X X X

[Reeves to Carson]
13th August '45
Monday Night

My Darling,
Hi-de-hi! Ho-de-ho! A bit of good news. This thing has been on the griddle since I have been here but I didn't dare mention it as I didn't wish to dash any hopes either of us would get up.

Well, I'm in. On Wednesday or Thursday I leave for Camp Richie, Maryland. That is the very ritzy and up-to-date Military Intelligence Training Center. Strategic, Tactical and Combat Intelligence. It would have been intensely important and interesting to me three years ago when I tried to get a course there. But it is just as interesting now: Richie is four hours from New York—two from Washington. I will be there for six weeks for a course of study beginning August 25th. My orders read that on completion of course I will return to my "proper" station, Viz., Camp Wheeler. But I may be able to pull some strings by then. The separation policy for permanent limited service men may go into effect by October 15 when I will be through there. In any event I can get away from the awful heat and from the South. The first two things I thought of on getting my orders were—I would be closer to you—I could get away from the South.

This thing doesn't lead to much now that the war is almost over—it doesn't commit me to overseas duty, unless I would volunteer—which I haven't. I would have been very keen about this before. Joseph probably went to school there.

In '42 I was at Richie for a short course and it is a very pleasant army post—if army posts can be allowed that adjective. It is up high near the Pennsylvania Pocono mountains with cool lakes around. It won't be like the usual crowded army camp and if you would like to come for a week or two in September I am all for it. I will G-2 the situation as soon as I get there and let you know. Oh! Dear Carson I am so happy about this.

We will see each other *this* month; I had resigned myself to 5 or 6 dreary, lonely months without being with you. You can't know how much I want to look at you and hold you close to me. It might have been a hundred years since I drove down the lane and waved goodbye to you.

In case you are making plans to stay in Yaddo for the winter—or part of it—I would say not cancel those plans because, Precious, I just can't possibly say where I will be, whether I will be in or out of the army. The army is as perverse as fate itself.

I will telephone you just as soon as I get to Maryland and find out what gives.

Hope you are half as happy as I am.

Your,

Reeves

[Reeves to Carson]
21 November 1945
Wednesday Night

Carson, Dear—

I wonder how my darling is tonight. It was good to talk with you the other night and I am pleased to know that you can sit by the fire.

I must have sounded a bit goofy on the telephone, but you see, I had to take the call in the Registrar's office and there were lots of people standing around.

You can't imagine how good it is to know that you have improved so much (you mentioned that William said 85%). You must not try to do too much and give yourself time to get completely well, for when I get there I want you healthy, fat and sassy. We will have such a good celebration, won't we?

My papers aren't back yet so I shan't make next week's board. At the earliest it will be December 6–7 before I can get there. The adjutant agrees that the unreasonable delay is a bit ridiculous even for the army and he is sending another tracer to Washington Friday. I have a feeling they have sent some chap paddling back to France in a canoe to look for any records that might have been left on the continent.

We will just have to be patient, my Precious. We will be together soon. These last few month's separation seem longer than when I was overseas, though.

My routine is still the same and I am disgustingly healthy. Read a strange, rambling little book the other day—"The Unquiet Grave" by Cyril Connolly also one by Philip Wylie full of pus, bite and venom: "Generation of Vipers." Right now I am absorbed in rereading some of Virginia Woolf's works.

The countryside here is so beautiful these days. It is good to be off by oneself to take it in. Today has been rainy and overcast and I have thought of you, wishing we could be sitting together before a fire talking and drinking.

Late this afternoon I became depressed and walked across the river to get some whiskey, but I won't drink much. Everyone here has gone somewhere for the week-end and I am the only one left in the ward.

It has stopped raining and the wind has risen. Dark, angry clouds are shuttling to the southwest. Tomorrow should be pleasant and cold.

I don't know if you noticed the enclosed clipping from last Sunday's Times or not. Please don't think I am hipped or fey on the subject of getting back to Germany, but there's something in me that says go to Europe for the next two years. Of course, if I could get what I want here in the States in factory management it would be best for me to stay. But my getting what I want just at this time is problematical. This business mentioned in the clipping is the most practical way for me to get to Europe. It is likely that you can get over on your own quite easily—but I do want us to be together. I need you. I hope I am able to offer what you need. I feel that there is so much before us; we are in the full growth and maturity of our lives. However, I have no intention of allowing us ever really to grow old. There is so much more for us to see, experience and do. And nothing I do or feel is good unless I can share it with you.

Be good to yourself and try not to fret about things. Do as your elders tell you.

Soon, my angel,
all my love,
R[eeves]
X X X X X X X X X X X X X X X

Appendices

Bibliography

Index

Appendix I
Outline of "The Mute"
(The Heart Is a Lonely Hunter)

The broad principal theme of this book is indicated in the first dozen pages.* This is the theme of man's revolt against his own inner isolation and his urge to express himself as fully as is possible. Surrounding this general idea there are several counter themes and some of these may be stated briefly as follows: (1) There is a deep need in man to express himself by creating some unifying principle or God. A personal God created by a man is a reflection of himself and in substance this God is most often inferior to his creator. (2) In a disorganized society these individual Gods or principles are likely to be chimerical and fantastic. (3) Each man must express himself in his own way—but this is often denied to him by a tasteful, short-sighted society. (4) Human beings are innately cooperative, but an unnatural social tradition makes them behave in ways that are not in accord with their deepest nature. (5) Some men are heroes by nature in that they will give all that is in them without regard to the effort or to the personal returns.

Of course these themes are never stated nakedly in the book. Their overtones are felt through the characters and situations. Much will depend upon the insight of the reader and the care with which the book is read. In some parts the underlying ideas will be concealed far down below the surface of a scene and at other times these ideas will be shown with a certain emphasis. In the last few pages the various motifs which have been recurring from time to time throughout the book are drawn sharply together and the work ends with a sense of cohesive finality.

The general outline of this work can be expressed very simply. It is the story of five isolated, lonely people in their search for expression

*Originally published in Oliver Evans's *The Ballad of Carson McCullers* and reprinted in *The Mortgaged Heart*, edited by Margarita G. Smith.

163

and spiritual integration with something greater than themselves. One of these five persons is a deaf mute, John Singer—and it is around him that the whole book pivots. Because of their loneliness these other four people see in the mute a certain mystic superiority and he becomes in a sense their ideal. Because of Singer's infirmity his outward character is vague and unlimited. His friends are able to impute to him all the qualities which they would wish for him to have. Each one of these four people creates his understanding of the mute from his own desires. Singer can read lips and understand what is said to him. In his eternal silence there is something compelling. Each one of these persons makes the mute the repository for his most personal feelings and ideas.

This situation between the four people and the mute has an almost exact parallel in the relation between Singer and his deaf-mute friend, Antonapoulos. Singer is the only person who could attribute to Antonapoulos dignity and a certain wisdom. Singer's love for Antonapoulos threads through the whole book from the first page until the very end. No part of Singer is left untouched by this love and when they are separated his life is meaningless and he is only marking time until he can be with his friend again. Yet the four people who count themselves as Singer's friends know nothing about Antonapoulos at all until the book is nearly ended. The irony of this situation grows slowly and steadily more apparent as the story progresses.

When Antonapoulos dies finally of Bright's disease Singer, overwhelmed by loneliness and despondency, turns on the gas and kills himself. Only then do these other four characters begin to understand the real Singer at all.

About this central idea there is much of the quality and tone of a legend. All the parts dealing directly with Singer are written in the simple style of a parable.

Before the reasons why this situation came about can be fully understood it is necessary to know each of the principal characters in some detail. But the characters cannot be described adequately without the events which happen to them being involved. Nearly all of the happenings in the book spring directly from the characters. During the space of this book each person is shown in his strongest and most typical actions.

Of course it must be understood that none of these personal characteristics are told in the didactic manner in which they are set down here. They are implied in one successive scene after another—and it is only at the end, when the sum of these implications is considered, that the real characters are understood in all of their deeper aspects.

CHARACTERS AND EVENTS

John Singer

Of all the main characters in the book Singer is the simplest. Because of his deaf-mutism he is isolated from the ordinary human emotions of other people to a psychopathic degree. He is very observant and intuitive. On the surface he is a model of kindness and cooperativeness—but nothing which goes on around him disturbs his inner self. All of his deeper emotions are involved in the only friend to whom he can express himself, Antonapoulos. In the second chapter Biff Brannon thinks of Singer's eyes as being "cold and gentle as a cat's." It is this same remoteness that gives him an air of wisdom and superiority.

Singer is the first character in the book only in the sense that he is the symbol of isolation and thwarted expression and because the story pivots about him. In reality each one of his satellites is of far more importance than himself. The book will take all of its body and strength in the development of the four people who revolve about the mute.

The parts concerning Singer are never treated in a subjective manner. The style is oblique. This is partly because the mute, although he is educated, does not think in words but in visual impressions. That, of course, is a natural outcome of his deafness. Except when he is understood through the eyes of other people the style is for the main part simple and declarative. No attempt will be made to enter intimately into his subconscious. He is a flat character in the sense that from the second chapter on through the rest of the book his essential self does not change.

At his death there is a strange little note from the cousin of Antonapoulos found in his pocket:

DEAR MR. SINGER,
No address on corner of letters. They all sent back to me. Spiros Antonapoulos died and was buried with his kidneys last month. Sorry to tell same but no use writing letters to the dead.
Yours truly,
CHARLES PARKER

When the man is considered in his deepest nature (because of his inner character and peculiar situation) his suicide at the death of Antonapoulos is a necessity.

Mick Kelly

Mick is perhaps the most outstanding character in the book. Because of her age and her temperament her relation with the mute is more accentuated than in any other person's. At the beginning of the second part of the work she steps out boldly—and from then on, up until the last section, she commands more space and interest than anyone else. Her story is that of the violent struggle of a gifted child to get what she needs from an unyielding environment. When Mick first appears she is at the age of thirteen, and when the book ends she is fourteen months older. Many things of great importance happen to her during this time. At the beginning she is a crude child on the threshold of a period of quick awakening and development. Her energy and the possibilities before her are without limits. She begins to go forward boldly in the face of all obstacles before her and during the next few months there is great development. In the end, after the finances of her family have completely given way, she has to get a job working ten hours a day in a ten-cent store. Her tragedy does not come in any way from herself—she is robbed of her freedom and energy by an unprincipled and wasteful society.

To Mick music is the symbol of beauty and freedom. She has had no musical background at all and her chances for educating herself are very small. Her family does not have a radio and in the summer she roams around the streets of the town pulling her two baby brothers in a wagon and listening to any music she can hear from other people's houses. She begins reading at the public library and from books she learns some of the things she needs to know. In the fall when she enters the Vocational High School she arranges to have rudimentary lessons on the piano with a girl in her class. In exchange for the lessons she does all the girl's homework in algebra and arithmetic and gives her also fifteen cents a week from her lunch money. During the afternoon Mick can sometimes practice on the piano in the gymnasium—but the place is always noisy and overcrowded and she never knows when she will be interrupted suddenly by a blow on the head from a basketball.

Her love for music is instinctive, and her taste is naturally never pure at this stage. At first there is Mozart. After that she learns about Beethoven. From then on she goes hungrily from one composer to another whenever she gets a chance to hear them on other people's radios—Bach, Brahms, Wagner, Sibelius, etc. Her information is often very garbled but always the feeling is there. Mick's love for music is intensely creative. She is always making up little tunes for herself—and she plans to compose great symphonies and operas. Her plans are always definite in a certain way. She will conduct all of her music herself and her initials will always be written in big red letters on the curtains of the stage. She will conduct her music either in a red satin evening dress or else she will wear a real man's evening suit. Mick is thoroughly egoistic—and the crudely childish side of her nature comes in side by side with the mature.

Mick must always have some person to love and admire. Her childhood was a series of passionate, reasonless admirations for a motley cavalcade of persons, one after another. And now she centers this undirected love on Singer. He gives her a book about Beethoven on her birthday and his room is always quiet and comfortable. In her imagination she makes the mute just the sort of teacher and friend that she needs. He is the only person who seems to show any interest in her at all. She confides in the mute—and when an important crisis occurs at the end of the book it is to him that she wants to turn for help.

This crisis, although on the surface the most striking thing that happens to Mick, is really subordinate to her feelings for Singer and to her struggle against the social forces working against her. In the fall when she enters Vocational High she prefers to take "mechanical shop" with the boys rather than attend the stenographic classes. In this class she meets a fifteen-year-old boy, Harry West, and gradually they become good comrades. They are attracted to each other by a similar intensity of character and by their mutual interest in mechanics. Harry, like Mick, is made restless by an abundance of undirected energy. In the spring they try to construct a glider together in the Kellys' backyard and, although because of inadequate materials they can never get the contraption to fly, they work at it very hard together. All of this time their friendship is blunt and childish.

In the late spring Mick and Harry begin going out together on Saturday for little trips in the country. Harry has a bicycle and they go out about ten miles from town to a certain creek in the woods. Feelings that neither of them fully understands begin to come about between them. The outcome is very abrupt. They start to the country one Saturday afternoon in great excitement and full of childish animal energy— and before they return they have, without any premeditation at all, experienced each other sexually. It is absolutely necessary that this facet of the book be treated with extreme reticence. What has happened is made plain through a short, halting dialogue between Mick and Harry in which a great deal is implied but very little is actually said.

Although it is plain that this premature experience will affect both of them deeply, there is the feeling that the eventual results [will] be more serious for Harry than for Mick. Their actions are rather more mature than would be expected. However, they both decide that they will never want to marry or have the same experience again. They are both stunned by a sense of evil. They decide that they will never see each other again—and that night Harry takes a can of soup from his kitchen shelf, breaks his nickel bank, and hitchhikes from the town to Atlanta where he hopes to find some sort of job.

The restraint with which this scene between Mick and Harry must be told cannot be stressed too strongly.

For a while Mick is greatly oppressed by this that has happened to her. She turns to her music more vehemently than ever. She has always looked on sex with a cold, infantile remoteness—and now the experience she has had seems to be uniquely personal and strange. She tries ruthlessly to forget about it, but the secret weighs on her mind. She feels that if she can just tell some person about it she would be easier. But she is not close enough to her sisters and her mother to confide in them, and she has no especial friends of her own age. She wants to tell Mr. Singer and she tries to imagine how to go about this. She is still taking consolation in the possibility that she might be able to confide in Mr. Singer about this when the mute kills himself.

After the death of Singer, Mick feels very alone and defenseless. She works even harder than ever with her music. But the pressing economic condition of her family which has been growing steadily worse all through the past months is now just about as bad as it can be. The two elder children in the family are barely able to support themselves and can be of no help to their parents. It is essential that Mick get work of some kind. She fights this bitterly, for she wants to go back at least one more year to High School and to have some sort of chance with her music. But nothing can be done and at the beginning of the summer she gets a job working from eight-thirty to six-thirty as a clerk in a ten-cent store. The work is very wearing, but when the manager wants any of the girls to stay overtime he always picks Mick—for she can stand longer and endure more fatigue than any other person in the store.

The essential traits of Mick Kelly are great creative energy and courage. She is defeated by society on all the main issues before she can even begin, but still there is something in her and in those like her that cannot and will not ever be destroyed.

Jake Blount

Jake's struggle with social conditions is direct and conscious. The spirit of revolution is very strong in him. His deepest motive is to do all that he can to change the predatory, unnatural social conditions existing today. It is his tragedy that his energies can find no channel in which to flow. He is fettered by abstractions and conflicting ideas—and in practical applications he can do no more than throw himself against windmills. He feels that the present social tradition is soon to collapse completely, but his dreams of the civilization of the future are alternately full of hope and of distrust.

His attitude toward his fellow man vacillates continually between hate and the most unselfish love. His attitude toward the principles of communism are much the same as his attitude toward man. Deep inside him he is an earnest communist, but he feels that in concrete application all communistic societies up until the present have degenerated into bureaucracies. He is unwilling to compromise and his is the attitude of all or nothing. His inner and outward motives are so contradictory at times that it is hardly an exaggeration to speak of the man as being deranged. The burden which he has taken on himself is too much for him.

Jake is the product of his peculiar environment. During the time of this book he is twenty-nine years old. He was born in a textile town in South Carolina, a town very similar to the one in which the action of this book takes place. His childhood was passed among conditions of absolute poverty and degradation. At the age of nine years (this was the time of the last World War) he was working fourteen hours a day in a cotton mill. He had to snatch for himself whatever education he could get. At twelve he left home on his own initiative and his self-teachings and wanderings began. At one time or another he has lived and worked in almost every section of this country.

Jake's inner instability reflects markedly on his outer personality. In physique he suggests a stunted giant. He is nervous and irritable. All of his life he has had difficulty in keeping his lips from betraying his emotions—in order to overcome this he has grown a flourishing mustache which only accentuates this weakness and gives him a comic, jerky look. Because of his nervous whims it is hard for him to get along with his neighbors and people hold aloof from him. This causes him either to drop into self-conscious buffoonery or else to take on an exaggerated misplaced dignity.

If Jake cannot act he has to talk. The mute is an excellent repository for conversation. Singer attracts Jake because of his seeming stability and calm. He is a stranger in the town and the circumstance of his loneliness makes him seek out the mute. Talking to Singer and spending the evening with him becomes a sedative habit with him. At the end, when the mute is dead, he feels as though he had lost a certain inner ballast. He has the vague feeling that he has been tricked, too, and that all of the conclusions and visions that he has told the mute are forever lost.

Jake depends heavily on alcohol—and he can drink in tremendous quantities with no seeming ill effect. Occasionally he will try to break himself of this habit, but he is as unable to discipline himself in this as he is in more important matters.

Jake's stay in the town ends in a fiasco. As usual, he has been trying during these months to do what he can to right social injustice. At the end of the book the growing resentment between the Negroes and the white factory workers who patronize the show is nourished by several trifling quarrels between individuals. Day by day one thing leads to another and then late on Saturday night there is a wild brawl. (This scene occurs during the week after Singer's death.) All the white workers fight bitterly against the Negroes. Jake tries to keep order for a while and then he, too, loses control of himself and goes berserk. The fight grows into an affair in which there is no organization at all and each man is simply fighting for himself. This brawl is finally broken up by the police and several persons are arrested. Jake escapes but the fight seems to him to be a symbol of his own life. Singer is dead and he leaves the town just as he came to it—a stranger.

Dr. Benedict Mady Copeland

Dr. Copeland presents the bitter spectacle of the educated Negro in the South. Dr. Copeland, like Jake Blount, is warped by his long years of effort to do his part to change certain existing conditions. At the opening of the book he is fifty-one years old, but already he is an old man.

He has practiced among the Negroes of the town for twenty-five years. He has always felt, though, that his work as a doctor was only secondary to his efforts at teaching his people. His ideas are laboriously thought out and inflexible. For a long while he was interested mainly in birth control, as he felt that indiscriminate sexual relations and haphazard and prolific propagation were responsible in a large part for the weakness of the Negro. He is greatly opposed to miscegenation—but this opposition comes mainly from personal pride and resentment. The great flaw in all of his theories is that he will not admit the racial culture of the Negro. Theoretically he is against the grafting of the Negroid way of living to the Caucasian. His ideal would be a race of Negro ascetics.

Parallel with Dr. Copeland's ambition for his race is his love for his family. But because of his inflexibility his relations with his four children are a complete failure. His own temperament is partly responsible for this, too. All of his life Dr. Copeland has gone against the grain of his own racial nature. His passionate asceticism and the strain of his work have their effect on him. At home, when he felt the children escaping from his influence, he was subject to wild and sudden outbreaks of rage. This lack of control was finally the cause of his separation from his wife and children.

While still a young man Dr. Copeland suffered at one time from pulmonary tuberculosis, a disease to which the Negro is particularly susceptible. His illness was arrested—but now when he is fifty-one years old his left lung is involved again. If there were an adequate sanatorium he would enter it for treatment—but of course there is no decent hospital for Negroes in the state. He ignores the disease and keeps up his practice—although now his work is not as extensive as it was in the past.

To Dr. Copeland the mute seems to be the embodiment of the control and asceticism of a certain type of white man. All of his life Dr. Copeland has suffered because of slights and humiliations from the white race. Singer's politeness and consideration make Dr. Copeland pitiably grateful. He is always careful to keep up his "dignity" with the mute—but Singer's friendship is of great importance to him.

The mute's face has a slightly Semitic cast and Dr. Copeland thinks that he is a Jew. The Jewish people, because they are a racially persecuted minority, have always interested Dr. Copeland. Two of his heroes are Jews—Benedict Spinoza and Karl Marx.

Dr. Copeland realizes very fully and bitterly that his life work has been a failure. Although he is respected to the point of awe by most of the Negroes of the town his teachings have been too foreign to the nature of the race to have any palpable effect.

In the beginning of the book Dr. Copeland's economic situation is very uncertain. His house and most of his medical equipment are mortgaged. For fifteen years he had received a small but steady income from his work as a member of the staff of the city hospital—but his personal ideas about social situations have led to his discharge. As a pretext for dismissal he was accused, and rightly, of performing abortions in certain cases where a child was an economic impossibility. Since the loss of this post, Dr. Copeland has had no dependable income. His patients are for the most part totally unable to pay fees for treatment. His illness is a hindrance and he steadily loses ground. At the end the house is taken away from him and after a lifetime of service he is left a pauper. His wife's relations take him out to spend the short remaining part of his life on their farm in the country.

Biff Brannon

Of the four people who revolve around the mute Biff is the most disinterested. It is typical of him that he is always the observer. About Biff there is much that is austere and classical. In contrast with the driving enthusiasms of Mick and Jake and Dr. Copeland, Biff is nearly always coldly reflective. The second chapter of the book opens with him and in the closing pages his meditations bring the work to a thoughtful and objective finish.

Biff's humorous aspects are to be brought out in all the parts dealing with him. Technically he is a thoroughly rounded character in that he will be seen completely from all sides. At the time the book opens he is forty-four years old and has spent the best part of his life standing behind the cash register in the restaurant and making his own particular observations. He has a passion for detail. It is typical of him that he has a small room in the back of his place devoted to a complete and neatly catalogued file of the daily evening newspaper dating back without a break for eighteen years. His problem is to get the main outlines of a situation from all the cluttering details in his mind, and he goes about this with his own painstaking patience.

Biff is strongly influenced by his own specific sexual experiences. At forty-four years he is prematurely impotent—and the cause of this lies in psychic as well as physical reasons. He has been married to Alice for twenty-three years. From the beginning their marriage was a mistake, and it has endured mainly because of economic necessity and habit.

Perhaps as a compensation for his own dilemma Biff comes to his own curious conclusion that marital relations are not the primary functions of the sexual impulse. He believes that human beings are fundamentally ambi-sexual—and for confirmation he turns to the periods of childhood and senility.

Two persons have a great emotional hold on Biff. These are Mick Kelly and a certain old man named Mr. Alfred Simms. Mick has been coming in the restaurant all through her childhood to get candy with her brother and to play the slot machine. She is always friendly with Biff, but of course she has no idea of his feelings for her. As a matter of fact, Biff is not exactly clear himself on that point, either. Mr. Simms is a pitiable, fragile old fellow whose senses are muddled. During middle life he had been a wealthy man but now he is penniless and alone. The old man keeps up a great pretense of being a busy person of affairs. Every day he comes out on the street in clean ragged clothes and holding an old woman's pocket-book. He goes from one bank to another in an effort to "settle his accounts." Mr. Simms used to like to come into Biff's restaurant and sit for a little while. He always sat at a table quietly and never disturbed anyone. With his queer clothes and the big pocket-book clutched against his chest he looked like an old woman. At that time Biff did not have any particular interest in Mr. Simms. He would kindly pour him out a beer now and then, but he did not think much about him.

One night (this was a few weeks before the opening of the book) the restaurant was crowded and the table where Mr. Simms was sitting was needed. Alice insisted that Biff put the old man out. Biff was used to ejecting all sorts of people from the place and he went up to the old man without thinking much about it and asked him if he thought the table was a park bench. Mr. Simms did not understand at first and smiled up happily at Biff. Then Biff was disconcerted and he repeated the words in a much rougher way than he had intended. Tears came to the old man's eyes. He tried to keep up his dignity before the people around him, fumbled uselessly in his pocket-book and went out crushed.

This little episode is described here in some detail because of its effect on Biff. The happening is made clear in a chapter in the second part of the book. All through the story Biff's thoughts are continually going back to the old man. His treatment of Mr. Simms comes to be for him the embodiment of all the evil he has ever done. At the same time the old man is the symbol of the declining period of life which Biff is now approaching.

Mick brings up in Biff nostalgic feelings of youth and heroism. She is at the age where she possesses both the qualities of a girl and of a boy. Also, Biff has always wanted to have a little daughter and of course she reminds him of this, too. At the end of the book, when Mick begins to mature, Biff's feelings for her slowly diminish.

Toward his wife Biff is entirely cold. When Alice dies in the second part of the book, Biff feels not the slightest pity or regret for her at all. His only remorse is that he did not ever fully understand Alice as a person. It piques him that he could have lived so long with a woman and still understand her so confusedly. After her death Biff takes off the crepe paper streamers from under the electric fans and sews mourning tokens on his sleeves. These gestures are not so much for Alice as they are a reflection of his own feeling for his approaching decline and death. After his wife dies certain female elements become more pronounced in Biff. He begins to rinse his hair in lemon juice and to take exaggerated care of his skin. Alice had always been a much better business manager than Biff and after her death the restaurant begins to stagnate.

In spite of certain quirks in Biff's nature he is perhaps the most balanced person in the book. He has that faculty for seeing the things which happen around him with cold objectivity—without instinctively connecting them with himself. He sees and hears and remembers everything. He is curious to a comic degree. And nearly always, despite the vast amount of details in his mind, he can work his way patiently to the very skeleton of a situation and see affairs in their entirety.

Biff is far too wary to be drawn into any mystic admiration of Singer. He likes the mute and is of course very curious about him. Singer occupies a good deal of his thoughts and he values his reserve and common sense. He is the only one of the four main characters who sees the situation as it really is. In the last few pages he threads through the details of the story and arrives at the most salient points. In his reflections at the end Biff himself thinks of the word "parable" in connection with what has happened—and of course this is the only time that this designation is used. His reflections bring the book to a close with a final, objective roundness.

Subordinate Characters

There are several minor characters who play very important parts in the story. None of these persons are treated in a subjective manner—and from the point of view of the novel the things that happen to them are of more importance in the effects on the main characters than because of the change that they bring about among these characters.

Spiros Antonapoulos. Antonapoulos has been described with complete detail in the first chapter. His mental, sexual and spiritual development is that of a child of about seven years old.

Portia Copeland Jones, Highboy Jones, and Willie Copeland. A great deal of interest is centered around these three characters. Portia is the most dominant member of this trio. In actual space she occupies almost as much of the book as any one of the main characters, except Mick—but she is always placed in a subordinate position. Portia is the embodiment of the maternal instincts. Highboy, her husband, and Willie, her brother, are inseparable from herself. These three characters are just the opposite of Dr. Copeland and the other central characters in that they make no effort to go against circumstances.

The tragedy that comes to this group plays an important part on all the phases of the book. At the beginning of the second section Willie is arrested on a charge of burglary. He was walking down a side alley after midnight and two young white boys told him they were looking for someone, gave him a dollar, and instructed him to whistle when the person they were looking for came down the alley. Only when Willie saw two policemen coming toward him did he realize what had happened. In the meantime the boys had broken in a drug store. Later in the fall Willie is sentenced along with them for a year of hard labor. All of this is revealed through Portia as she tells this great trouble to the Kelly children. "Willie he so busy looking at that dollar bill he don't have no time to think. And then they asks him how come he run when he seen them police. They might just as soon ask how come a person jerk their hand off a hot stove when they lays it there by mistake."

This is the first of their trouble. Now that the household arrangements are disturbed, Highboy begins keeping company with another girl. This too is told by Portia to the Kelly children and Dr. Copeland: "I could realize this better if she were a light-colored, good-looking girl. But she at least ten shades blacker than I is. She the ugliest girl I ever seen. She walk like she has a egg between her legs and don't want to break it. She not even clean."

The most brutal tragedy in the book comes to these three people. Willie and four other Negroes were guilty of some little misbehavior on the chain-gang where they were working. It was February and the camp was stationed a couple of hundred miles north of the town. As punishment they were put together in a solitary room. Their shoes were taken off and their feet suspended. They were left like this for three full days. It was cold and as their blood did not circulate the boys' feet froze and they developed gangrene. One boy died of pneumonia and the other four had to have one or both of their feet amputated. They were all manual laborers and of course this completely took away their means for future livelihood. This part is of course revealed by Portia, too. It is told in only a few blunt broken paragraphs and left at that.

This happening has a great effect on the main characters. Dr. Copeland is shattered by the news and is in delirium for several weeks. Mick feels all the impact of the horror. Biff had formerly employed Willie in his restaurant and he broods over all the aspects of the affair.

Jake wants to bring it all to light and make of it a national example. But this is impossible for several reasons. Willie is terribly afraid—for it has been impressed upon him at the camp to keep quiet about what has been done to him. The state has been careful to separate the boys immediately after the happening and they have lost track of each other. Also, Willie and the other boys are really children in a certain way—they do not understand what their cooperation would mean. Suffering had strained their nerves so much that during the three days and nights in the room they had quarreled angrily among themselves and when it was over they had no wish to see each other again. From the long view their childish bitterness toward each other and lack of cooperation is the worst part of the whole tragedy.

Highboy comes back to Portia after Willie returns and, handicapped by Willie's infirmity, the three of them start their way of living all over again.

The thread of this story runs through the whole book. Most of it is told through Portia's own vivid, rhythmic language at intervals as it happens.

Harry West. Harry has already been briefly described in the section given to Mick. During the first part of the year, when he and Mick started their friendship, he was infatuated with a certain little flirting girl at High School. His eyes had always given him much trouble and he wore thick-lensed glasses. The girl thought the glasses made him look sissy and he tried to stumble around without them for several months. This aggravated his eye trouble. His friendship with Mick is very different from his infatuation with the other little girl at High School.

Harry has the exaggeratedly developed sense of right and wrong that sometimes is a characteristic of adolescence. He is also of a brooding nature. There is the implication that his abrupt experience with Mick will leave its mark on him for a long time.

Lily Mae Jenkins. Lily Mae is an abandoned, waifish Negro homosexual who haunts the Sunny Dixie Show where Jake works. He is always dancing. His mind and feelings are childish and he is totally unfit to earn his living. Because of his skill in music and dancing he is a friend of Willie's. He is always half starved and he hangs around Portia's kitchen constantly in the hopes of getting a meal. When Highboy and Willie are gone Portia takes some comfort in Lily Mae.

Lily Mae is presented in the book in exactly the same naive way that his friends understand him. Portia describes Lily Mae to Dr. Copeland in this manner: "Lily Mae is right pitiful now. I don't know if you ever noticed any boys like this but he cares for mens instead of girls.

When he were younger he used to be real cute. He were all the time dressing up in girls' clothes and laughing. Everybody thought he were real cute then. But now he getting old and he seem different. He all the time hungry and he real pitiful. He loves to come set and talk with me in the kitchen. He dances for me and I gives him a little dinner."

The Kelly Children—Bill, Hazel, Etta, Bubber, and Ralph. No great interest is focused on any of these children individually. They are all seen through the eyes of Mick. All three of the older children are confused, in varying degrees, by the problem of trying to find their places in a society that is not prepared to absorb them. Each one of these youngsters is seen sharply—but not with complex fullness.

It is Mick's permanent duty to nurse Bubber and the baby during all the time when she is not actually at school. This chore is something of a burden for an adventurous roamer like Mick—but she has a warm and deep affection for these youngest children. At one time she makes these rambling remarks concerning her sisters and brothers as a whole: "A person's got to fight for every single little thing they ever get. And I've noticed a lot of times that the farther down a kid comes in a family the better the kid really is. Youngest kids are always the toughest. I'm pretty hard because I have a lot of them on top of me. Bubber—he looks sick but he's got guts underneath that. If all this is true Ralph sure ought to be a real strong one when he's big enough to get around. Even though he's just thirteen months old I can read something hard and tough in that Ralph's face already."

Interrelations of Characters

It can easily be seen that in spirit Dr. Copeland, Mick Kelly and Jake Blount are very similar. Each one of these three people has struggled to progress to his own mental proportions in spite of fettering circumstances. They are like plants that have had to grow under a rock from the beginning. The great effort of each of them has been to give and there has been no thought of personal returns.

The likeness between Dr. Copeland and Jake Blount is so marked that they might be called spiritual brothers. The greatest real difference between them is one of race and of years. Dr. Copeland's earlier life was spent in more favorable circumstances and from the start his duty was clear to him. The injustices inflicted on the Negro race are much more plainly marked than the ancient vastly scattered mismanagements of capitalism as a whole. Dr. Copeland was able to set to work immediately in a certain narrow sphere, while the conditions which

Jake hates are too fluid for him to get his shoulder to them. Dr. Copeland has the simplicity and dignity of a person who has lived all of his life in one place and given the best of himself to one work. Jake has the jerky nervousness of a man whose inner and outer life has been no more stable than a whirlwind.

The conscientiousness of both of these men is heightened by artificial stimulation—Dr. Copeland is running a diurnal temperature and Jake is drinking steadily every day. In certain persons the effects of these stimulants can be very much the same.

Dr. Copeland and Jake come into direct contact with each other only once during the book. Casual encounters are not considered here. They meet and misunderstand each other in the second chapter when Jake tries to make the doctor come into Biff's restaurant and drink with him. After that they see each other once on the stairs at the Kelly boarding house and then on two occasions they meet briefly in Singer's room. But the only time they directly confront each other takes place in Dr. Copeland's own house under dramatic circumstances.

This is the night in which Willie has come home from the prison hospital. Dr. Copeland is in bed with an inflammation of the pleura, delirious and thought to be dying. The crippled Willie is on the cot in the kitchen and a swarm of friends and neighbors are trying to crowd in through the back door to see and hear of Willie's situation. Jake has heard of the whole affair from Portia and when Singer goes to sit with Dr. Copeland during the night Jake asks to accompany him.

Jake comes to the house with the intention of questioning Willie as closely as possible. But before the evening is over he is drawn to Dr. Copeland and it is he, instead of Singer, who sits through the night with the sick man. In the kitchen Willie is meeting his friends for the first time in almost a year. At first in the back of the house there is a sullen atmosphere of grief and hopelessness. Willie's story is repeated over and over in sullen monotones. Then this atmosphere begins to change. Willie sits up on the cot and begins to play his harp. Lily Mae starts dancing. As the evening progresses the atmosphere changes to a wild artificial release of merriment.

This is the background for Jake's meeting with Dr. Copeland. The two men are together in the bedroom and the sounds from the kitchen come in during the night through the closed door. Jake is drunk and Dr. Copeland is almost out of his head with fever. Yet their dialogue comes from the marrow of their inner selves. They both lapse into the rhythmic, illiterate vernacularisms of their early childhood. The inner purpose of each man is seen fully by the other. In the course of a few hours these two men, after a lifetime of isolation, come as close to each other as it is possible for two human beings to be. Very early in the morning Singer drops by the house before going to work and he finds them both asleep together, Jake sprawled loosely on the foot of the bed and Dr. Copeland sleeping with healthy naturalness.

The interrelations between the other characters will not have to be described in such detail. Mick, Jake and Biff see each other frequently. Each one of these people occupies a certain key position in the town; Mick is nearly always on the streets. At the restaurant Biff comes in frequent contact with all the main characters except Dr. Copeland. Jake is constantly watching a whole cross-section of the town at the show where he works—later when he drives a taxi he becomes acquainted with nearly all of the characters, major and minor, in the book. Mick's relations toward each of these people are childish and matter of fact. Biff, except for his affinity for Mick, is coldly appraising. Certain small scenes and developments take place between all of these people in a variety of combinations.

On the whole the interrelations between the people of this book can be described as being like the spokes of a wheel—with Singer representing the center point. This situation, with all of its attendant irony, expresses the most important theme of the book.

GENERAL STRUCTURE AND OUTLINE

Time

The first chapter serves as a prelude to the book and the reckoning of time starts with Chapter Two. The story covers a period of fourteen months—from May until the July of the following year.

The whole work is divided into three parts. The body of the book is contained in the middle section. In the actual number of pages this is the longest of the three parts and nearly all of the months in the time scheme take place in this division.

Part I. The first writing of Part I is already completed and so there is no need to take up this section in detail. The time extends from the middle of May to the middle of July. Each of the main characters is introduced in detail. The salient points of each person are clearly implied and the general direction each character will take is indicated. The tale of Singer and Antonapoulos is told. The meetings of each one of the main characters with Singer are presented—and the general web of the book is begun.

Part II. There is a quickening of movement at the beginning of this middle section. There will be more than a dozen chapters in this part, but the handling of these chapters is much more flexible than in Part 1. Many of the chapters are very short, and they are more dependent upon each other than the first six chapters. Almost half of the actual space is devoted to Mick, her growth and progress, and the increasing intensity of her admiration for Singer. Her story, and the separate parts developed from her point of view, weave in and out of the chapters about the other characters.

This part opens with Mick on one of her nocturnal wanderings. During the summer she has been hearing concerts under unusual circumstances. She has found out that in certain wealthier districts in the town a few families get fairly good programs on their radios. There is one house in particular that tunes in every Friday evening for a certain symphony concert. Of course the windows are all open at this time of the year and the music can be heard very plainly from the outside. Mick saunters into the yard at night just before the program is to begin and sits down in the dark behind the shrubbery under the living room window. Sometimes after the concert she will stand looking in at the family in the house for some time before going on. Because she gets so much from their radio she is half in love with all of the people in the house.

It would take many dozens of pages to go into a synopsis of this second part in complete detail. A complete and explanatory account would take actually longer than the whole part as it will be when it is completed—for a good book implies a great deal more than the words actually say. For convenience it is best to set down a few skeleton notations with the purpose of getting the sequence of events into a pattern. These rough notes mean very little in themselves and can only be understood after a thorough reading of the part of these remarks which goes under the heading of Characters and Events. This rough outline is still in a tentative stage and is only meant to be indicative of the general formation of this central part.

Late Summer:
Mick's night wandering and the concert. Resumé of the growth that is taking place in Mick this summer. On the morning after the concert Portia tells Mick and the other Kelly children of Willie's arrest. Mick's morning wanderings.
Jake Blount's experience at the Sunny Dixie Show.

Autumn:

Mick's first day at Vocational High.

Dr. Copeland on his medical rounds. Another visit from Portia in which she tells her father that Highboy has left her.

Mick becomes acquainted with Harry West.

Biff's wife, Alice, dies—his meditations.

Mick and her music again. Mick's sister, Etta, takes French leave of her family and tries to run away to Hollywood, but returns in a few days. Mick goes with the little girl who teaches her music to a "real" piano lesson. She experiences a great embarrassment when she boldly tells the teacher she is a musician and sits down to try to play on a "real" piano. (This takes place at the house where Mick was listening to the concert at the opening of this section—and Mick already knows this teacher and her family quite well after watching them through the window during the summer.)

Winter:

Christmas. Dr. Copeland gives his two annual Christmas parties— one in the morning for children and another in the late afternoon for adults. These parties have been given by him every year for two decades and he serves refreshments to his patients and then makes a short talk. The relation between Dr. Copeland and the human material with which he works is brought out clearly.

Singer visits Antonapoulos.

Jake Blount's experience in the town as a ten-cent taxi driver.

Mick and Singer. Mick begins plans for the glider with Harry West.

The tragedy of Willie and the other four boys is told by Portia in the Kelly kitchen to Mick, Jake Blount and Singer.

Spring:

Further meditations of Biff Brannon—and scene between Mick and Biff at the restaurant.

Mick and her music again—Mick and Harry work on the glider.

Willie returns. The meeting of Dr. Copeland and Jake.

The experience between Harry and Mick comes to its abrupt fulfillment and finish. Harry's departure. Mick's oppressive secret. The Kelly's financial condition. Mick's energetic plans and her music.

Singer's death.

This outline does not indicate the main web of the story—that of the relations of each main character with the mute. These relations are so gradual and so much a part of the persons themselves that it is impossible to put them down in such blunt notations. However, from these notes a general idea of the time scheme and of sequence can be gathered.

Part III. Singer's death overshadows all of the final section of the book. In actual length this part requires about the same number of pages as does the first part. In technical treatment the similarity between these sections is pronounced. This part takes place during the months of June and July. There are four chapters and each of the main characters is given his last presentation. A rough outline of this conclusive part may be suggested as follows:

Dr. Copeland. The finish of his work and teachings—his departure to the country. Portia, Willie and Highboy start again.

Jake Blount. Jake writes curious social manifestoes and distributes them through the town. The brawl at the Sunny Dixie Show; Jake prepares to leave the town.

Mick Kelly. Mick begins her new work at the ten-cent store.

Biff Brannon. Final scene between Biff, Mick and Jake at the restaurant. Meditations of Biff concluded.

PLACE — THE TOWN

This story, in its essence, could have occurred at any place and in any time. But as the book is written, however, there are many aspects of the content which are peculiar to the America of this decade—and more specifically to the southern part of the United States. The town is never mentioned in the book by its name. The town is located in the very western part of Georgia, bordering the Chattahoochee River and just across the boundary line from Alabama. The population of the town is around 40,000—and about one third of the people in the town are Negroes. This is a typical factory community and nearly all of the business set-up centers around the textile mills and small retail stores.

Industrial organization has made no headway at all among the workers in the town. Conditions of great poverty prevail. The average cotton mill worker is very unlike the miner or a worker in the automobile industry—south of Gastonia, S. C., the average cotton mill worker has been conditioned to a very apathetic, listless state. For the most part he makes no effort to determine the causes of poverty and unemployment. His immediate resentment is directed toward the only social group beneath him—the Negro. When the mills are slack this town is veritably a place of lost and hungry people.

TECHNIQUE AND SUMMARY

This book is planned according to a definite and balanced design. The form is contrapuntal throughout. Like a voice in a fugue each one of the main characters is an entirety in himself—but his personality takes on a new richness when contrasted and woven in with the other characters in the book.

It is in the actual style in which the book will be written that the work's affinity to contrapuntal music is seen most clearly. There are five distinct styles of writing—one for each of the main characters who is treated subjectively and an objective, legendary style for the mute. The object in each of these methods of writing is to come as close as possible to the inner psychic rhythms of the character from whose point of view it is written. This likeness between style and character is fairly plain in the first part—but this closeness progresses gradually in each instance until at the end the style expresses the inner man just as deeply as is possible without lapsing into the unintelligible unconscious.

This book will be complete in all of its phases. No loose ends will be left dangling and at the close there will be a feeling of balanced completion. The fundamental idea of the book is ironic—but the reader is not left with a sense of futility. The book reflects the past and also indicates the future. A few of the people in this book come very near to being heroes and they are not the only human beings of their kind. Because of the essence of these people, there is the feeling that no matter how many times their efforts are wasted and their personal ideals are shown to be false, they will someday be united and they will come into their own.

Appendix II
Chronology

1917
February 19   Lula Carson Smith, daughter of Lamar and Marguerite Waters Smith, born at 423 13th Street, Columbus, Georgia.

1919
May 13   Lamar Smith, Jr., Lula Carson's brother, born.

1921
September   Lula Carson begins kindergarten at Sixteenth Street School, Columbus, Georgia.

1922
August 2   Margarita Gachet Smith, Lula Carson's sister, born.

1923
February   Lula Carson enters first grade.
November 21   Lula Caroline Carson Waters, Lula Carson's maternal grandmother and namesake, with whom the Smith family lives, dies.

1925
Summer   Lamar Smith, Sr., buys Whippet Coupe and moves family to rented house at 2417 Wynnton Rd., Columbus, Georgia.
September   Lula Carson transfers to third grade at Wynnton School.
November 21   Lula Carson joins First Baptist Church of Columbus.

1926

	Lula Carson begins piano lessons with Mrs. Kendrick Kierce.
January	Smith family buys house at 1519 Starke Avenue.
May 30	Lula Carson baptized at First Baptist Church of Columbus.

1930

February 3	Lula Carson enters eighth grade at Columbus High School.
July	Lula Carson visits uncle and aunt, the Elam Waters, in Cincinnati and drops Lula from name.
August	Colonel Albert S. J. and Mary Tucker (Carson's future piano teacher) transferred to Fort Benning.
Fall	Carson ends piano study with Mrs. Kierce.
October	Carson begins piano study with Mary Tucker.

1931

| June | James Reeves McCullers, Jr., (born 11 August 1913) graduates from Wetumpka High School (Wetumpka, Alabama). |
| November 3 | Reeves McCullers enlists in army at Fort Benning, Georgia. |

1932

| Winter | Carson, stricken with rheumatic fever (incorrectly diagnosed), ill for several weeks; tells friend Helen Harvey of decisions to write and give up plans for the concert stage. |

1933

| | Carson reads voraciously, writes plays, and writes first short story, "Sucker." |
| June | Carson graduates from Columbus High School. |

1934

| Spring | Carson meets Edwin Peacock. |
| June | Tucker family transferred to Fort Howard, |

	Maryland. Carson tells Mary Tucker of decision to write.
September	Carson, age seventeen, travels by boat from Savannah to New York.
November 2	Reeves McCullers completes three-year enlistment in army and re-enlists for three additional years. Edwin Peacock introduces Reeves to Smith family.
1935	
February–June	Carson enrolls in creative-writing courses with Dorothy Scarborough and Helen Rose Hull at Columbia University.
Mid-June	Carson returns to Columbus by bus. Edwin Peacock introduces Carson to Reeves McCullers. Peacock, Reeves, and Carson make summer visits to Max Goodley's.
August	Carson works as reporter for *Columbus Ledger.*
September	Carson returns to New York, enrolls at Washington Square College of New York University and studies writing for two semesters with Sylvia Chatfield Bates.
November	John Vincent Adams, a friend of Reeves and Peacock, moves to New York and urges Reeves to leave army, join him in New York, and dedicate himself to writing.
1936	
January	Reeves inherits Alabama Harbor bonds, purchases discharge from army.
February–June	Carson continues study at New York University with Sylvia Chatfield Bates.
June	Carson returns briefly to Columbus.
July	Carson returns to New York to study with Whit Burnett at Columbia.
September	Reeves enrolls at Columbia University and takes courses in journalism and anthropology.
November	Carson seriously ill. Reeves withdraws from Columbia (November 12) and takes Carson home to Georgia.
Winter	Put to bed for the winter, Carson begins

	story of a deaf mute, titled "The Mute" (later *The Heart Is a Lonely Hunter*).
December	"Wunderkind" published in *Story*. "Like That" also purchased by *Story*, remains unpublished during Carson's lifetime.

1937

	On a trip to Charleston with Reeves, Carson introduced to the writing of Isak Dinesen by John Zeigler and Edwin Peacock.
March	Carson spends three and a half weeks with Reeves in Goldens Bridge at Lake Katona, New York, before returning sick to Columbus.
Summer	Carson teaches music courses in Columbus.
September 20	Carson marries James Reeves McCullers, Jr., and moves to Charlotte, North Carolina, where Reeves has job with credit agency. Their first apartment is at 311 East Boulevard.
Fall	Carson and Reeves move to 806 Central Ave. in Charlotte, North Carolina.

1938

March	Carson and Reeves move to Rowan Street apartment in Fayetteville, North Carolina, after Reeves receives raise and promotion. Carson works on "The Mute."
April	Carson submits outline of "The Mute" to enter Houghton Mifflin fiction contest.
July	Carson visits family in Columbus, Georgia.
Fall	Carson and Reeves move to 119 North Cool Spring Street in Fayetteville.

1939

Spring	Carson finishes "The Mute" (now titled *The Heart Is a Lonely Hunter*) and writes "Army Post" (later published as *Reflections in a Golden Eye*). Carson returns twice to Columbus alone and unsuccessfully tries to publish "Sucker" and "Court in the West Eighties."

Fall	Carson returns to Columbus and begins to conceive *The Member of the Wedding*.
1940	
June 4	*The Heart Is a Lonely Hunter* published by Houghton Mifflin.
Mid-June	Carson and Reeves leave Fayetteville for New York City and move into apartment at 321 W. 11th St. in Greenwich Village.
July	Carson meets Klaus and Erika Mann, W. H. Auden, and Annemarie Clarac-Schwarzenbach.
August	Carson sells *Reflections in a Golden Eye* to *Harper's Bazaar.*
August 14	Carson attends Bread Loaf Writers' Conference for two weeks where she meets Louis Untermeyer and Eudora Welty.
August 29	Carson visits editor Robert Linscott and the Houghton Mifflin offices in Boston.
September	Carson separates from Reeves and moves with George Davis and W. H. Auden to 7 Middagh Street in Brooklyn Heights.
October–November	*Reflections in a Golden Eye* published in *Harper's Bazaar.*
Thanksgiving	Chasing fire engine with Gypsy Rose Lee, Carson has inspiration for "The Bride and Her Brother" (published as *The Member of the Wedding*).
Winter	Ill, Carson returns to Columbus to recuperate where she faces hometown reactions to *Reflections in a Golden Eye.*
November	Annemarie Clarac-Schwarzenbach hospitalized for mental illness. Clarac-Schwarzenbach flees from hospital and Carson returns to New York.
December	"Look Homeward, Americans" published in *Vogue.*
1941	
	Carson meets cousin Jordan Massee and his companion Paul Bigelow.
January 1	"Night Watch Over Freedom" published in *Vogue.*

February	Carson stricken with first cerebral stroke, radically impaired vision, and stabbing head pains. Although sight returns, Carson not ambulatory for over a month.
February 14	*Reflections in a Golden Eye* published in book form by Houghton Mifflin. Carson, visiting Columbus, continues writing projects.
March	"Brooklyn Is My Neighborhood" published in *Vogue*.
April	Reeves, seeking reconciliation, goes to Columbus and returns with Carson to New York City to W. 11th St. apartment. "Books I Remember" published in *Harper's Bazaar*.
May 2	Carson and Reeves meet composer David Diamond, beginning complicated three-way love affair with him.
June 14–August 22	Carson at Yaddo Arts Colony in Saratoga Springs, New York; meets Katherine Anne Porter and Newton Arvin and writes *The Ballad of the Sad Cafe*.
July–November 14	Reeves lives with David Diamond in Rochester, New York, and works at Samson United chemical plant.
July	Reeves forges checks on Carson's account and she considers divorce. "The Russian Realists and Southern Literature" published in *Decision*.
July 15	"We Carried Our Banners—We Were Pacifists Too" published in *Vogue*.
August 22–30	Carson accompanies Newton Arvin, Granville Hicks and his family to Quebec. On return trip, Carson visits Smith College with Newton Arvin in Northampton, Massachusetts.
August 23	"The Jockey" published in the *New Yorker*.
Late Summer	Carson receives series of letters from Clarac-Schwarzenbach.
September 4–30	Carson return to New York from Yaddo and initiates divorce proceedings.
October	Diamond dedicates ballet, *The Dream of Audubon*, to Carson and Reeves.
Mid-October	Carson returns to Columbus.

November–December	"The Twisted Trinity," Carson's first published poem, appears in *Decision;* the poem set to music by David Diamond.
December–January	Carson critically ill with pleurisy, strep throat, and double pneumonia.
Winter	Carson writes short stories "Madame Zilensky and the King of Finland" and "Correspondence."

1942

Mid-February	Carson recuperated enough to resume work on "Bride" manuscript. She interrupts work on "The Bride" to write "A Tree. A Rock. A Cloud."
February 7	"Correspondence," short story, published in the *New Yorker.*
March	Carson tells David Diamond that "Bride" manuscript is finished but quickly realizes that it must undergo revision before publication.
March 19	Reeves, now divorced, re-enlists in army.
March 24	Carson notified that she has been awarded a Guggenheim Fellowship.
Spring	Carson visits Columbus.
April 26	Carson visits Warm Springs, Georgia.
Late June	Carson travels to New York from Georgia, then to Yaddo.
July 2–January 17	Carson works at Yaddo.
November	Carson completes *The Ballad of the Sad Cafe.* "A Tree. A Rock. A Cloud" published in *Harper's Bazaar* and selected by Herschel Brickell for annual anthology, *O. Henry Memorial Prize Stories of 1942.*
November 5	Carson moves to Pine Tree studio at Yaddo.
November 15	Annemarie Clarac-Schwarzenbach dies in Sils, Switzerland.
November 29	Reeves receives army commission at Camp Upton, New York.
December 1	Carson learns of Clarac-Schwarzenbach's death while at Yaddo.

1943

January–February	Carson ill from "a mean grippy cold" and

	an infection due to broken jaw bone (broken accidentally by dentist during molar extraction).
January	*The Ballad of the Sad Cafe* sold to *Harper's Bazaar* for publication in August.
January 17	Carson leaves Yaddo and moves back to 7 Middagh Street, Brooklyn Heights.
February	Marguerite Smith travels from Columbus to Middagh Street to nurse daughter and accompany her to Columbus.
February 23	Reeves writes Carson conciliatory letter from Camp Forrest, Tennessee.
April	"Love's Not Time's Fool" published in *Mademoiselle.*
April 2	Reeves writes to Carson from Camp Forrest, Tennessee.
April 9	Carson learns that she will receive an Arts and Letters Grant of $1,000 from the American Academy of Arts and Letters and the National Institute of Arts and Letters.
April 22	Carson returns to Columbus.
April 25	Reeves writes to Carson from Camp Forrest, Tennessee.
May 3	Reeves writes to Carson from Camp Forrest, Tennessee.
May 5	Carson reunites with Reeves in Atlanta. A week later he joins her in Columbus for a five-day leave.
May 16	Reeves writes to Carson from Camp Forrest, Tennessee.
May 31	Reeves writes to Carson from Camp Forrest, Tennessee.
June 1	Carson returns briefly to 7 Middagh Street.
June 8–August 12	Carson at Yaddo.
August	*The Ballad of the Sad Cafe* published in *Harper's Bazaar.*
August 15–September	Carson spends a few days in New York City, visits David Diamond, returns to Columbus due to father's illness.
September 1	Reeves writes to Carson from Camp Forrest, Tennessee.

September 8	Reeves writes to Carson from Fort Pierce, Florida.
October 5	Reeves writes to Carson from Fort Dix, New Jersey.
October 15	Reeves writes to Carson from Fort Dix, New Jersey.
October 16	Reeves writes to Carson from Fort Dix, New Jersey.
October 20	Reeves writes to Carson from Fort Dix, New Jersey.
October 21–30	Carson stays with Reeves at Fort Dix. They consider remarriage but decide against it.
November 2	Reeves writes Carson from Fort Dix, New Jersey.
November 13	Reeves writes Carson from "Eastern U.S."
November 15	Reeves writes Carson.
November 16	Reeves writes Carson.
November 28	Reeves embarks from Fort Dix for Europe.
December 5	Reeves writes Carson from England.
Winter	Carson, in Columbus, begins to refer to manuscript of "The Bride" as *The Member of the Wedding*.

1944

January–February	Carson ill with influenza and pleurisy, suffers severe nervous attack, and fears for Reeves's safety in combat.
February 19	Reeves writes Carson.
February	Carson learns that Reeves has fractured wrist in a motorcycle accident in England.
March 4	Reeves writes Carson from England.
March 9	Reeves writes Carson.
March 27	Reeves writes Carson.
March	Carson's sister, Rita Smith, moves to New York City to write and find a job in publishing.
Spring	Carson tries to get job as a war correspondent.
June	Rita Smith begins working for George Davis at *Mademoiselle*.
June 1	Carson receives cable from Reeves training

	in England for Normandy invasion; first word from Reeves for over two months.
June 6	Reeves wounded in the Normandy invasion.
June 10	Reeves writes Carson form letter from abroad U.S.S. Texas.
June 15–August 2	Carson at Yaddo.
June 20	Reeves writes Carson from France.
June 24	U.S. Army cables Carson regarding Reeves's injury.
June 25	Carson receives cable regarding Reeves's injury at Normandy.
June 27	Reeves writes Carson from France.
July 9	Reeves writes Carson from France.
July 10	Reeves writes Carson from France.
July 14	Reeves writes Carson from France enclosing newspaper clipping.
August 1	Carson's father dies in Columbus and she returns to Columbus for funeral.
August 5	Reeves writes Carson from France.
August 21	Reeves writes Carson from France.
September 4	Carson, Rita, and their mother move to Nyack, New York, and rent apartment at 127 South Broadway (Graycourt Apartments).
September 13	Reeves writes Carson from France.
September 14	Reeves writes Carson from France.
October 5	Reeves writes Carson two letters from "somewhere in Europe."
October 10	Reeves writes Carson two letters from Luxembourg.
October 17	Reeves writes Carson from Luxembourg.
November 8	Reeves writes Carson from Luxembourg.
Early November	Carson briefly visits Yaddo to see Newton Arvin and Elizabeth Ames.
November 12	Carson writes Reeves from Nyack, New York.
November 21	Carson writes Reeves from Nyack, New York.
November 22	Reeves writes Carson from Germany.
November 22	Carson writes Reeves from Nyack, New York.

December	Carson suffers acute eye strain and is unable to work. *The Ballad of the Sad Cafe* included in Martha Foley's *The Best American Short Stories of 1944.*
December 3	Carson writes Reeves from Nyack, New York.
December 3	Reeves writes Carson two letters from Belgium.
December 4	Reeves writes Carson from Belgium.
December 5	Carson writes Reeves from Nyack, New York.
December 8	Reeves writes Carson from Germany.
December 9	Reeves wounded in Rotgen, Germany.
December 12	Reeves writes Carson from Paris.
December 13	Carson writes Reeves from Nyack, New York.
December 15	Carson writes Reeves from Nyack, New York.
December 17	Reeves writes Carson from England.
December 18	Carson writes Reeves.
December 19	Carson writes Reeves two letters.
December 20	U.S. Army cables Carson regarding Reeve's injury.
December 21	Carson writes Reeves two letters.
December 25	Carson, at Yaddo, writes Reeves.
December 26	Reeves writes Carson from England.
December 27	Carson writes Reeves.
December 28	Carson writes Reeves two letters.
Late December	Carson returns to Nyack from Yaddo.

1945

January	Carson ill with influenza during much of January.
January 1	Carson writes Reeves from Nyack, New York.
January 6	Carson writes Reeves from Nyack, New York, after receiving letter from Reeves (first since injury) in England.
January 7	Carson writes Reeves from Nyack, New York.
January 7	Carson cables Reeves in London from Nyack, New York.

January 8	Carson writes Reeves from Nyack, New York.
January 9	Carson writes Reeves from Nyack, New York.
January 10	Carson cables Reeves in London from Nyack, New York. Carson writes Reeves from Nyack, New York.
January 11	Carson writes Reeves from Nyack, New York.
January 14	Carson writes Reeves from Nyack, New York.
January 17	Carson writes Reeves from Nyack, New York.
January 18	Carson writes Reeves from Nyack, New York.
January 24	Carson cables Reeves in London from Nyack, New York. Carson writes Reeves from Nyack, New York. Reeves cables Carson "may be home soon."
January 27	Carson writes Reeves from Nyack, New York.
February 4	Carson writes Reeves from Nyack, New York.
February 8	Carson writes Reeves from Nyack, New York.
February 10	Reeves leaves England by ship for the United States.
February 15	Marguerite Smith receives money from husband's estate and looks for house to buy in Nyack.
February 19	Carson writes Reeves from Nyack, New York.
February 24	Carson meets Reeves in New York City on return from England.
March 19	Carson and Reeves remarry in a civil ceremony in New City, New York.
April 2	Carson writes Reeves from Nyack, New York.
May 8	Carson writes Reeves from Nyack, New York.
May 15	Carson's mother buys house at 131 South Broadway, Nyack, New York.

Mid-July	Reeves recommended for medical discharge from army.
June 26–August 31	Carson works at Yaddo on *The Member of the Wedding.*
August 3	Reeves writes Carson from Camp Wheeler, Georgia (near Macon).
August 5	Reeves writes Carson from Camp Wheeler, Georgia.
August 7	Reeves writes Carson from Camp Wheeler, Georgia.
August 9	Reeves writes Carson from Camp Wheeler, Georgia.
August 13	Reeves writes Carson from Camp Wheeler, Georgia.
August 31	Carson returns to Nyack from Yaddo having completed *The Member of the Wedding.*
November	"Our Heads Are Bowed" published in *Mademoiselle.*
November 21	Reeves writes Carson.
Christmas	Reeves returns to Nyack on terminal leave from temporary assignment at Camp Wheeler, Georgia.

1946

January	Part 1 of *The Member of the Wedding* published in *Harper's Bazaar.*
February	Reeves promoted to captain.
February 19	Book Basement, book store owned by John Zeigler and Edwin Peacock, opens in Charleston on Carson's birthday.
March 16	Reeves granted physical disability discharge from army.
March 19	*The Member of the Wedding* published by Houghton Mifflin.
March 23–May 31	Carson returns to Yaddo.
April 15	Carson awarded second Guggenheim Fellowship. Reeves and Carson plan to live in France.
June	Carson spends several weeks in Nantucket with Tennessee Williams and begins adaptation of *The Member of the Wedding.*

June 29	Carson briefly returns to Nyack from Nantucket.
July 4	Carson and Reeves return to Nantucket. Reeves stays only a few days; Carson remains until midsummer.
November 22	Carson and Reeves sail for Europe on the *Ile de France*.

1947

April	Carson goes on skiing expedition in Italian Tyrol and visits Natalia Danesi Murray in Rome.
May	Stage version of *The Member of the Wedding* entangled in lawsuit; Carson plans trip to Key West with Tennessee Williams. Carson meets attorney Floria Lasky.
Late Summer	Carson and Reeves depart for Paris.
August	Carson suffers severe stroke; hospitalized in the American Hospital in Paris.
November	Carson has second serious stroke in Paris, which destroys lateral vision in right eye and paralyzes left side; hospitalized for three weeks at the American Hospital in Paris under the care of Dr. Robert Myers.
December 1	Carson and Reeves flown home on stretchers from Paris; Reeves suffers from delirium tremens, Carson from paralysis of stroke.
December 1–25	Carson hospitalized at Neurological Institute at Columbia Presbyterian Hospital.
December 17	*Quick* magazine names Carson one of the best postwar writers in America.

1948

January	Carson named one of the ten most deserving women in America for 1947 and receives *Mademoiselle* Merit Award.
February	Reeves moves from Nyack to New York City.
February 28	Carson writes letter to Columbus Public Library protesting its racial segregation policy.

March	Carson attempts suicide; hospitalized briefly at Payne Whitney Psychiatric Clinic in Manhattan.
Spring–Fall	Carson hires part-time secretary for dictation and revises play, *The Member of the Wedding.*
Spring	Audrey Wood becomes Carson's agent, replacing Ann Watkins.
May 19	Carson attends national psychiatric convention in Washington, D.C., and meets Hervey Cleckley.
August	Carson and Reeves reconcile. Carson's health worsens.
September	"How I Began to Write" published in *Mademoiselle.* "The Mortgaged Heart" and "When We Are Lost" (poems) published in the literary journal *New Directions.*
October	Carson publicly supports Harry Truman for president.

1949

January	Carson spends a month with Reeves in apartment at 105 Thompson Street in Manhattan.
March 13	Carson returns with mother to Georgia for two weeks, first to Columbus, then to Macon (March 17) to visit cousin Jordan Massee.
March 21	Carson returns to New York City because of controversy regarding Elizabeth Ames (Yaddo director) and the Communist Party. On way to New York City, Carson inter-viewed in Atlanta by Ralph McGill of the *Atlanta Constitution.*
May 13	Carson and Reeves visit friends Edwin Peacock and John Zeigler in Charleston, South Carolina, continuing Carson's aborted trip south.
December	*The Member of the Wedding* (play) published by New Directions. "Home for Christmas" published in *Mademoiselle.*
December 19	"Loneliness, an American Malady"

	published in *This Week Magazine* of the New York *Herald Tribune*.
December 22	*The Member of the Wedding* opens at the Walnut Theatre in Philadelphia for its pre-Broadway run.

1950

January 5	*The Member of the Wedding* opens on Broadway; wins Drama Critics' Circle Award and Donaldson Award.
Spring	Carson and Reeves move temporarily into the Dakota building at 72nd St. and Central Park West.
April	"The Vision Shared" published in *Theatre Arts*.
A pril 24	Carson reunited with former piano teacher Mary Tucker.
May	"The Sojourner" published in *Mademoiselle*.
May 20	Carson sails for Ireland to visit Elizabeth Bowen.
Early June	Reeves flies to meet Carson in London.
July	Carson and Reeves return to Bowen Court to visit Elizabeth Bowen.
August 2	Carson and Reeves return to New York and separate. Reeves takes an apartment and Carson stays with friends in New York City.
Summer–Fall	Carson visits Tucker family in Virginia.

1951

March	Screen rights to *The Member of the Wedding* sold to Stanley Kramer. Carson buys Nyack home from mother.
March 17	*The Member of the Wedding* closes after 501 performances.
May 24	*The Ballad of the Sad Cafe and Other Works* published by Houghton Mifflin.
June 28	Carson (and Reeves as stowaway) sail on the *Queen Elizabeth* for England.
Summer	Carson visits Edith Sitwell in London.
October	Carson returns to America.
Fall	Carson begins work on "The Pestle" (part of the novel *Clock Without Hands*).

December	Carson completes poem, "The Dual Angel," in Nyack and continues work on *Clock Without Hands*. Carson and Reeves travel to New Orleans.

1952

January 30	Carson and Reeves sail on the *Constitution* for Naples, Italy.
February 6–April	Carson and Reeves stay in Rome.
April	Carson and Reeves drive to Paris and buy house at Bachvillers near Paris.
May 28	Carson inducted in absentia into the National Institute of Arts and Letters.
Mid-Summer	*The Ballad of the Sad Cafe and Collected Short Stories* published by Houghton Mifflin.
Summer	Carson and Reeves return to Nyack to see Marguerite Smith, who suffered a heart attack and a fall.
July	"The Dual Angel: A Meditation on Origin and Choice," a poem, published in *Mademoiselle*.
September	Carson and Reeves go to Rome; Carson works on film script for David O. Selznik's *Terminal Station*. "The Dual Angel" printed in Italian literary journal *Botteghe Oscure*.
Late Summer	Marguerite Smith ill again. Carson returns to Nyack alone.
Summer–Fall	Lamar Smith, Jr., moves from Florida to Columbus, Georgia. Marguerite Smith returns to Columbus with son and his family. Nyack house cared for by Reeves's mother and sister.
Mid to Late October	Carson hospitalized for a week at Salvador Mundi Clinic in Rome.
November	Carson and Reeves return to Bachvillers.
Thanksgiving	Carson and Reeves host friends from American Hospital in Paris for Thanksgiving dinner at Bachvillers.
Christmas	Carson and Reeves guests of friends at American Hospital for Christmas.

1953

July	"The Pestle" (Part I of *Clock Without Hands*)

	simultaneously published in *Mademoiselle* and *Botteghe Oscure*.
Late Summer	Reeves tries to convince Carson to commit suicide with him. Carson flees to the United States. Marguerite Smith returns to Nyack from visit to Columbus to care for Carson.
November 18	Reeves commits suicide in Paris.
November 19	Reeves's body found in Paris hotel. Carson hears of Reeves's death while visiting author Lillian Smith in Clayton, Georgia.
November 21–25	Carson visits Dr. Hervey Cleckley in Augusta, Georgia.
November 25	Carson returns to Nyack.
November 27	Reeves's obituary appears in the *New York Times*.
December 3	Carson returns to the South.
December 15	Carson's favorite aunt, Martha Waters Johnson, dies in Columbus. Carson returns from South to Nyack to be with mother.
December 27	"The Invisible Wall," television adaptation of short story "The Sojourner," broadcast on Ford Foundation program *Omnibus*.

1954

February–May	Carson makes lecture appearances with Tennessee Williams.
February 17	Carson lectures on fiction writing and drama at Goucher College.
Late February	Carson travels to Charleston to visit friends.
Spring	Marguerite Smith breaks hip. Carson returns to Nyack from Yaddo. Marguerite admitted to nursing home.
Late March	Carson travels to Charlotte, North Carolina, to visit friends.
April 19	Carson returns to Yaddo from Charlotte.
May 8	Carson lectures at Poetry Center of the Young Men and Young Women's Hebrew Association in New York City.
April 20–July 3	Carson completes first draft of *The Square Root of Wonderful* at Yaddo.

Summer	Carson meets Marilyn Monroe in New York City.
Fall	Carson spends time in New York City at the home of Robert and Hilda Marks. Marguerite Smith returns to Nyack home from nursing home. Ida Reeder hired as housekeeper.

1955

April	Carson vacations with Tennessee Williams in Key West; works on three manuscripts then in progress: dramatization of *The Ballad of the Sad Cafe*, *The Square Root of Wonderful*, and *Clock Without Hands*. Carson and Williams spend weekend in Cuba.
May 25	"Who Has Seen the Wind?" a short-story version of *The Square Root of Wonderful*, completed.
June 10	Carson's mother, Marguerite Waters Smith, dies in Nyack.
June 13	Marguerite Waters Smith's obituary appears in the *New York Times*.
November	"The Haunted Boy" published simultaneously in *Mademoiselle* and *Botteghe Oscure*.

1956

	Carson ill during much of year, paralyzed left arm becomes increasingly painful and drawn. She works with Saint Subber on the revision of play *The Square Root of Wonderful*.
September	"Who Has Seen the Wind?" published in *Mademoiselle*.

1957

February	"Mick" published in *Literary Cavalcade*.
February 16	*The Member of the Wedding* opens at the Royal Court Theatre, London.
July	Poem, "Stone Is Not Stone," published in *Mademoiselle*.
September 2	*The Square Root of Wonderful* goes into rehearsal.

October 10	Ten-day pre-Broadway run at the McCarter Theatre in Princeton, New Jersey, begins.
October 13	"Playwright Tells of Pangs" published on October 13 in the *Philadelphia Inquirer.*
October 23	George Keathley called in to replace director Jose Quintero for production of *The Square Root of Wonderful.*
October 30	*The Square Root of Wonderful* opens at the National Theatre on Broadway.
December 7	*The Square Root of Wonderful* closes after forty-five performances.

1958

January	Carson suffers depression after *The Square Root of Wonderful* closes.
February	Carson begins therapy with Dr. Mary Mercer and undergoes a series of operations on left arm.
May	Carson makes sound recording with Jean Stein Vanden Heuvel entitled "Carson McCullers Reads from *The Member of the Wedding* and Other Works."
July	Carson lectures at Columbia University and writes "A Personal Preface" to *The Square Root of Wonderful.*
August	Carson works on "Flowering Dream" manuscript.
August 19	Carson participates in a panel discussion on drama in the television production of "Lamp Unto My Feet."
December	*The Member of the Wedding,* translated by Andre Bay and William Hope, produced in French at the Alliance Francaise in Paris.

1959

	Carson undergoes two operations on left arm and wrist. Two more operations scheduled for the following year. Unable to work on manuscripts, writes children's verse.
January 21	Carson attends dinner meeting of the American Academy of Arts and Letters and the National Institute of Arts and

	Letters and meets Isak Dinesen. Carson later gives luncheon for Dinesen, Arthur Miller, and Marilyn Monroe.
December	"The Flowering Dream: Notes on Writing" appears in *Esquire*.

1960

April	Carson's third application for a Guggenheim denied because she has already received two earlier grants.
July	Edward Albee approaches Carson with the idea to adapt *The Ballad of the Sad Cafe* for the stage.
December 1	Carson finishes *Clock Without Hands* almost twenty years after beginning the novel.

1961

January	Screen rights to *The Heart Is a Lonely Hunter* bought by Thomas Ryan.
February	Carson corrects galley proofs of *Clock Without Hands*.
May	Kermit Bloomgarden acquires theater rights to *Clock Without Hands*.
June	Carson has surgery on left hand at Harkness Pavilion in New York.
July	"To Bear the Truth Alone" (Part II of *Clock Without Hands*) published in *Harper's Bazaar*.
September 18	*Clock Without Hands*, dedicated to Dr. Mary Mercer, published by Houghton Mifflin.
December	"A Child's View of Christmas" published in *Redbook*.

1962

Summer	Carson visits Mary Tucker in Virginia with Edward Albee.
Late Summer	Carson and Mary Mercer visit Edward Albee on Fire Island. Carson and Major Simeon Smith meet William Faulkner at West Point.
September	Carson has breast and hand operations at Harkness Pavilion.
October	Carson attends Cheltenham Festival and

Edith Sitwell's 75th birthday celebration in
England.

1963

January	"The Dark Brilliance of Edward Albee" published in *Harper's Bazaar.*
April 12	Carson and Mary Mercer travel to Charleston. Carson meets and begins friendship with Gordon Langley Hall in Charleston.
September	"Sucker," short story, published in *Saturday Evening Post.*
October 30	Edward Albee's adaptation of *The Ballad of the Sad Cafe* opens on Broadway at the Martin Beck Theatre.

1964

February 15	*The Ballad of the Sad Cafe* closes after 123 performances.
Spring	Carson breaks right hip and shatters left elbow in fall.
May 25	Dramatization of short story, "The Sojourner," presented by NBC television.
November 1	*Sweet as a Pickle and Clean as a Pig* published by Houghton Mifflin.
November 8	Carson signs last will and testament.
December 1	Selections from *Sweet as a Pickle and Clean as a Pig* published in *Redbook.*

1965

	Carson McCullers: Her Life and Work, first book-length study of McCullers's work, written by Oliver Evans, published in London by Peter Owen.
July 14	Carson undergoes exploratory surgery and has broken hip reset. Remains in hospital three months.
September	Carson has leg operation.
December 7	During a visit to Carson in Nyack, Margaret Sue Sullivan sees manuscript of "Illuminations Until Now."
December 18	Carson awarded the Prize of the Younger

	Generation by *Die Welt*, a newspaper published in Hamburg, Germany.
1966	
	Carson works with Mary Rodgers on musical adaptation of *The Member of the Wedding* and works on a manuscript referred to as "Illuminations and Night Glare."
October	Filming begins on *Reflections in a Golden Eye* at Mitchell Field on Long Island.
November	University of Mississippi awards Carson a Grant for the Humanities.
1967	
February 19	Carson celebrates fiftieth birthday with a stay at the Plaza Hotel in New York. Carson interviewed by Rex Reed.
March	"The March," a short story, appears in *Redbook*.
April 1	Carson and Ida Reeder visit John Huston in Ireland.
April 16	Interview with Rex Reed, "Frankie Addams at 50," Carson's final interview, appears in the *New York Times*.
April 18	Carson and Ida Reeder return from Ireland. Carson continues dictating autobiography titled "Illumination and Night Glare."
April 30	Carson named winner of the 1966 Henry Bellamann Award, a $1,000 grant, in recognition of "outstanding contribution to literature."
July 31	Carson writes final letter to John Huston.
August 15	Carson suffers final stroke, a massive brain hemorrhage; comatose for forty-seven days.
August 19	A tracheotomy performed on Carson at Nyack Hospital.
September 8	Tennessee Williams visits Carson in hospital.
September 27	An advanced screening of film adaptation of *Reflections in a Golden Eye* presented.
September 29	Carson dies in the Nyack Hospital.

September 30   Carson's obituary appears in the *New York Times*.

October 2   Shooting begins on the film adaptation of *The Heart Is a Lonely Hunter*.

October 3   Carson buried in Oak Hill Cemetery overlooking the Hudson River in Nyack.

October 4   Details of Carson's funeral reported in the *New York Times*.

October 11   *Reflections in a Golden Eye* film adaptation released.

October 15   (Scheduled date for leg amputation.)

December   "A Hospital Christmas Eve" published in *Redbook*.

1968

Film version of *The Heart Is a Lonely Hunter* released.

1971

The Mortgaged Heart, edited by Margarita G. Smith, published by Houghton Mifflin.

Appendix III
Editorial Apparatus and Practices and
List of Emendations and Corrections

This edition of "Illumination and Night Glare" is based on
the two extant typescripts of the work housed at the Harry Ransom
Humanities Research Center at the University of Texas at Austin. Typescript "A" includes 128 pages and typescript "B" includes 111 pages
(the "B" manuscript is missing the final 17 pages). The two typescripts
were emended separately. This edition includes the emendations and
corrections from both typescripts.

The number preceding each entry in the following list refers to the
page where the correction or emendation appears. A word or words
before a right bracket in the list of emendations and corrections repre-
sent changes indicated by editorial marks in the typescripts of the autobiography. The words or words following the right bracket are text
as it appeared in the typescript of the autobiography. Example: Flan-
nery] Flattery.

¶   Indicates insertion of a paragraph break.
A: Correction/change appearing only in 128-page typescript
       ("A" manuscript).
B: Correction/change appearing only in 111-page typescript
       ("B" manuscript).
A/B: Correction/change that appears in both copies of type-
       script but not identically (not a change made with carbon
       paper).
a/b: Carbon correction/change identical in both manuscripts
       (change made with carbon paper).

LIST OF EMENDATIONS AND CORRECTIONS

3   [Illumination and Night Glare] BIOGRAPHY / by / CARSON McCULLERS / First Draft / ILLUMINATION AND NIGHT GLARE

3   A/B: easy, nor has love, may I add.] easy.

3   A: working life] adolescence

3   A/B: at] from

3   A/B: novel] work

3   A/B: unfocussed] blurred in my mind

3   A: write these] write out these

3   A/B: creation] work

4   [Straightaway] Straightway

4   B: fresh] new

4–5   [¶The broad principal theme of this book . . . in all of their deeper aspects.] QUOTE PASSAGE, GET FROM LEON.

5   B: ¶The next] The next

5   B: book:] book.

5   B: "In . . . together."] In . . . together.

5   B: For a year or so] From then on

5   [Mifflin] Miflin

5   B: novel.] novel, I submitted about a hundred or more pages to them.

5   ["The Mute"] The Mute

5   [although] altho

5   B: That outline was a moral support to me, altho I have never before or again worked so closely with an outline. That outline appears in the appendix.] already completed. It did not win

5   [Houghton Mifflin] H.M.

5   B: H.M.] they

5   B: almost as] almost just as

5   A/B: in 1937 in my] in my

5   B: not? In doing so, I felt I had to confess to my parents. I told them . . .]not? I told them . . .

5   B: my parents] them

5   B: marry him until] marry until

5   B: my parents I didn't want to marry him until I first had experienced sex with him] them I didn't want to marry until I first had a sexual experience

5   B: confess to my parents. I said marriage. . . . . . .as well as incredible. ¶I told my parents] confess to my parents. ¶I told my parents . . .

6   [Chatterley's] Chatterly's
6   B: I]¶I
6   B: my parents] them
6   A/B: who was living] at his home
6   A/B: in Goldens Bridge for the Winter.] in Westchester, while he was taking courses at Columbia in N.Y.
6   A: They] My parents
6   A: let me go. ¶The sexual] let me go. The sexual
6   A/B: explosions or colored lights,] explosions,
6   A/B: out of season.] out of season, and working together we were pretty good cooks.
6   A/B: about "The Mute," my working title for "The Heart Is A Lonely Hunter"] about the Mute,
6   A/B: writing for both of us.] work.
6   A/B: work. In Sylvia Bates' class,] work. In the meantime, and in Sylvia Bates' class,
6   A: my first] a
6   B: published in 1936 in] published in
6   A/B: *Story Magazine*] Story Magazine
6   A: WUNDERKIND. (It is hard to realize the prestige & importance that *Story Magazine* had at that time for young authors.) Exhilarated] WUNDERKIND. Exhilarated
6   ["Wunderkind"] WUNDERKIND
6   B: a writer] an author
6   [1937] 1936
6   A/B: On September 20, 1936] In September (check year
6   A/B: "The Mute."] the Mute.
6   [N.Y.,] NY.
6   B: philosophy, psychology, in NY. etc.,] psychology, etc.,
6   B: Reeves] he
6   ["The Mute,"] The Mute
6   [Is] is
6   B: title, later was changed to "The Heart is a Lonely Hunter" by my publisher, a title which I was pleased with, took] title, took
6   B: ... loved hard. Directly after "Heart" was finished in 1939, I immediately began another work which was "Reflections in a Golden Eye." ¶The pattern ...] ... loved hard. ¶The pattern ...
6   B: pattern of love had] pattern had
6   B: adored] loved
6   B: sachet.] sachet and whom I adored.

7	["Bring] "bring
7	[kumquats] cumquats
7	[fits.] <u>fits</u>.
7	B: fits.] <u>fits</u>.
7	B: illnesses,] illness,
7	[Woman's Christian Temperance Union] WCTU
7	[They] There
7	B: serious] many
7	[Lamar] Lemar
7	[POP,] "POP",
7	[Lamar] Lemar
7	[Daddy] daddy
7	["Is] "is
7	[Lamar] Lemar
7	[Lamar] Lemar
7	[brothers] <u>brothers</u>
7	B: <u>brothers</u>.] brothers
7	B: every day to] every day except Sunday to
9	B: Tieh's,] Lieh's
9	[Tieh] Teih
9	B: Teih] Leih
9	[scuppernong] Scupernong
9	[Tupelo] Tuppelo
9	[gardener] gardner
9	[Tieh] Teih
9	B: Teih] Leih
9	[When I was calm that afternoon] WHEN I WAS CALM THAT AFTERNOON
9	B: WHEN I WAS CALM THAT AFTERNOON Mother] Mother
9	["She's] "she's
9	[Kissing is for live people.] KISSING IS FOR LIVE PEOPLE.
9	B: people. KISSING IS FOR LIVE PEOPLE."] people."
9	[The floors creaked in the way of old houses.] THE FLOORS CREAKED IN THE WAY OF OLD HOUSES.
9	B: Georgia. THE FLOORS CREAKED IN THE WAY OF OLD HOUSES. She owned] Georgia. She owned
9	B: properties] houses
9	B: It was in this house that] That was the house where
9	[missing text]
12	[it?"] it"
12	[fuck,"] fuck"
12	[said.] said

12   [times."] times"
12   [fuck,"] fuck
12   B: 5] six
12   [in] IN
12   B: old IN 1922, my] old my
13   [Then I swung into "Yes, We Have No Bananas."] THEN I
        SWUNG INTO "YES, WE HAVE NO BANANAS."
13   B: THEN I SWUNG INTO "YES, WE HAVE NO BANANAS."
13   B: at age thirteen] at this age
13   [grown] GROWN
13   B: GROWN] adult
13   A/B: Karl] Carl
13   B: that was . . . about justice.] that probably was the dawn of
        social consciousness in me.
13   [Depression] depression
13   [Negroes] Negros
13   B: something fearful] somethingfearful
13   B: I] It
13   ["in love,"] "in love",
13   B: my] the
13   B: joy to] joy of my life to
14   [Juilliard] Juillard
14   [great] GREAT
14   B: GREAT] great
15   B: The next book] This time the book
15   ["Brown River."] 'Brown River'.
15   ["Sons and Lovers."] 'Sons and Lovers'
15   ["fast"] 'fast'
15   [traveled] travelled
15   B: marvels,] marvels
15   B: fact, she had] fact, had
15   [In the daytime I'd got to Macy's and just sit in a telephone
        booth where I knew I was safe. Then back to the horror of a
        sleepless night.] IN THE DAYTIME I'D GOT TO MACY'S
        AND JUST SIT IN A TELEPHONE BOOTH WHERE I KNEW
        I WAS SAFE. THEN BACK TO THE HORROR OF A SLEEP-
        LESS NIGHT.
15   B: strange men. IN THE DAYTIME I'D GOT TO MACY'S AND
        JUST SIT IN A TELEPHONE BOOTH WHERE I KNEW I WAS
        SAFE. THEN BACK TO THE HORROR OF A SLEEPLESS
        NIGHT. ¶Finally] strange men. ¶Finally
15   B: Finally,] Then finally,

15   B: ... men. ¶Finally ...] ... men. I could not sleep at night. ¶Finally ...
15   B: had the sense to] thought I would
15   B: "17,"] "Seventeen,"
15   [Girl's] GIRL'S
15   B: Women's] GIRL'S
15   B: twenty-four] twenty
16   [*More Fun and New Comics.*] 'More Fun and New Comics.'
16   ["front man"] 'front man'
16   [Field] Fields
16   B: "salesman."] salesman.
16   B: getting sour cream for Mrs. Fields, which she would eat] that Mrs. Fields would send me out for sour cream. She would eat the sour cream
16   [Field] Fields
16   [Field] Fields
16   [1935] 1936
16   B: June of 1936 I] June I
16   B: It] There
16   B: her beautiful records.] her records of music.
16   [Coke] coke
16   B: was] is
17   [doctor] Doctor
17   B: "It turned out to be a childhood attack of Rheumatic fever, but was never properly diagnosed, as such - (Continue on back of page to page 40 of writing [illegible word]" is inserted following "at home." The illegible word, perhaps "Important," is underlined three times.
17   [such.] such
17   B: his] Reeves'
17   B: Fearful & ill,] Stuck in the bed on Doctor's orders,
18   B: their] his
18   B: patience & understanding.] patience.
18   B: in 1937 in the] in the
18   [Mother] mother
18   [mothers] mother's
18   [Daddy] daddy
18   [said, "What] said "what
18   [said,] said
18   ["We'd] "we'd
18   ["Do] "do
18   [stuck] stuck

18 B: stuck] stuck
19 [me moral support] me moral support
19 B: me moral support] me moral support
19 A: wrang] rang
19 [other] other
19 B: other.] other
19 [led] lead
20 [husband] husband
20 B: husband] husband
20 [and] snd
20 B: recognized] recognize
20 [Klein's] Kleins
20 A/B: Kleins] kleins
20 [Erika] Erica
21 [Erika's] Erica's
21 [Myshkin's] Myschkin's
21 [Nastasya Filippovna] Natasha Philopla?
21 [Erika] Erica
21 [couturiers] coutouriers
21 [Annemarie] Anna Marie
21 [Annemarie] Anna Marie
22 [said.] said,
22 [Mademoiselle Schwarzenbach?"] Madamoiselle Schwartzen-
bach?" (Check spelling in Reflections)
22 [struggle up,] struggle up,
22 B: struggle up,] struggle up,
23 [have gotten on] of gotten on
23 B: gotten on] gotten on
23 [*Harper's Bazaar*] Harper's Bazaar
23 ["Since] "since
23 [brownstone] Brownstone
23 [agency,] Agency,
23 [brownstone] Brownstone
23 [Middagh] Minaugh
23 A/B: Auden,] Aughden
23 B: Pears. In turn they had good friends. Louis MacNiece,
Christopher Isherwood, Richard Wright Aaron Copeland
Jane & Paul Boles. Thank goodness] . . . Pears. Thank goodness . . .
23 [Britten] Britton
23 A/B: friend] frien
23 [friends:] friends.

23	[MacNeice] MacNiece
23	[Wright,] Wright
23	[Copland,] Copeland
23	[Bowles] Boles
23	B: his] their
23	[party] (party)
23	[Vreeland] Vreeland (Check spelling in Harpers).
23	A: Vreeland] Vrelind
23	[Wystan] Wyston
23	A/B: Auden,] Aughden,
23	[Kierkegaard] Kierkeard (poet, check spelling)
23	A: Kierkeard] Kierkegard
23	B: Kierkeard] Kierkergaard
23	[Dichterliebe] Dieterlieber. (Check spelling)
23	B: Dieterlieber] Dichtelieber
24	[Annemarie.] Anna Marie.
24	a/b: Marie. ¶In spite] Marie. In spite
24	[Saratoga Springs,] Saratoga,
25	[doctor] Doctor
25	[*New Yorker*] New Yorker
25	[*New Yorker*] New Yorker
25	[*New Yorker*] New Yorker
25	[*New Yorker*] New Yorker
25	[*New Yorker*] New Yorker
25	B: playwright] playwrite
26	A: 1946] 1943
26	[von] Van
26	[Annemarie's] Anna Marie's
26	[haute] haut
26	[possessed] Possessed
26	[Audrey] Audry
26	[Lasky] Laskey
26	[has] had
26	B: had] had
26	[Lasky] Laskey
26	[Annemarie] Anna Marie
27	B: tide] emotion
27	B: of war] of the war
27	[*New Yorker*] New Yorker
27	[was as weird] was weird
27	A: Flannery] Flattery
27	B:] Flattery

27	[Mother] mother
27	[Mother] mother
27	B: could,] could
27	[Mother] mother
27	[Breuer] Brewer
30	["Second] "second
30	A: vulgar."] vulger."
30	["We're] "we're
30	A/B: Poor,] Poors,
30	[doctor] Doctor
30	["Men] men
31	A: imaginary,] imaginative,
31	[Ku] Klu
31	B: Klu] Ku
31	["We] "we
31	[erysipelas] erysipalis
31	[shrubbery] shrubery
31	[tote a few tokens] <u>tote a few tokens</u>
31	B: <u>tote a few tokens</u>] tote a few tokens
31	[doctor's] Doctor's
31	[*Crime and Punishment*] "Crime and Punishment"
31	[doctor] Doctor
31	B: disappeared almost as] disappeared as
32	[*Vogue*] Vogue
32	[Sand] Sands
32	[Copland] Copeland
33	[he] He
33	[said.] said,
33	[he?"] he,"
33	[gangster."] ganster.
34	[Edwin Peacock] Edwin
34	[Erika] Erica
34	[Annemarie] Anna Marie
34	[Annemarie's] Anna Marie's
34	[Annemarie] Anna Marie
34	[von] Van
34	[Annemarie] Anna Marie
34	A: into] to
34	[I] "I
34	[Annemarie] Anna Marie
34	[crippled?] crippled?"
34	[life?"] life?

34   [Annemarie's] Anna Marie's
35   [Annemarie] Anna Marie
35   B: DeGaulle forces in the Congo,] them at Brazzavia (CHECK
      SPELLING),
35   [deity] diety
35   [have] of
35   A/B: ¶"When] "When
36   ['Reflections In A Golden Eye.'] "Reflections In A Golden Eye."
36   [as] ad
36   [Annemarie,] Annamarie,
36   [a correspondent] correspondant
36   [Annemarie's] Annamarie's
37   [have] of
37   ["Pipe] "pipe
37   [Brother] brother
37   A/B: "illumination"] "illimination"
37   [me: in] me; In
37   [Is] is
38   B: random when my] random my
38   [book.] book?
38   [Is] is
39   [accompanies] accompanys
39   B: most welcoming.] delighted.
40   [belonged. There also] belonged. (NOTE HER 75th ANNIVER-
      SARY—TO COME LATER) There also
40   [Gascoyne] Gascogne
40   A: strokes] dtrokes
43   [Presbytere,"] Presbyter
43   A/B: curé] cure
43   [soufflé] souffle
43   [*dépendances*] "Dependence."
43   [dreadfulness] dreadfullness
43   [Presbytere] Presbyter
44   ["It's] "I'ts
44   [said.] said,
44   [the Wedding,"] The Wedding",
44   B: ¶My] My
44   A: Breuer,] Bruer,
44   A: plainly] Plainly
45   [*Alice in Wonderland*] Alice in Wonderland
45   [*Sundown Beach*] Sundown Beach
45   [Audrey Wood.] Wood.

45	[Miss Ethel Waters] Miss Waters
45	[men."] men.
45	[¶"Mrs. McCullers] Mrs. McCullers
45	[man. She's] man." "She's
45	[director was] director (CHECK NAME), was
45	[asked.] asked (CHECK THEIR NAMES)
45	[parents'] parents
45–46	B: us all." ¶ I had . . . try-outs. Of course . . . them myself. The Philadelphia . . . means ecstatic. I made . . . its' life. ¶But when] us all. ¶But when . . .
46	[night's] nights
46	[minute] min
46	[its] its'
46	[January 5,] June 5,
46	[lobster] lobester
46	[Newburg] newburg
46	["Member"] Member
46	B: Member] It
46	[Critics'] Critics
46	[Award."] Award." (Insert from back of page)
46	[hell] Hell
46	[Mother] mother
46	[said. "It] said, "it
46	[the] The
46	[something,"] something"
47	[psychiatrist,] pshchiatrist,
47	[immediately.] immediately,
47	[gynecologist] gynocologist
47	[William Mayer] William
47	[on."] on.
47	[marvelous] mervelous
47	[strength.] strength. (Continue on page 68)
47	A: Rodgers,] Rogers
47	[Barer,] Barerd (Check Spelling),
47	A: Barerd] Berard
47	[lyricist] lyrisist
47	[and] an
48	[it.] it. (Check Credits)
48	[September] Sept
48	B: Sept] July
48	[I'm] I'M

48   [André] Andre
48   ["Painting in Movement"] "Pictures in Motion"
48   [André] Andre
50   a/b: bad.] bad,
50   a/b: Not] {Tab} Not
50   [its] it's
50   [Chinese] chinese
50   [*New York Times*] New York Times
51   [7,] 4,
51   ["The Vamp"] "The Vamp" (CHECK NAME OF PLAY)
51   [acquiesced] acquieced
51   [said. "Go] said, "go
51   [and] And
52   ["It] "it
52   [led] lead
52   [Mercer.] Mercer. ¶ TO BE INSERTED IN PROPER PLACE
52   [d'art] d'arte
52   [my] mu
52   [hors d'oeuvres] h'ors d'oeuvres
52   ["Just] Just
53   [*Gone with the Wind.*] "Gone With The Wind." ¶NOTE: AT-
      LANTA LUNCHEON AND HOMESICKNESS. MOTHER
      SAID, "I WAS AMBASSADOR TO THE WORLD, BUT WHAT
      AN AMBASSADOR.
53   [limpet] limpid
53   [Wystan] Wyston
53   [Wystan] Wyston
53   [Wystan] Wyston
54   [Rasputin.] "Rasputin."
54   B: chaise] chez
54   [My Life,] "My Life,"
54   [Isadora] Isador
54   [Depression] depression
54   [Lamar] Lemar
56   ["tip toe to the window."] "Tip Toe to the Window."
56   [You're] you're
56   [Mother] mother
56   B: pretty good liberal] pretty liberal
56   [Daddy] daddy
56   [Daddy] daddy
56   B: about] bout
57   B: baby as a teenager,] baby,

57	B: at the birth.] at birth.
57	[its] it's
57	[Daddy and Mother] daddy and mother
57	[Methodist Church] methodist church
57	[Daddy] daddy
58	[Daddy] daddy
58	[Nursey] Mursey
58	[girls."] girls.
58	[Mother] mother
58	[Mother] mother
59	[Dostoevsky] Dostoeveski
59	[*The Idiot,*] "The Idiot,"
59	[Nastasya Filippovna.] Natasya Filippovnas.
59	[Nastasya] Natasya
59	[Nastasya] Natasya
59	[Ganya] Gana
59	[*True Story*] "True Story"
59	[war] War
59	[Sebastopol,] Sabastopol (?),
59	[*War and Peace*] "War and Peace"
59	[canvases] canvasses
60	B: Mercer] Mrecer
60	[*Where Angels Fear to Tread.*] "Where Angels Fear To Tread."
60	A: Forster,] Forster
60	[Woolf,] Wolf,
60	A: Woolf] Wolf
60	B: asked] saked
60	[*The Death of the Heart,*] "The Death of The Heart,"
60	[*Death of the Heart*] "Death of the Heart"
60	B: bathtub] bathroom
60	[its] it's
60	[she] She
60	A: Afterwards She lived] She now lives
60	[Ewald] Ewold
60	A: Ewold] (CHECK NAME)
60	[Baroness] Countess
61	[she] shw
61	[Denys Finch-Hatton] Denis Finch-Hatten
61	[Tanya] Tania
61	A: Tania] Tanya
61	A: jewel-like] liquid eyes
61	[kohl] Kohl

61   A:I] you
61   A: I] one
61   A/B: this] that
61   ["No] "no
62   A: make do] do
62   [soufflés] souffles
62   [Britten] Britton
62   [the] The
62   [Tanya] Tania
62   [Tanya] Tania
62   [beautiful beech tree,] beautiful———tree,
62   [*Reflections in a Golden Eye*] "Reflections In a Golden Eye"
62   [*The Heart Is a Lonely Hunter,*] "The Heart is a Lonely Hunter,"
62   [Negro,] negro,
62   [Zeigler] Ziegler
62   [*Out of Africa,*] "Out Of Africa,"
62   [*Out of Africa,*] "Out Of Africa,"
62   [*Seven Gothic Tales.*] "Seven Gothic Tales."
62   [*Out of Africa*] "Out Of Africa"
62   [*Out of Africa*] "Out Of Africa"
62   [Tanya] Tania
62   [Negroes] negros
64   [*Black Boy,*] "Black Boy,"
64   [Negro.] negro.
64   [Negroes] negros
64   [Negro] negro
64   [Negro] negro
64   [*clef*] cle
64   [course] Course
64   A: dining room. There . . . fountain. When . . . first."] dining
      room. ("There . . . " and "When . . . " sentences inserted in
      typescript A only)
64   A: visit me at the American Hospital] take me to Paris
64   A: Brooklyn,] Brooklyn
64   [Negro,] negro,
64   A: art, nor his independence either,] art,
64   [the] The
65   A: stead. Adequate . . . them. This . . . aware of this, but this
      unfortunately, . . .] stead, but this unfortunately, . . .
65   [Negro] negro
65   [Negroes] negros

65	A: out. My house . . . Christ] out. ("My house . . . " sentence inserted in typescript A only)
65	A: out. ¶Among] out. Remorse and regret are hard things to live with but it's equally difficult to find a logical solution. ¶Among . . .
65	[*New Yorker* magazine,] New Yorker Magazine,
65	[*Atlanta Constitution*] "Atlanta Constitution"
65	[*Reflections in a Golden Eye.*] "Reflections In A Golden Eye."
65	[*Reflections in a Golden Eye,*] "Reflections In A Golden Eye,"
65	[actors."] actors.
65	[Zorro David.] (Japanese servant?)
66	[*Reflections*] "Reflections"
66	[Chapman Mortimer] Mortimer?
66	[but I said,] but said,
66	B: elevator at the Plaza] elevator
66	[its] it's
66	A: Her bread . . . tasted.] ("Her bread . . . " sentence inserted in typescript A only)
67	[house.] house, (Veronica? Countess?)
67	a/b: ¶In] In
67	[*Reflections in a Golden Eye.*] "Reflections In A Godlen Eye."
67	[*Irish Times*] Irish Times
67	A: handsomely] beautifully
68	A: Harkness Pavilion] the hospital
68	A: patient, at least the nurses heard him singing it over & over.] patient.
68	[printed. ¶New York] printed. ¶TO BE INSERTED IN PROPER PLACE ¶ New York
68	[going.] going?
68	[*Square Root*] "Square Root"
69	[rosé] Rose
69	[look,"] look"
70	[Baudelaire] Beaudelaire
70	[Baudelaire] Beaudelaire
70	[André] Andre
71	[Markses] Marks'
71	[Your] your
71	[Markses] Marks'
71	[Isabel] Isabelle
71	[Jordan Massee,] Jorden Massey,
71	[Jordan] Jorden

71　[*Dubliners.*] "Dubliners."
71　[*A Portrait of the Artist as a Young Man,*] "The Portrait Of An Artist As A Young Man,"
71　[*Ulysses,*] "Ulysses,"
72　[*Finnegans Wake,*] "Finnegan's Wake,"
72　["Anna Livia Plurabelle"] "Anna Lavia Plura Bella"
72　[its] it's
72　[*Dubliners*] "Dubliners"
72　[*Ulysses*] "Ulysses"
72　[sister,] sisters,
72　[Church.] church.
72　[lovable,] loveable,
72　[*Tender Is the Night,*] "Tender Is The Night,"
72　[*Papa Hemingway.*] "Papa Hemingway."
73　[*New York Times,*] New York Times,
73　[Hammerschlag] Hammerschlag (?)
74　[*Member of the Wedding,*] "Member of The Wedding,"
76　[hollered. "Take] hollered, "take
76　[Hervey Cleckley] Harvey Cleckely
76　[*The Mask of Sanity,*] "The Mask of Sanity,"
78　[*Heart,*] "Heart,"
78　[*Reflections in a Golden Eye.*] "Reflections In A Golden Eye."
78　[Daddy] daddy
78　[have] of
78　[*Heart*] "Heart
78　[*Reflections.*] "Reflections."
78　[*Heart*] "Heart"

Bibliography

WORKS BY CARSON McCULLERS

The Heart is a Lonely Hunter. Boston: Houghton Mifflin, 1940.
Reflections in a Golden Eye. Boston: Houghton Mifflin, 1941.
The Member of the Wedding. Boston: Houghton Mifflin, 1946.
The Ballad of the Sad Cafe: The Novels and Stories of Carson McCullers. Boston: Houghton Mifflin, 1951.
The Member of the Wedding. (Play) New York: New Directions, 1951.
The Square Root of Wonderful. (Play) Boston: Houghton Mifflin, 1958.
Collected Short Stories and the Novel "The Ballad of the Sad Cafe." Boston: Houghton Mifflin, 1961.
Clock Without Hands. Boston: Houghton Mifflin, 1961.
Sweet as a Pickle and Clean as a Pig. Boston: Houghton Mifflin, 1964.
The Mortgaged Heart. Edited and introduced by Margarita G. Smith. Boston: Houghton Mifflin, 1971.
Collected Stories of Carson McCullers: Including "The Member of the Wedding" and "The Ballad of the Sad Cafe." Introduced by Virginia Spencer Carr. Boston: Houghton Mifflin, 1987.

WORKS ABOUT CARSON McCULLERS

Bloom, Harold, ed. *Carson McCullers.* Modern Critical Views Ser. New York: Chelsea House, 1986.
Carr, Virginia Spencer. *The Lonely Hunter: A Biography of Carson McCullers.* Garden City: Doubleday, 1975.
Carr, Virginia Spencer. *Understanding Carson McCullers.* Columbia, S.C.: University of South Carolina Press, 1990.
Cook, Richard. *Carson McCullers.* New York: Ungar, 1975.
Critical Essays on Carson McCullers. New York: G. K. Hall, 1996.
Edmonds, Dale. *Carson McCullers.* Austin: Steck-Vaughn, 1969.
Evans, Oliver. *The Ballad of Carson McCullers.* New York: Coward-McCann, 1966.
Graver, Lawrence. *Carson McCullers.* Minneapolis: University of Minnesota Press, 1969.

James, Judith Giblin. *Wunderkind: The Reputation of Carson McCullers, 1940–1990*. Columbia, S.C.: Camden House, 1995.

Kiernan, Robert F. *Katherine Anne Porter and Carson McCullers: A Reference Guide*. Boston: G. K. Hall, 1976.

McDowell, Margaret B. *Carson McCullers*. Boston: Twayne, 1980.

Shapiro, Adrian M., et al. *Carson McCullers: A Descriptive Listing and Annotated Bibliography*. New York: Garland, 1980.

Westling, Louise. *Sacred Groves and Ravaged Gardens: The Fiction of Eudora Welty, Carson McCullers, and Flannery O'Connor*. Athens: University of Georgia Press, 1985.

Index

Note: For individual works of Carson McCullers, see their individual titles.

227

William L. Andrews
General Editor

Robert F. Sayre
The Examined Self: Benjamin Franklin, Henry Adams, Henry James

Daniel B. Shea
Spiritual Autobiography in Early America

Lois Mark Stalvey
The Education of a WASP

Margaret Sams
Forbidden Family: A Wartime Memoir of the Philippines, 1941–1945
Edited, with an introduction, by Lynn Z. Bloom

Journeys in New Worlds: Early American Women's Narratives
Edited by William L. Andrews

Mark Twain
Mark Twain's Own Autobiography:
The Chapters from the "North American Review"
Edited, with an introduction, by Michael J. Kiskis

American Autobiography: Retrospect and Prospect
Edited by Paul John Eakin

Charlotte Perkins Gilman
The Living of Charlotte Perkins Gilman: An Autobiography
Introduction by Ann J. Lane

Caroline Seabury
The Diary of Caroline Seabury: 1854–1863
Edited, with an introduction, by Suzanne L. Bunkers

Cornelia Peake McDonald
A Woman's Civil War: A Diary with Reminiscences of the War, from March 1862
Edited, with an introduction, by Minrose G. Gwin

Marian Anderson
My Lord, What a Morning
Introduction by Nellie Y. McKay

American Women's Autobiography: Fea(s)ts of Memory
Edited, with an introduction, by Margo Culley

233